COLLARD
the
HONITON & DORSET
POTTER

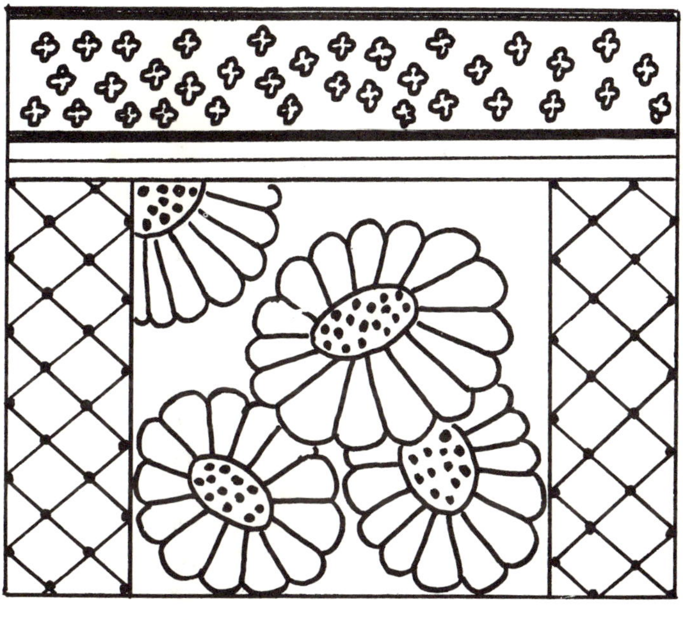

Carol & Chris Cashmore

First published 1983 by the authors
5 Sussex Road, Brentwood, Essex

ISBN 0 9508828 0 1

Printed and bound in Great Britain by
Anchor Brendon Ltd
Tiptree, Essex

CONTENTS

"Factories have practically driven folk-art out of England; it survives only in out of the way corners even in Europe, and the artist-craftsman, since the days of William Morris, has been the chief means of defence against the materialism of industry and its insensibility to beauty."

"To dig a single clean clay in the vicinity of the kilns was the habit of the old country potters, and it is one which can be recommended to the potter of today . . . he should not want to standardise, or to depend entirely upon those reliable but uninteresting substances which the potter's merchant offers to the trade."

from *'A Potter's Book'* by Bernard Leach.

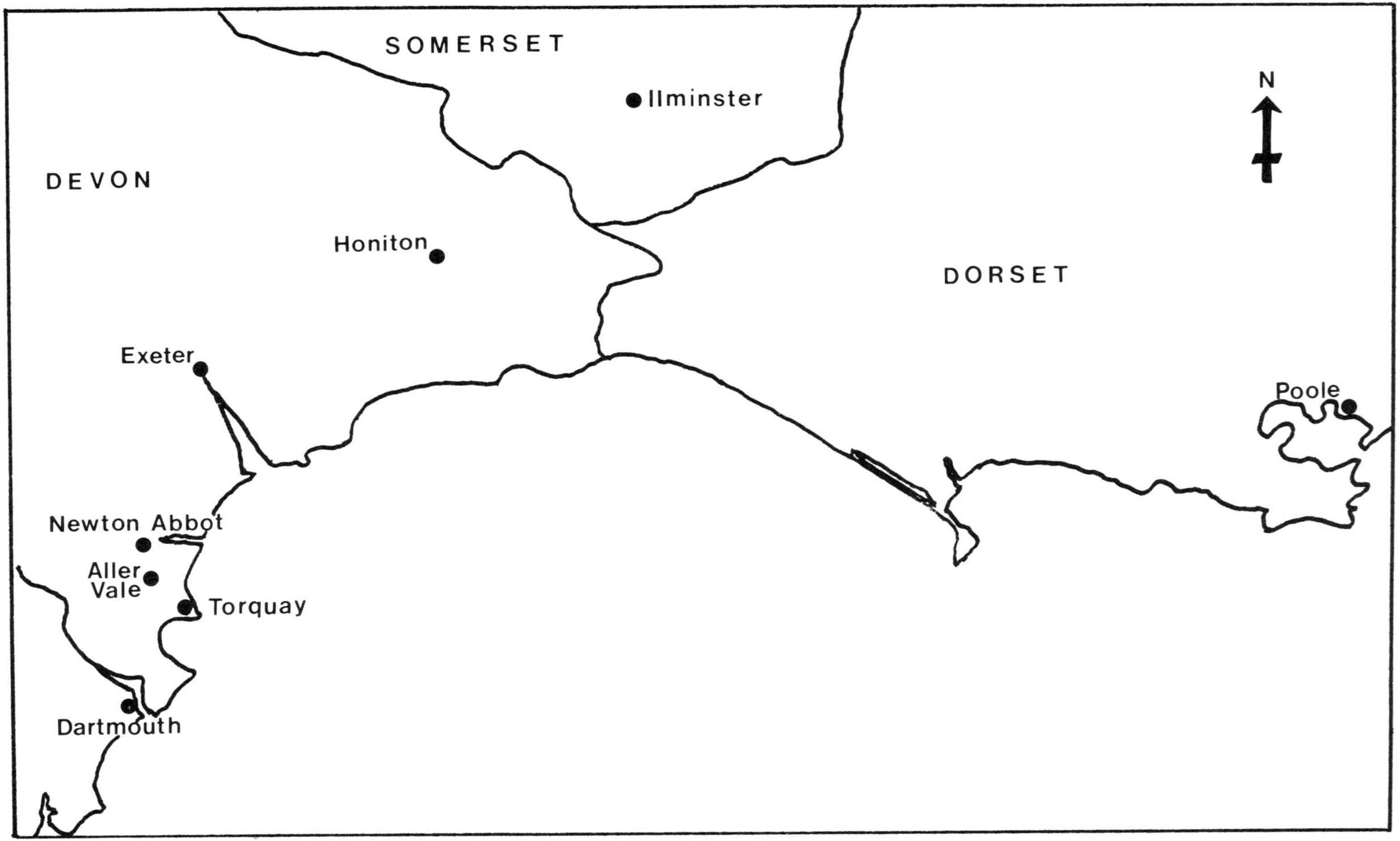

SOMERSET
Ilminster
N
DEVON
Honiton
DORSET
Exeter
Poole
Newton Abbot
Aller Vale
Torquay
Dartmouth

Acknowledgements

So very many people have helped us to write this book by giving us freely of their time, memories and knowledge; this has made the undertaking such a great pleasure.

We thank all those who sent us valuable snippets of information, and in particular the following who had connections with the potteries:

CROWN DORSET. Mrs Cobb (née Stephens), Mrs Clee (née Lambert), Mrs Cartridge (née Knight), H. J. O'Donnell, A. Hawkes, F. J. Main, Mrs May, Mrs Wigmore and the Way family.

HONITON. Mrs Clancy, Mrs Phelps and her daughters, Mrs F. Richards (née Loving), Mrs E. Richards (née Readhead), Mrs Freemantle, A. Nott, E. Carnell, D. Hickmott, Mr Auckland.

We are very grateful for the help of members of the Torquay Pottery Collectors Society who have shared their knowledge with us, especially Mr and Mrs Barber, Mrs Furzeland, J. Mills, J. Knight, J. Marsh, K. Paull and I. Green, and also for the help of the Crown Dorset collectors Mr and Mrs Willis.

Finally our special thanks to Miss Collard without whose help this book would not have been possible.

PART I
ALLER VALE

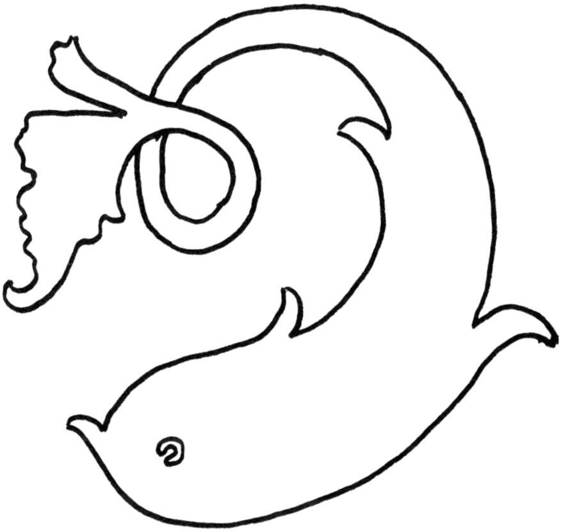

Introduction

"All things must yield to industry and time
None cease to rise but those who cease to climb"

This Victorian aphorism written on one of the earliest pieces of Aller Vale pottery sums up the life and work of Charles Collard. Born the youngest of seven children of a poulterer he rose to become one of the leading decorators at the Aller Vale Pottery, Torquay and had some of his work presented to the future King and Queen. Subsequently he ran his own potteries at Poole (The Crown Dorset Art Pottery) and the better known one at Honiton. Both potteries were commercial and artistic successes and indeed Honiton was probably the last true art pottery in England. Thus the principles of the nineteenth century arts and crafts movement that so influenced Collard at Aller Vale survived well into the middle of the twentieth century. This book attempts to outline his life, the pottery he made, the techniques he used and the artistic influences that led to his unique style. There is no doubt that the Crown Dorset pottery has been sadly neglected and in fact standard works on ceramics make no reference to its existence. Honiton Pottery is better known but has wrongly been thought of as an imitator of the better known Poole Pottery of Carter, Stabler and Adams. In fact the techniques and decoration used at Honiton were quite distinctive. Honiton Pottery of the Collard period was entirely hand made and hand painted and represents a promising field for the collector.

Charles Henry Fletcher Collard was the rather imposing name given by Francis Collard and his wife Elizabeth to their youngest child born on 1st September, 1874 at 11, Pennsylvania Terrace, Torquay. Fletcher was his mother's family name and apparently all of her sons were christened Fletcher so that they could adopt this name, rather than that of Collard, in later life if they so wished. Charles' father, Francis, came from a family of small tenant farmers in South Devon but was himself a poulterer, eventually aspiring in the 1900s to running his own business in Teignmouth Road, Torquay. The family is believed to have come from Belgium originally and to include the well-known piano manufacturers.

Being the youngest child Charles did not really know his brothers as they had left home before he grew up; one joined the navy, one was killed in the First World War and the other emigrated to Australia and kept in touch with Charles by letter. He also had three sisters of whom he was very fond, two of whom visited him regularly in later life. One sister married and settled in Ipplepen, about twelve miles West of Torquay, Ipplepen was also the home of some cousins of the family and one of the highlights of Collard's childhood was the occasional visit by pony and trap to visit them. He loved the countryside all his life and was obviously pleased even as a child to leave the town and stay for a while on a farm.

By the time he was of school age the family had moved from Pennsylvania Terrace to Warren Road, Torquay and he was sent to the pay school in Abbey Road until he was twelve years old. Then in 1886 by some good chance, or possibly at his own wishes, his parents decided to send him as an apprentice to the Aller Vale pottery. Collard loved his work at the pottery and had a great affection for Mr Phillips its proprietor. John Phillips seems to have been seen almost as a father figure at the works rather than as an employer, much as Collard himself was viewed in later years at Honiton. Collard mastered all the processes of potting at an early age. This knowledge proved invaluable when running his own pottery and indeed when the need arose there was no aspect of the work from preparing the clay to decorating glazed wares to which he could not, or would not, turn his hand. Nevertheless his greatest skill was as a decorator and this was also his greatest love. In his period at Aller Vale he became a skilled and valued artist, to such an extent that ex-colleagues at Aller

Vale, who had moved to their own potteries at Exeter and Longpark, were keen to obtain his services.

In order to understand the nature of the training and influence of Aller Vale on Collard both in technique and ethos, it is necessary to know something of the ideals of John Phillips which were based upon the belief that art was a necessary part of life and that no one, however humble, was beneath studying it and all who desired should have the facilities to do so in their spare time. To this end he helped found art schools and when he formed his own art pottery he put his ideals into practice, this work is outlined in the following chapter.

Chapter 1

The Crank at Aller

John Phillips' Aller Vale Pottery Works

Today Aller is the beginning of Torquay to people driving South on their summer holidays, a housing estate in a valley between Dartmoor and the sea linked to Torquay by Kingskerswell. Just over a hundred years ago it was a village whose inhabitants depended on farming for their livelihood, then a pottery was formed which was to change the lives of many of the younger inhabitants. Pottery making was traditional in the Vale of Aller because of the existence of suitable clays, and in the 1860s Francis Buckland ran an ochre works at Moor Park, Aller. This business was bought in the early 1870s by John Phillips a clay merchant who lived at 3 Peamore Place, Devon Square, Newton Abbot. For some years Phillips ran the business as a clay and ochre works as well as running his previous business in Quay Road, Newton Abbot, but he obviously considered the business at Aller to be the major one as by 1873 he and his unmarried sister had moved to Aller to live. Phillips took a keen interest in local affairs and local history and he was a member of the council of the Devonshire Association. He was also an enthusiastic supporter of Cottage Art Schools and gave lectures on the potter's skill from an arts and crafts point of view.

In 1870 an art school had been founded in Newton Abbot with the assistance of Phillips and like-minded people. Eleven years later, in 1881, a major art exhibition was held in Newton Abbot in association with the art schools of the town, at which Phillips' sister won first prize for decorative pottery with a vase. The competition was noticeably strong and was judged by two members of the Royal Academy, and therefore her success was no mean feat.

This major event seems to have given a new impetus to Phillips' philanthropic works and to the art classes held in the villages of King's and Abbotskerswell which Phillips had helped to found on a small scale a few years earlier. Prior to this these classes existed to give drawing lessons to young farm workers during the long winter evenings. Rapidly however these classes were reorganised under Phillips' leadership into Cottage Art Schools and the subjects covered expanded to include art lectures, modelling, carpentry, woodcarving, metalwork and even cookery. Phillips tried to hold the classes in what he described as "a pleasant evening atmosphere" rather than the formal surroundings of the Board Schools of which his pupils might have unpleasant memories! In Kingskerswell a large room was hired, but in Abbotskerswell Phillips could not find a suitable room and was forced to use the living rooms of Mary Bulley and her neighbour John Brimblecombe. Later Phillips attributed part of the success of the schools to the fact that they were held in a homely atmosphere and when in 1888 another school opened in Coffinswell Phillips used the living room of John Easterbrook. The homely atmosphere was created by log fires burning in the hearth and every evening finished with 'glee songs and choruses' two of the favourites being the 'Farmer's Boy' and 'Hearts of Oak'. Phillips' sister wrote a special song for his students which was also popular, and is reproduced below:

SONG OF THE 'THREE WELLS'

Swiss Air

When stars shine bright,
And Cynthia's light
Falls gently over hill and plain;
When hushed to rest
Each quiet nest,
And shadows deepen in the lane,
Then comes the hour, the mystic hour,
When Arts and Crafts assume their power,

In Coffinswell and Kingskerswell!
And so in Abbotskerswell too!
For here we merry craftsmen dwell,
And wondrous is the work we do!

This county blest,
That in the West,
Lies softly 'twixt the balmy seas;
In days of old,
As we are told,
Was famed throughout the world, for these
Our Arts and Crafts, which here we ply
When winter nights go swiftly by.
There's Coffinswell! and Kingskerswell!
And so there's Abbotskerswell too!
And here we merry craftsmen dwell,
And wondrous is the work we do!

Should storms assail,
Or floods prevail,
We speed across the rugged ground;
For in our lore
'Tis reason more,
That at our trysting-place we're found;
Thus helping on, with heart and hand,
The glory of our native land.
Here's Coffinswell and Kingskerswell!
And here's for Abbotskerswell too!
'Tis where we merry craftsmen dwell,
And wondrous is the work we do!

The last line was no idle boast as the reader will learn.

Formation of the Art Pottery

Art pottery might not have been produced at Aller but for a fire at Phillips' premises. In 1881, ten years after he had bought them, the buildings were badly damaged by fire and Phillips decided to take the opportunity to re-open as an art pottery. He had presumably noticed the success of the nearby Watcombe Pottery formed in 1869 and of the Torquay Terra-Cotta Company formed in 1875. The Watcombe Pottery was already well established employing eighty workers or more and making all types of vases and statuettes in terracotta. Such was its standing that the firm had displayed its work at the International Exhibition in London in 1872 and at the

Philadelphia Exhibition four years later, and had been the subject of an article in the Art Journal following the London exhibition in which it was described as "one of the happiest issues of speculative venture that has ever been arrived at in so short a time".

Naturally Phillips decided to employ the local students of King's and Abbotskerswell in his new pottery and he hired a 'gipsy' as a thrower to teach them. The word gipsy in this context means an itinerant pottery worker. These workers were quite common around this period and moved round the country working for one pottery for a short spell and then moving on to another. All work at the art schools had begun with drawing, both "plain and colour", and only when a student could work out designs on paper was he allowed to apply them to wood, metal or any other material to be worked, and this was a good beginning for a training in the decoration of pottery. The students studied and drew different ornaments and patterns so that when they began to decorate pottery "they had acquired sufficient freedom of hand and skill in the use of colour to proceed at once to decorate any given piece without sketching the design first on the pot". So said Cosmo Monkhouse writing an article on the pottery in the Magazine of Art in 1891. Phillips provided his students with all types of different designs and pots to study, from different periods and from different cultures, Egyptian, Turkish, Persian, French, Japanese, Italian, etc.. Monkhouse was rather scathing about this idea, saying "that the culture with which Phillips hopes to permeate the agricultural classes is perhaps the greatest of all enemies to original production".

Despite Monkhouse's depressing view the idea seems to have worked very well and Phillips, influenced by the arts and crafts movement, in turn influenced his students. They absorbed the designs of foreign cultures into their Devonshire minds and produced original ideas and pieces. In fact Phillips prided himself that at the Aller Vale Pottery all the work, apart from being done entirely by hand, was also completely original and that no other contemporary pottery's designs or shapes were copied; though other potteries copied them subsequently.

The Cottage Art Schools Exhibition, 1890

Both of Phillips' ventures, the pottery and the art schools, were very successful. The schools were so popular that by Christmas 1888, two years after Collard joined the pottery, sixty-four young people were attending twice a week at the three villages, their ages ranging from eleven to twenty-three. In 1887 the Kingskerswell Cottage Art Schools, as they were known, held their first annual exhibition at which their work was displayed for the public to admire. It was the fourth annual exhibition, however, held in Torquay itself which really brought the schools to the notice of the public. Phillips managed to get Queen Victoria's daughter, Princess Louise, to open the exhibition in her capacity as the President of the Recreative Evening Schools.

Judging by reports in the Torquay Times and South Devon Advertiser of 9th May, 1890 the whole town considered this a great event and every street was hung with bunting. Mr Shapcott, it reports, an ironmonger had two stars and the letters V.R. in gas jets as decoration of his premises. Gas was a popular form of decoration but the Torquay Times themselves went one better and displayed a "handsome bouquet of flowers" in each of their five windows and in the centre of each bouquet were two incandescent electric lamps the existence and beauty of which seemed almost to overwhelm the reporter! After the atmosphere of the town the atmosphere of the exhibition, held in the Bath Rooms, may have appeared rather sombre as there was nothing inside to detract from the work exhibited. The first exhibit the visitor would see, we are told by the newspaper report, "is a large collection of very quaint pitchers, pots and models made for South Kensington by 'Sam', who can also be seen plying his potter's wheel, which is the original Barnet Common type". The 'Sam' referred to is Sam Main who worked at the Aller Vale Pottery and who left in 1905 to work with Charles Collard at Poole. He was quite a young lad in 1890 but a very skilled workman and his work received much attention; Princess Louise watched him working at the wheel and afterwards autographed a model he had made and presented it to him. Sam's name was already well known because prior to this he had made "a few crates of his quaint pots for the South Kensington museum and being much pleased with his order, and to prevent any mistake, rudely inscribed on the bottom of each 'Sam made it' ". He can be seen at Aller Vale in plate 40 and working at the Dorset Art Pottery in plate 43.

Many potteries were represented at the exhibition, Brannam of Barnstaple exhibited his sgraffito ware, and work from his pottery by J. S. Dewdney, W. S. Baron and T. Liverton. The Torquay Terra-Cotta Company had an extensive show including several beautiful statuettes of classical subjects, a replica of Focardi's 'You Dirty Boy', and some new enamelling after the manner of Linthorpe, called Stapleton ware. Sir E. Elton, Bart of Clevedon Court showed a magnificent collection of pottery as did Mr de Morgan of Great Malborough Street. Unfortunately the Watcombe Pottery refused to exhibit, this caused considerable disappointment and regret.

Of course the relatively new Aller Vale Pottery was represented with examples of all their styles of pottery, the highlights of which were three terracotta vases two and a half feet high thrown and finished on the wheel by Thomas Lewis, and decorative sgraffito plaques by Senor Marcucci. The reporter for the Pottery Gazette was particularly struck by the Aller Vale slip work including vases and tiles by Mr C. Butler-Stoney, a well known exhibitor at the Royal Academy, and hon. secretary of the exhibition. The correspondent said that he "has discovered some fascination in clay slips and produces very charming effects in his flower pieces and in the depicting of Brixham trawlers". Miss Phillips, John Phillips' sister, exhibited some pieces on the stand including the vase with which she won first prize at the Newton Abbot Exhibition in 1881 and a small vase exhibited in the South Kensington collection which had recently been bought by the government for the South Kensington museum. The latter had been made at the Aller Vale pottery and was decorated in "Oriental design under glaze". The Cottage Art Classes themselves showed a splendid display of ironwork made by the local smiths in addition to work in other metals, notably brass and copper repoussé work. Needlework, carved work and an entirely handmade forty hour clock of very complicated mechanism (which received special attention) were also exhibited.

"The chef d'oeuvre of the exhibition and of the potter's art" according to the Pottery Gazette "was the bas relief in terracotta by the Princess Louise. It was a large piece taken from the Idylls of the Kings, the scene depicted being AEnid driving through the woods the horses of the slain robber, while the jealous Gerant — her husband — follows at a distance". Perhaps it was this exhibit which led her husband the Marquis of Lorne to say that it was the "best exhibition of decorative art that he had ever seen in the provinces".

After opening and inspecting the exhibition Princess Louise moved on to lay the foundation stone of the new pier which she did with surprising skill according to the newspaper report. Possibly it was not really surprising as one of her main interests and hobbies was sculpturing! This was not the end of her links with the pottery and schools, she became a patroness and made several useful suggestions from time to time which included the following inscription for a loving cup:

Come fill me full of liquor sweet,
For that is good when friends do meet,
But pray take care don't let me fall,
Lest you lose your liquor jug and all.

By this period the work of organisations such as the Home Arts and Industries Association, the Recreative Evening Schools and locally the Devon Arts and Crafts Society had grown by leaps and bounds. John Phillips gave a lecture at Barnstaple on the subject in 1890 in which he sums up his philosophy and that of the societies. "Amid the din of political and other strife there is arising a healthier tone, one of greater contentment, and of greater enjoyment of life, from a growing appreciation and the use of the good things around us, given us for our enjoyment, and a growing sympathy that is fostered by these societies between the cultured and refined mind and the uncultured."

An article in the Pottery Gazette of 1903 written by a close acquaintance sums up particularly well Phillips' personality and life's work. "He was an enthusiast — some called him a 'crank'. The world is deeply indebted to its cranks. I remember how earnest he was when — seated in my own room — he related to me the difficulties he experienced in getting workmen to work just as he wanted them to work, and how, as a consequence, he adopted the same method as that pursued by the late Henry Doulton — he took young boys and girls and trained them to do what their elders could do, but would not. He founded the School of Art at Newton Abbot, and so interested the Princess Louise in his scheme of training young artistic workers, that she went down and opened the school, making several purchases of Mr Phillips' goods. If Mr Phillips had possessed commercial keenness equal to his artistic ability, he would have become a millionaire. But he did not. Like many others he cared little for the commercial side of his work. He was bent on producing artistic but inexpensive pieces to take the place of the incongruous ornaments that then abounded in so many homes. He produced them, and was surprised that the production did not pay him!"

Processes

Because of the ideals behind the formation of the Aller Vale pottery and the influence of the arts and crafts movement all processes were carried out in the traditional manual way and all materials used were obtained locally. There were deposits of clay all around Aller and, once dug, the clay was cleaned by means of a water wheel; this drove a drum with spikes which churned up the clay while a small stream flowed over it. The clay dissolved in the water and was carried away leaving the gravel and other impurities which sank to the bottom and could easily be removed. The water carrying the clay was taken to settling pits and then put into drying flues in order to get the clay to the normal fairly solid state.

The first stage in pot making is to take a lump of clay and to shape it on a potter's wheel. The craftsman who does this is known as a thrower, and at Aller Vale the wheel was a metal disc which was made to revolve by ropes connected to a large wooden wheel worked by a boy. This was the traditional method and somewhat wasteful of labour and had been replaced at most potteries by wheels driven by the potter's foot, but at Aller they preferred the traditional method "for fear of degrading the hand work ideal". These processes are described in an article in Country Life, 1901. It states that a competent thrower could throw about twenty-four large vases, eighteen inches high, in one day, and that at that time five throwers were employed. Standard shapes of pots were of course produced but no two pots are likely to be exactly identical in shape. A record of the weight of clay to produce a particular shape was kept, the weighed ball of clay was then drawn up by hand on the wheel and could be measured by gauges to check the required height and width. This can be seen in plates 43 and 53 showing throwers at work at Crown Dorset and Honiton at the beginning of this century. The pots were then removed from the wheel by sliding a wire underneath (the wiremarks can often be seen on the base of the finished pot) and then left to dry 'leather dry'.

When the pots were dry enough to be handled, the turners polished them off on a lathe, smoothing and finishing the items that needed it, such as cups, and making sure that teapot lids were a good fit; again the machines were driven by boys who operated the treadles. This was obviously part of the boys' education; while they were providing the energy they were learning by watching experts at work.

The next stage was normally to dip the exterior of the pot into a thin coloured slip, the inside was left unslipped so that the clay can nearly always be seen on the inside of the pieces. The mottoes and sgraffito patterns could be scratched if required through the slip when dry and then decoration was applied. The decoration was applied by brush and was normally of coloured clays or slips, of a fairly thick consistency which left the pattern raised on the finished article.

Once decorated the pots were put into oval clay boxes, called saggars, these were piled up in the kiln where they stayed for twenty-four hours during firing. The Aller Vale biscuit kiln could hold up to 1,000 saggars. After this the articles looked like flower pots in texture, they were then dipped into coloured glazes. Aller Vale had some very good glazes which were made on the premises of local materials, and even the enamel colours were derived from local minerals which were chemically treated and oxidised at the works. It was very unusual indeed for a pottery of this size to produce its own glazes. The glazed pottery was then put into box ovens where the colour of the glaze changed in the firing process.

By the end of the century between fifty and sixty men and boys were employed by the pottery. No women were employed. The ware was exported all over the world, to Australia, the United States, Germany, etc.. However, recession was just around the corner and styles were beginning to change away from the arts and crafts ideas of hand-made articles towards mass production and soon the pottery would be forced to change its ideas and produce cheap items for the tourist market.

There is no doubt that the principles put into practice by John Phillips at Aller Vale had a lasting influence on Charles Collard's working methods. Years later when he ran the Honiton Pottery he was still implementing these ideals, thus the pottery dug its own clay, made its own glazes and all the pots were entirely hand-made. This is not to say that he was backward looking, he was one of the first to use an oil kiln in place of a coal one and was a great innovator of new methods where they did not conflict with his ideals.

Chapter 2

Aller Ware

Styles and Designs

In 1886, when Collard joined Aller Vale as an apprentice at the age of twelve, the pottery was just beginning to develop its own distinctive styles. Some of the very early wares had been terracotta, following the examples of Watcombe and the Torquay Terra-Cotta Company, but these were quickly displaced by glazed pottery much of which was liberally decorated. This was the fashion of the time and probably also appealed to the students more than the rather drab terracotta pieces.

Barbotine

One of the earliest styles was known as Barbotine, a term which was French in origin and meant designs drawn by means of a slip of creamy consistency (of white pipe clay) freely trailed on in the manner of icing sugar on a cake. The application of this technique to earthenware was developed by Ernest Chaplet in 1871 at the Laurin factory at Bourg-la-reine and presumably spread to England in the 1880s. The Barbotine decoration at Aller Vale was nearly always a painting of flowers usually done on a rough textured or stippled surface which sometimes looks like the surface of an orange. Although most of the pieces produced at Aller Vale were of red clay, some white clay ware was made particularly during the earlier years. Presumably white clay was used because it had a greater plasticity and was therefore more suitable for some shapes than the red clay. Sometimes, too, a mixture of white and red clay was used which produced a body that looks a pinky-buff in colour. Many of the Barbotine vases were made with this mixture of clay and appear buff in colour, the remainder were produced in white clay. These vases were sometimes small (three inches high) and simple in shape but more often were larger more important pieces of more elaborate design.

Usually the flowers were naturalistic paintings of roses, moondaisies, convolvuli, etc., sometimes however the painter let his fantasies run riot and some vases have very exotic looking flowers drawn either from the imagination or from the eastern pottery the students were given to study. These flowers were painted on different coloured grounds, the most popular of which was a dullish mid blue, this was closely followed in popularity by a bright yellow; dark green and peach were also used. Very often the ground shaded from dark to light from the base to the top of the vase. A very fine example of this ware can be seen in plate 1, which has perhaps a significant similarity to the Jacobean pattern produced many years later by the Collards at Honiton, see plate 18. The flowers were normally painted on the front of the vase only and the back was plain except for a stem and leaf design which looks rather like a palm tree. This distinctive design can be found on many of the Barbotine vases and can be a guide to identification although it must be noted that similar designs did appear on vases produced by other potteries. Sometimes the 'palm tree' was replaced by ears of corn, a butterfly or dragonfly. The vase pictured in plate 2 is an unusual Barbotine pattern with a dragonfly on one side and star-like flowers on the other on a peach ground. It is marked on the base with a scratched 'CC', this presumably stands for Charles Collard. Signed or initialled pieces of Aller Vale pottery are very rare indeed and only test pieces or pieces made as presents are normally signed on the base with the maker's name or initials.

Much of the early Aller Vale ware does not bear a pottery mark and is therefore difficult to identify unless one is familiar with the pottery. However, sometimes small impressed marks, believed to be turners' marks, can be found on the base if one looks closely. Four marks have been identified by Mrs Pat Barber, an expert on Aller Vale pottery; they are a crescent, a Maltese cross, a letter 'T' and a shape which can be best described as resembling a bow-tie. The pottery mark when it does appear on these early pieces is impressed and has the words ALLER VALE in serif capitals, see appendix I, mark 5.

The Barbotine pattern is one of the very few Aller Vale patterns without a code number, presumably because each piece was unique and could not really be reordered in that an identical piece could not be made later by simply knowing the pattern number because of the variation in the flower decoration. It is true that these were early pieces on the whole, the majority being made in the 1880s, but as one is pictured in C. Monkhouse's article in the Magazine of Art of 1891 and as another is signed 'CC' it seems likely that production of this pattern continued until the mid 1890s by which time the pattern number system was well under way. There were of course other pieces that were done as 'one offs' and not given a code. The design of dragonflies, stylised birds and trailing leaves has been seen on several pieces, one of which is pictured in plate 32. It can also be seen in the photograph taken in 1897 on the vase on the ground nearest the left hand side, plate 40. Presumably this design was not used regularly enough to warrant a pattern number. On the other hand, the coronation pattern used later for Edward VII's coronation was given a code number, M2; this seems rather strange as it could not be a pattern that was repeated and in any case could be identified quite easily without the aid of a code.

Persian Pattern

Virtually all the other patterns became standardised and were given a code number. These were introduced around 1890 and therefore earlier pieces do not bear code numbers. In addition to pattern codes shape numbers were introduced at the same time; the shape numbers ran well beyond 1,000 by the time the pottery closed which indicates the variety of pieces made. The pattern codes are a letter of the alphabet followed by a number. The first, and Collard's favourite pattern, being A1, is known as the Persian pattern; the name is misleading because it was actually derived from Turkish pottery rather than Persian. The Ottoman Empire reached its peak artistically during the sixteenth century and one of its greatest forms of expression was in the pottery produced at Isnik. The Ottoman style par excellence was the 'quatre-fleurs' pattern, a piece of Isnik pottery decorated in this design is illustrated in plate 34. Again the name, 'quatre-fleurs', is in error because the design often exceeded four flowers, however the four most popular flowers used in the decoration which typify the style were tulips, carnations, hyacinths and roses. As can be seen from the plate these are stylised rather than natural flowers, arranged in patterns, with borders decorated with arabesques or scrolls. The early Isnik decorations were in deep cobalt blue, turquoise and green on a white ground; later a rich brown-red colour was added known as Armenian bole, this had to be applied thickly and was consequently raised above the other decoration. Many of the pieces in the British Museum come from the Henderson bequest of 1878, including the plate shown in this book, and these may well have been the pieces studied by Collard and his colleagues at Aller Vale. It is certain that the students at Aller Vale studied the 'quatre-fleurs' design amongst the other ancient pottery supplied by Phillips because the A1 pattern is almost identical in the shape and colour of the flowers.

Collard was fascinated all his life by Isnik pottery; he often borrowed books with plates of Turkish pottery from the library to study. What is believed to be his apprentice piece, a mug illustrated in plate 3, was decorated with the A1 pattern, and he used and developed the pattern all his life and was still using it forty years later at Honiton as can be seen from plate 21. This Honiton pot is interesting because it incorporates the Isnik 'Saz' pattern which was hardly ever used at Aller Vale and so proves that Collard was still studying pottery and altering his styles quite late on in his life. The 'Saz' style gets its name from the reed pen (saz) with which the Turkish drew pictures, the design looks rather like a long feather or leaf with a serrated edge. Isnik pottery was very popular towards the end of the last century but has now been largely forgotten because it relies for its appeal on its decoration rather than on the structure and texture of the pot which is fashionable today. Amongst other people to be inspired by it were William de Morgan and the Frenchman Teodore Deck. However interest has been revived to some extent recently with an exhibition held in 1982 of the decorative arts from the Ottoman Empire and its accompanying book 'Tulips, Arabesques and Turbans'.

The very early pieces of A1 are on a pale honey-beige background and the leaves appear to swirl around much as seaweed might in water, this effect is heightened by a tendency for the colours to run slightly under the glaze. Gradually the ground became paler until late pieces are almost white; in addition the blue tulips and other flowers are usually decorated with coloured blobs of slip in red-brown on early pieces in this pattern made before about 1892; but after this the colour of these blobs changes to a pale yellow. These differences can be seen in plates 3 and 4. All A1 pieces have tulips and hyacinths painted in slip in blue, normally a mid to dark blue, and carnations and roses in a red-brown. Apart from the green leaves, yellow highlights and a dark brown used for outlining, these are the only colours used. The flowers developed over the years and by the later period, 1892-1902, a rather attractive blue rosette shaped flower was introduced and a seed head outlined in red-brown appears quite often; see plate 4. (Some earlier pieces bear a very faintly outlined seed head.) The clay used at Aller Vale for this pattern was almost always white but when the design was reproduced later at other potteries it was nearly always done on red clay which was then covered in a white slip.

Collard's Early Training

It is difficult to be certain when this Persian pattern was introduced at Aller, but it is thought to be during the mid 1880s and was still in production when Collard left the pottery in 1902 although its popularity seems to have declined in the late 1890s. Occasionally pieces were produced well into the twentieth century; it was still being advertised amongst other patterns in an advertisement in the Pottery Gazette during 1921. The pattern may have been in use before Collard joined the firm, and was certainly used before he became a decorator, but he took it over and became its greatest exponent at the pottery. When he first joined the firm at the age of twelve he started as was the custom by learning the processes. He did this so thoroughly that not only could he perform all the different pottery processes, but he understood them so that he was able to take them and adapt them, for instance by building his own kilns when he founded his own pottery subsequently. On a different level he had his own allotment as a boy at the pottery. Phillips was keen to encourage the lads to grow their own flowers and vegetables so that they acquired a knowledge of agriculture as well as of manufacturing; to this end he gave every boy a piece of land on which to grow whatever he liked, the results of which could be exhibited at a summer show held every year for that purpose. Apart from gardening Collard also used his spare time for reading and studying art all of which helped to further his knowledge. As late as the 1899/1900 session of the Torquay School of Science and Art, when he was twenty six, he was awarded the Committee prize for success in the Art Examination and chose as his prize 'Lessons on Decorative Design' by Frank Jackson. By this time he was established as a decorator which initially was his greatest interest, this may well have been because he had the good fortune to study under the guidance of Senor Marcucci, a man he much admired.

Senor Marcucci, an Italian, probably joined Aller Vale in the autumn of 1889 and was employed both as a decorator and as a teacher at the Cottage Art Schools. Collard, by now fifteen, had probably learnt most of the pottery processes and carried out his apprenticeship cleaning the clay, weighing the balls of clay, operating the throwing and turning wheels, etc., and had probably just begun decorating when Senor Marcucci joined the business that winter. We can first judge the influence of Marcucci on the Aller Vale pottery by the pieces he exhibited at the Cottage Art Schools Exhibition in 1890; where we are told he exhibited "his new and beautiful designs", these included "majolica ware in the Italian style" which he introduced at Aller Vale and a range of decorative plaques in "coloured sgraffito". His new designs and knowledge of techniques helped to inspire Collard and his fellows and as a consequence the range of designs and their technical execution kept on improving throughout the 1890s. A jardiniere stand made by Senor Marcucci, and signed by him, is shown in plate 33. This very fine piece is fired and painted but not glazed and must have been made by him soon after he joined Aller Vale, and it demonstrates clearly the influence he had at the pottery. The scrolls change into patterns which resemble dolphins, this idea was used and developed by the Aller Vale decorators in the 1890s. Both scroll and dolphin patterns are discussed later in this chapter. They came originally of course from Renaissance designs, for instance some of the chased stonework in the church of Sta Maria dei Miracoli,

Venice is very similar to Aller Vale painted scrollwork. Some panels from this church are reproduced in Owen Jones' Grammar of Ornament, a book which Phillips probably made available to the students at the pottery.

Other patterns

Returning to the designs produced by Aller Vale, A2 represents a floral pattern similar to the Persian A1 but painted in slip on a blue ground, rather than a creamy white one, in a range of colours which include flesh pink. A3 is the same pattern on a green ground.

The codes starting with the letter B represent patterns of leafy scrolls similar to Marcucci's work in plate 33. Whether Marcucci was the originator of these designs is uncertain because the first multi-coloured versions appear to have been made in the late 1880s prior to the introduction of the coding system, these were non standard in colour for instance scrolls of pink, brown, pale blue and green on a ground of mustard yellow. About the same time a design called the Renaissance pattern was developed which consisted of white leaves and scrolls on a coloured ground, usually dark blue, when the coding system developed this colour combination of the pattern became B5. An example of the Renaissance pattern decorated by Joseph Bening was exhibited at the 1890 Cottage Art Schools Exhibition. From these early examples coded scroll patterns evolved, thus B1 represents a pattern of scrolls painted in combinations of brown, beige, blue, white, green and yellow on a cream ground, B2 on a green ground and B3 on a dark blue ground. There are other colour combinations of the scroll pattern, these and all the patterns are listed in appendix II. Usually the scrolls terminate in a flower head of three petals, which on the earlier pieces tend to appear to be almost wilting, on later examples the centre petal becomes larger than the other two and the flower looks firmer, as in plate 37. The decorator at Aller Vale particularly noted for this ware was apparently Samuel Bradford who is pictured in plate 40 sitting second from the left in the second row up. However Collard obviously also decorated in this style, as can be seen from plate 39 taken in 1901, where he is decorating some large vases with a scroll type decoration. He also continued to use this pattern throughout his career, as can be seen for example in plates 9 and 10. Both of these plates show the rather distinctive style of scrolls that Collard developed later where highlights are achieved by shading; to achieve this the colour is applied thickly in some areas of the decoration and allowed to thin as the brush gradually runs out of paint. This allowed the terminals to be finished in a graceful and delicate manner; whereas in the normal Aller Vale scrolls, painted in a rather thick slip, the shading effect cannot be achieved and highlights were made by superimposing a different coloured slip.

A plain version of the scroll pattern, which consists of mid-blue scrolls on a white ground became very popular with the public and many examples of it can be found by the collector. One of the reasons for its popularity was that the Princess of Wales, later Queen Alexandra, saw this ware on a visit to the pottery and placed a special order for it. It is claimed that she was very pleased with the execution of the work and at her request this design became known as Sandringham ware. This pattern is rather surprisingly coded C1.

Another Aller Vale pattern which Collard used later at Poole was the D1 pattern of a stylised narcissus surrounded by scroll type leaves, this can be seen in plate 5. The decoration appears always to be in yellows, creams and a pinky-brown on a dark blue ground on Aller Vale pieces.

A pattern which became popular later at Aller Vale, perhaps as a replacement for the Barbotine style, was the K2 pattern, early versions of this exist but the majority were made in the late 1890s. K2 stands for flowers in slip on a green ground, usually a dark green. One of the flowers often used in the K2 pattern, presumably because of the attractive colour contrast, was the daffodil, many of these are cream rather than yellow and often the trumpets were painted in a different shade to the petals. The daffodil design remained popular and was used afterwards by Watcombe (later part of the same company as Aller Vale), Longpark and by Collard when he first went to Poole. However the Aller Vale K2 is in no way restricted to daffodils, many different types of flowers can be found by the collector. Usually the flowers are painted in slip, but very occasionally a sgraffito design can be found. In addition to the most popular ground, green, K1 represents flowers on a cream ground, K3 ginger, K4 blue and K5 on a chocolate ground.

Another pattern that appears on a dark green ground is the M3 pattern of a heron or stork standing on one leg in shallow water amongst reeds. This pattern is rare and normally appears on large vases some of which are not marked with a code on the base. Many of these birds must have been painted by Collard and he was obviously still very proud of them years later as can be seen from his letter heading at Poole, plate 51, where a vase decorated with a bird in the Aller Vale style is included in the photograph.

By contrast the Q1 pattern as it became known was entirely different to most of the other Aller Vale designs in technique and style. Some Q1 pieces are early, obviously predating the coding system, and therefore are not incised Q1 on the base, but the pattern was popular and continued in production until the beginning of this century. It was probably introduced by Senor Marcucci and is a design of flowers and scrolls outlined, through a cream ground, in sgraffito. The design was then lightly washed in with different colours principally cobalt blue, dark leaf green and mustard yellow under a transparent glaze, whereas of course the vast majority of Aller Vale designs were painted in slip. This decoration was used on both small and large pots, the design changing to suit the size and shape of the piece sometimes to such an extent that the design was purely abstract. In any case bands of abstract decoration often formed borders around the piece vertically as well as horizontally, being used vertically to split up the main floral design from a sgraffito motto or verse, as can be seen in plate 35. This style of decoration in similar colours including the vertical bands was used by Collard at the Honiton Pottery in the 1930s, the only difference being that the scrolls and flowers were replaced by a geometric floral design illustrated in plate 27.

Occasionally the Q1 sgraffito pattern was elaborated and the scrolls turned into a leaping dolphin. Dolphins were also used as a decoration on non-sgraffito pieces; for instance a vase, whose neck fanned out to hold a series of flowers individually, was ingeniously decorated with a dolphin swimming downwards on the vase so that its tail led upwards and became the fan shaped neck of the vase. Dolphins decorated jardinieres as well as vases, sometimes in such a stylised form that only their heads are recognisable, see plate 36. The idea for this design would appear to have been introduced by Senor Marcucci as some of the scrolls in plate 33 resemble dolphins. It is thought that many of the Aller Vale dolphin patterns were painted by Collard because there is considerable similarity between these, especially in the drawing of the dolphin's eye, and the work he did later at other potteries involving dolphins and other sea creatures.

All of the previous patterns discussed were used on major pieces but Aller Vale did not neglect the cheaper end of the market and produced many designs on small items aimed at the tourist memento market and also cheap practical pieces aimed towards local working people. This may have been done to make the business more commercially viable, but knowing Phillips' character it was probably done to give the less able boys a chance to achieve something worthwhile. The majority of these pieces had a design in slip on one side and a motto scratched through the slip on the other. Some of the mottoes were just a couple of words, others were as long as four or even six lines of verse, and they generally expressed the Victorian virtues of hard work and sober living, in a lighthearted rather than a pious manner. Mottoes had been included on some of the early Aller Vale pieces mainly on the sgraffito Q1 pattern and on the Abbotskerswell (I4) pattern, which consists of slip applied in simple strokes to represent a daisy pattern. Unfortunately it is outside the scope of the book to discuss all of the Aller Vale patterns in detail, however a full list of all the known pattern codes appears in appendix II.

It is interesting to note that some of the mottoes are quotations from Charles Kingsley, for example:

> Do the work that's nearest,
> Though its dull at whiles;
> Helping, when you meet them,
> Lame dogs over stiles.

Some pieces of the Q1 pattern have been found marked on the

base Westward Ho Faience rather than Aller Vale, it seems likely that these pieces were made at Aller Vale and it is possible that Kingsley inspired this series much as Thomas Hardy, the Dorset writer, inspired Collard to produce a series of 'Hardy ware' later at the Crown Dorset pottery.

The main use, however, for mottoes on small pieces was on the patterns coded N1, N2 and N3. These patterns later became synonymous with South Devon pottery generally and were copied by nearly all of the local potteries, notably Watcombe, Longpark and Hart and Moist. Perhaps the word 'copied' is rather harsh because these were patterns done by decorators who probably moved on to other potteries subsequently, taking their painting skills with them. These patterns were also taken by Collard to Poole and used during his first year or so there.

N1 stands for Scandy and was probably developed from the earlier Aller Vale pattern called Rhodian, this was a misnomer because the design is believed to have been developed from Isnik pottery again and not from pottery from Rhodes. The Scandy pattern developed and changed as it was taken from pottery to pottery and each developed its own slightly different variation. The typical Aller Vale Scandy pattern can be seen in plate 38.

N2 stood for a coloured cockerel and N3 for a black cockerel. At Aller Vale most of the cockerels were coloured ones but later on at other potteries the majority were black. In addition to the motto on the reverse the Aller Vale cockerels usually have 'Good Morning' scratched sideways through the slip, so as to appear to be issuing from the cockerel's beak. The cockerels are painted in a variety of bright colours usually dark and light green, dark and pale blue and red-brown and appear particularly on items that might be used on an ordinary breakfast table, such as small jugs, mugs and plates.

It is interesting that at Aller Vale only one person was employed at one time to scratch the mottoes. This is in contrast to Collard's pottery at Poole subsequently, where all of the girl decorators were allowed to do this work. Furthermore at Aller Vale, with occasional exceptions, only two handwritings appear during the life of the pottery. The first handwriting which appears on early pieces only (normally red clay ware with unglazed bases), shows a somewhat introverted character, the writing leans backwards slightly, the letters are scratched thickly and are rather 'fuzzy' in appearance. About 1890 the second hand appears and continues to the closure of the Aller Vale pottery in 1924. Many of the workers including the motto scratcher were then transferred to Watcombe pottery and the same handwriting can then be found on Watcombe pieces for a few years. This is a very attractive hand, scratched deep into the clay, with rather fancy capital letters — it is no wonder that he kept the job for so many years.

Clays, Shapes and Marks

The pottery developed its own distinctive shapes as well as designs. One of the most popular was the jug with a large rim which is pierced by the handle passing through it, this can be seen in plate 50. This plate is not of an Aller Vale jug but of a piece made by Collard later at Poole and illustrates the influence that Aller Vale had upon him in his first years at Poole. Another Aller Vale shape that his pottery at Poole used was the four funnelled tulip vase, although at Poole some examples rather interestingly have only three funnels. This design came originally from eastern pottery and was copied by the throwers at Aller Vale, the first pieces they made were small with relatively large vertical funnels, complete copies of their eastern counterparts. Later, however, the style developed and was used on large vases such as the one pictured in plate 37. As in the photograph, these later pieces are most often decorated with a scroll design and look most attractive in the Sandringham pattern which shows off the shape clearly.

Nearly all of the Sandringham ware is made of white clay as is, of course, most of the ware with a white ground such as B1; with the exception of Barbotine, most of the other designs are done on red clay. This red clay is a distinctive orangey red and unmarked pieces of the pottery can be identified by the colour and texture of the clay, especially the early pieces which nearly always have an unglazed flat base. The later pieces have a glazed base and the colours in the glaze, especially the blues and greens, tend to mask the colour of the clay, which can appear under those conditions to be quite a darkish brown. Quite a few of these pieces have in addition a recessed base.

Some of the early pieces made of red clay with unglazed bases bear the mark MADE IN DEVON impressed on the base without any mention of the Aller Vale pottery. Others, if marked, have 'Aller Vale' scratched on the base in handwriting sometimes with the word 'Devon' as well. After the first few years the majority of pieces were marked and bore the impressed mark ALLER VALE in serif capitals, as mentioned earlier when discussing the Barbotine ware. Another mark was introduced about 1891 with ALLER VALE in small neat capitals sometimes with the words DEVON and/or ENGLAND added. The letters H. H. & Co were incorporated into this mark in 1897 when Hexter and Humpherson took over the business after Phillips' death. These marks can be seen in appendix I.

Collard as a Decorator

By the middle of the 1890s Collard had become one of the top, if not the top decorator, at Aller. This can be seen from an article in the Country Life in 1901 which has a picture, reproduced in plate 39, of him decorating vases. There are several other illustrations in the article including one of Collard's subsequent employee at Poole, James Main decorating mugs, and another of Thomas Lewis, whose work was exhibited at the 1890 Exhibition, throwing a large vase. Presumably these people were considered to be the best in their field at Aller.

Collard passed on his skills to the next generation by teaching art and decorating at the cottage school at Coffinswell in John Easterbrook's cottage. However he was not very keen on this because he did not like walking home through the dark country lanes late in the evening! In his youth he cycled from Torquay to Aller and back, a journey of about four miles each way, but later he took lodgings locally with Mr and Mrs Hancock of Kingskerswell. Perhaps this was to avoid the dark country lanes or possibly he was keen to get away from his family and stand on his own feet. The Hancocks treated Collard like a son and he was very fond of them, and it was whilst he was living in their house that the rumour went round the village that Collard had £100 in a trunk under his bed. Most of the lads at Aller Vale, including Collard, enjoyed backing the horses, but for some reason (perhaps a long string of losers!?) he decided to stop betting and save his money much to the amazement of his friends. His savings accumulated and he bought a trunk to keep them in and thus the rumour that he had £100 under his bed was true. If he had not started to save in this way he would not have been in a position to start his own pottery in later years.

It was through Phillips that Collard had one of his greatest decorating triumphs which was to decorate a tea service that Lord Clinton was to present to Prince George and Princess May (later Queen Mary). Lord Clinton was President of the Devonshire Association in 1890, this organisation had been formed in 1862 for the advancement of science, literature and art. Lord Clinton was obviously very impressed with the work of Phillips, and it was probably due to his influence that in the year of his presidency Phillips presented a paper to the Association on the work of the three village schools urging that more should be formed throughout the county. Perhaps as a result of his urging or perhaps the spreading of bureaucracy, the Technical Education Committee of Devonshire County Council took over his work at the schools in 1893. This was probably just as well as by then Phillips was fifty-seven and had only a few years left to live.

The Decline of Aller Vale and the merger with Watcombe

On February 25th 1897 John Phillips died, at the age of sixty-one. There is a tablet in commemoration in Abbotskerswell church "erected by the villagers, Sunday school teachers and children of this parish to commemorate his seventeen years of work amongst them". This obviously refers to his work for the cottage art school at Abbotskerswell.

A photograph, reproduced in plate 40, of all the Aller Vale workers was taken in 1897 in the grounds of Phillips' house at Moor Park, Aller. Judging by the vegetation in the photograph it must have been very shortly after Phillips' death, possibly as a record before the pottery was sold, and apart from showing the fifty-two workers illustrates one or two marvellous pieces of their work. Phillips' Moor Park residence can be seen in the background.

The death of Phillips was the beginning of the end for the

Aller Vale pottery, it was bought by Hexter, Humpherson and Company of Kingsteignton manufacturers of tiles and sanitary fittings. The pottery continued much as it had before for the next four years, expanding slowly, another ten employees were taken on and some very fine pottery was produced. Then Hexter, Humpherson bought the Watcombe pottery in nearby Torquay and the two potteries were combined under the name of the Royal Aller Vale and Watcombe Pottery Company. After this the two potteries produced similar wares and gradually the standard of work dropped as more and more of the top workers left. The change in public taste to mass produced rather than hand-made items that occurred around this period obviously accounted to some extent for the decline in standards at the pottery, and as it was now being run as a commercial organisation rather than a philanthropic venture meant that current taste had to be borne in mind when planning production. However, so many of the top employees left to join other companies or to start their own businesses during the first two or three years of this century that it must be assumed the pleasant working atmosphere and the freedom for the individual worker to decide what to produce and how it should be decorated, which was so much a hallmark of Philips' Aller Vale no longer existed under the new ownership.

After the merger of the two potteries the Watcombe pottery changed its style and for some time produced ware similar to that of Aller Vale, this included run of the mill lines such as motto ware decorated with scandies or cockerels which remained popular at Watcombe for many years. These of course were decorated in slip as were the new style pieces of better quality which included Aller Vale patterns such as scrolls, Persian (A1), daffodils and wading birds. Several Aller Vale workers were transferred to Watcombe to teach its employees the Aller shapes and designs; James Main was possibly one as it is thought that he worked there at some stage of his career. Collard moved to Watcombe in some senior capacity, probably in charge of decoration, and one or two fine pieces of his work from this period bear the Watcombe pottery mark.

The vase decorated with a wading bird, plate 6, is believed to have been painted by Collard as it is very similar to that shown in

Collard's Crown Dorset letter heading illustrated in plate 51. The jardiniere in plate 7 is decorated with an elaborate scroll pattern and although not signed by him can definitely be attributed to Collard because it incorporates so many characteristics of his painting. These include the intertwining stem and leaf on the left of the jardiniere which can clearly be seen in his work over the next year or so mainly at Hart and Moist, see page 43 and plates 8 and 41. Another such characteristic seen on this jardiniere is the 'crown' device discussed on page 60 and illustrated on a Crown Dorset piece in plate 10. The decoration on the jardiniere is clearly derived from Italian Renaissance designs and shows the strong influence that Marcucci had had upon Collard. The cherub is a most unusual form of decoration for Torquay pottery and seems entirely Italian in its inspiration.

Collard who had been such an admirer of Phillips and his ideals was obviously not happy under the new regime which offered no way for him to improve his position except by becoming manager. That would not have been a position to appeal to Collard as his interests lay in producing pottery himself and experimenting with new methods and designs. Therefore he had little choice and at the end of 1902 Collard left to go and work for Hart and Moist of Exeter. He left at Christmas that year and took with him a testimonial signed by Herbert Bulley, then the manager of Aller Vale and who was soon to become one of the owners of the Longpark pottery. He is pictured in plate 40 standing on the left hand end of the second row up. The testimonial that Bulley wrote on Christmas Eve 1902 for Collard said that he "has been in our employ for sixteen years and has at all times proved himself to be a most industrious and honest young man, he leaves our employ to better his position and we wish him well".

The Aller Vale pottery continued in production until 1924 producing mainly motto ware for the tourist market. Very few new designs were introduced, but those that were include cottages, windmills and boats; none of these carry a code number so presumably the code numbers ceased to be developed after the departure of many of the key employees around 1902/03, and it was only habit which made the remaining workers continue to use them for existing designs.

Chapter 3

The Turbulent Years

Hart and Moist and Longpark

The Hart and Moist Pottery

After leaving Aller Vale Collard found it very difficult to settle at other potteries. During 1903 and 1904 he tried working at Hart and Moist in Exeter and at Longpark in Torquay before deciding that he should be his own master and start his own pottery. The Hart and Moist Pottery that Collard joined in January 1903 had been in existence for seven years but had its origins in the earlier art potteries which were started in a rented malt-house at the junction of Exe Street and Napier Terrace in 1891. Two gentlemen by the name of Cole and Trelease put up the finance and the business traded under the name of the Exeter Art Pottery. Trelease appears to have been the manager of the pottery and Cole a sleeping partner. Their chief decorator was William Hart who had trained as a decorator at Aller Vale where he had of course met Charles Collard as a boy. Alfred Moist who was trained at the pottery in Bovey Tracey, and had also worked at Bristol and in the Staffordshire Potteries, joined the firm two years after its inception in 1893. For some reason the Exeter Art Pottery was terminated and Messrs Hart and Moist started the Devon Art Pottery in 1896 in St. Thomas, Exeter.

The wares produced by the Exeter Art Pottery had been of good quality and it appears that Messrs Hart and Moist took over the goodwill of the business as one piece has been seen bearing the impressed marks both of the Exeter Art Pottery and that of

Hart and Moist's new business. Surprisingly the old premises at 7 Exe Street remained unoccupied for quite a few years. The new pottery known either as the Devon Art Pottery, or more commonly just as Hart and Moist moved to purpose built premises. The two proprietors bought a field off Haven Road together with a cob barn and erected four new buildings, incorporating the original barn, around a courtyard. A year later Alfred's brother Joseph Moist moved down from Burslem to join the partnership.

Hart and Moist Wares

The pottery was not a very big affair and is thought never to have employed more than about ten workers, nevertheless it did produce some exceptionally fine pieces. During the remaining years of the nineteenth century most of their wares were similar in shape and design to those of the former Exeter Art Pottery. The most popular designs were flowers in a thick distinctive slip on grounds of dull blue, lime green, bottle green or brown under a thick glaze. Sometimes the flowers were replaced by scrolls, again applied in a thick slip. In addition they continued to produce a range of 'ancient wares' initiated by the Exeter Art Pottery, including tygs and three handled mugs which were decorated with simple brush strokes and sgraffito mottoes on a slip of dull green, pale blue or amber. All their wares were produced from red clay which was purchased from the Exeter Brick and Clay Company. Today the pottery can be recognised by this clay which is more brown than red in appearance and is fairly coarse containing noticeable black and white flecks. The base of the pottery is nearly always recessed and glazed, many pieces of the pottery are not marked but those that are are impressed in capitals 'H M EXETER'; see appendix I. One has to look hard on occasions to see this mark which is struck lightly and is often obscured by the thick glaze which most Hart and Moist pieces bear.

However at the beginning of this century their style of pottery changed and pieces more similar to those of Aller Vale were produced, presumably as the result of Aller Vale workers moving to join them. Their better production of this period is illustrated in plate 41 taken from an advertisement in the Pottery Gazette of January 1904 and as can be seen is some of the finest South

Devon art pottery. The production of pieces of this quality was very brief judging from their scarcity today and by the fact that their advertisements in the Pottery Gazette for the following years show no pieces of comparable quality. No more pieces were produced in the Aller Vale A1 (Persian) pattern after this brief spell and it seems certain that these pieces were decorated by Collard.

One fine example of Collard's work at Hart and Moist is seen in plate 8. The intertwining tendrils on the right of the vase are a distinctive characteristic of some of Collard's scrollwork and also appear on some of the Honiton scroll pieces that he very occasionally produced at that pottery in later years. They also appear on the Hart and Moist candlestick that appears in plate 41 and on the Watcombe jardiniere in plate 7. Other similarities in the scrollwork can be seen upon close inspection of the jardiniere and the large vases in plate 41.

Collard did not stay long at Hart and Moist, probably less than a year, but in that brief time he certainly left his mark on the pottery as can be seen from plate 41, just discussed. It is known that Collard was not happy at the pottery at Exeter, though this was not for personal reasons as he remained very friendly with Hart and saw him and his son, who became an Exeter estate agent, frequently in later life. Perhaps the reason he left was that the Moist brothers had picked up too many mechanised habits from the Potteries for his liking. It is quite possible that at this period the paints and glazes were bought from the potters' merchant's firm of Wengers of Etruria as they are believed to have been in later years. If this was so then Collard, brought up in the tradition of making paints and glazes in the pottery as was the custom at Aller, would have found this inconsistent with his views of what an 'art pottery' should be.

Some small items produced during this period at Hart and Moist were Aller Vale shapes, such as the jug with the large rim pierced by the handle, an example of this style of jug made later at the Dorset pottery can be seen in plate 50. Two other examples of Aller Vale shapes produced by Hart and Moist are a jug on which the lip is formed by making an indentation from the base to the rim on either side of the piece and secondly the typical four funnelled tulip vase, the Exeter version of which tends to have rather upright funnels. These pieces were often decorated in white slip on a dark blue ground with a scroll pattern being the most common design.

A quite common design but one believed unique to Hart and Moist is the 'daisy pattern'. This consists of a cream band on a dark green ground on which daisy heads in pale blue with brown eyes are painted in slip with their stems sweeping downwards through the green ground to cream coloured leaves below. Another design incorporating the cream band on a dark green ground (or very rarely a blue ground) is that of leafy scrolls terminating in stylised flowers with long flowing stamens. These are always painted in mid-green, cream, and red-browns and the cream band always bears a motto. For some reason this pattern and the previously discussed 'daisy pattern' are very rarely marked, though marked examples do exist. Lloyd Thomas in his book 'The Old Torquay Potteries' attributes this second pattern to the Brewer Broomhill Pottery at Torquay but it seems that most of the pieces encountered were made at Exeter. Two other patterns to be found with a brief accompanying motto are a Scandy pattern which is always in blue, red-brown and green and a rather shapely cockerel. These two latter patterns became the mainstay of Hart and Moist's production and continued to be popular until the business ran into financial difficulties and was forced to close in 1935. A black stamped mark 'Royal Devon Art Pottery' rather than the impressed company mark was used on some later pieces.

The Longpark Pottery

After leaving Hart and Moist Collard returned to Torquay and joined the Longpark Pottery which had been in existence since the 1880s. The ownership of this pottery had changed many times and appears to have changed yet again in 1903. It is thought that Herbert Bulley, the manager of the Aller Vale pottery who had given Collard such a glowing reference a year earlier, had bought the business with five other Aller Vale colleagues because they were not satisfied with life at Aller under the new proprietors. George Causey and Robert Skinner were two of the five partners who persuaded their respective brothers to leave Aller Vale and to come and work at the new Longpark

Pottery. George Bond was also a partner; it is not certain who the others were but it is likely that one of the five was Charles Collard.

It is not known precisely when Bulley and his colleagues took over Longpark but at an exhibition of ceramics, organised by the Royal Commission, which was held at St Louis in May 1904 a silver medal was awarded to H. E. Bulley, Longpark Potteries, Torquay for "a treatment of coloured clays or 'slips' on a 'raw clay' body, all pieces made and decorated by hand". Presumably Bulley and his partners must have taken over Longpark at least six months earlier to produce wares which they were happy to exhibit. It ought incidentally to be mentioned that Bulley was not himself a potter, he had started as a driver at Aller Vale and had worked his way up to become a sales representative and eventually the pottery manager. The fact that Bulley had no practical experience of making pottery seems to have been one of the reasons for Collard's brief stay at Longpark, as he thought Bulley a businessman rather than a potter. However even when he joined Longpark Collard probably had ideas of forming his own pottery. At first the new business was run as a partnership but on 28th February, 1905 it was incorporated as The Longpark Pottery Company Limited with a nominal share capital of £1,400, but it is unlikely that Collard was involved in the formation of the company as by this time he was well advanced with plans to start his own pottery at Poole. Unfortunately the records of the Longpark Company have been destroyed so it is uncertain who the shareholders were.

Collard's Work at Longpark

As at Hart and Moist Collard was soon making his mark upon their wares producing amongst other pieces the two handled vase decorated in the Aller Vale A1 (Persian) pattern seen in plate 42. The magnificent jardiniere with dolphin shaped handles seen in plate 9 was decorated by Collard with mythical sea creatures on each of the three sides. These are surrounded by scrolls which are very clearly painted in his distinctive style. He was to use sea creatures as decoration at Ilminster (see plate 16) and Poole subsequently, but as far as it is known this is the first time he had used them in this form, however vases decorated with dolphins had been produced earlier at Aller Vale by Collard, see plate 36.

In addition to these splendid pieces Collard also made a very humble inkpot which he sent to his sweetheart and future wife Emily Margaret Welsh. It is thought tht he first met her during the summer of 1902, while he was still at Aller Vale, when she was on holiday in Torquay with her sister, probably staying with friends of her family. She was then in her seventeenth year having been born on 24th September, 1885 and came from Standon near Ware in Hertfordshire where her father had a bakery business. They must have fallen in love almost at first sight and been very determined to marry because it was the start of a ten year courtship during which she lived in Standon and London and he in Torquay and later Poole. Perhaps her family thought that Charles Collard was not quite as good a match as she could make, or maybe, it was just the tradition in those days to wait until he had made his way in business before her parents allowed her to marry him. The inkpot Collard made and sent to Emily during 1904 bears the rather unusual impressed mark number 9 shown in appendix I and is scratched C.C. on the base. It is decorated with scrolls on a dark blue band above which is the message "jist zend a line tu lets know ow yu'm gwaine on", from which we can presume that she was not the most prolific of letter writers, and that possibly she made fun of his Devonshire accent. He used this idea of sending small pots with messages on them as mementoes a few years later when he had his own pottery at Poole.

Longpark Styles and Designs

The quality of the pottery produced under the new ownership was good. The decoration was above average under a glossy, rather yellow, glaze. The many new workers who joined Longpark at this period brought with them designs and patterns used at other local potteries. One of the first designs to be used and one which remained popular for so long that it typifies Longpark was its cockerel pattern. This was used on smaller items and may have been in existence before the Aller Vale men took over the pottery. Lloyd Thomas in his book 'The Old Torquay Potteries' records a piece decorated with a cockerel and marked 'Brewer Longpark Torquay', being the alleged mark of the previous proprietors. The piece to which the author refers does however bear a remarkable resemblance to cockerels bearing the mark 'H M Exeter'. The majority of the early 'Bulley'

Longpark cockerels were coloured and marked N2, later the N3 black cockerel became the norm. Thus the Aller Vale numbering system travelled with the pottery workers and Longpark Scandy pattern pieces bear the Aller Vale NI code. These Scandies differ slightly from the Aller Vale version, often having only three brush strokes in the centre and long thin side strokes which swing up around the centre which looks rather like the tail of a lyre bird. The Longpark workers seem to have felt that it rather resembled a 'peacock's feather' which is the name given to the Scandy pattern in 'Brunel's Tower' by Eden Philpotts. Whilst the book is a novel it is based on the Longpark Pottery and describes many of the patterns and processes of that pottery.

Further descriptions of the pottery produced at Longpark are outside the scope of this book because again Collard's stay was only a brief one and during the early months of 1905, just as the Longpark Company was being formed, he left to start his own pottery in Poole where he continued to use Torquay patterns such as Scandies and cockerels even with their Aller Vale pattern numbers in his first few years. The Longpark Pottery however remained in existence until 1957; the work produced was good until the 1930s when the management decided to concentrate mainly on the summer tourist trade at the expense of steady orders. From this point the struggle was always an uphill one, to such an extent that the employees often worked only three days a week in the winter and drew the dole on the remaining three days.

PART II
CROWN DORSET ART POTTERY

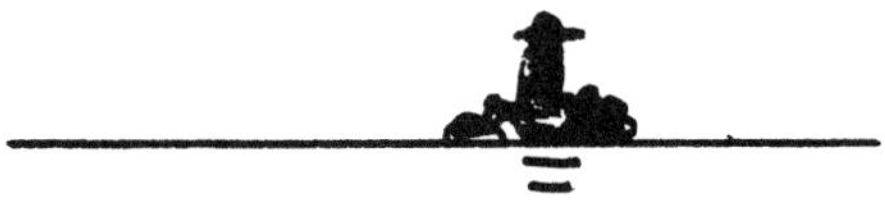

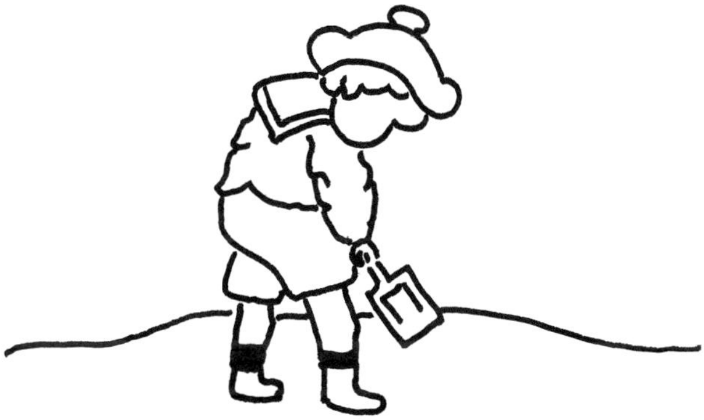

Vor Do'set dear

Chapter 4

A New Venture

Collard Poole Dorset

1903 and 1904, the years at Hart & Moist and Longpark had been unsettled ones for Collard, in fact he does not seem to have been entirely happy in his work since the death of John Phillips although he did produce some of his finest work during this period. It is known that he enjoyed the freedom that Phillips gave him to work on his ideas in his own way and that he was a fairly ambitious man who wished to succeed in life.

To solve the problem Collard decided to set up on his own. In order to do this he needed financial backing and of course a suitable pottery. He obtained the finance from the family of Whiteway Wilkinsons. William and John Whiteway Wilkinson were clay merchants. Whiteway and Co. of Kingsteignton had been in business for over a hundred years selling potters' blue ball, spur and ivory clays both to local potteries and those in Stoke on Trent and presumably it was through business connections that Collard knew the Whiteway Wilkinsons and sought their financial support.

The next problem was to find a pottery. Competition in the Torquay area was great with Aller Vale, Watcombe and Longpark in existence; Hart and Moist were of course producing wares in Exeter and on the north coast of Devon, at Barnstaple, Brannam, Baron and Lauder were all in existence at that time. Besides this he would be setting up and competing with ex colleagues.

Collard may have been pondering on the problem when he picked up the January 1905 copy of the Pottery Gazette, in which a correspondent wrote on Poole as a pottery centre. "Poole . . . is of no little interest to the potter, for it is situated on the confines of that interesting part of Dorset known as the Isle of Purbeck, from whence comes the well-known Dorset pottery clays; while around Poole itself are found many deposits of valuable pottery and stoneware clays." (An earlier article in the Pottery Gazette had stated that there was a twenty acre red clay pit adjacent to Poole Harbour.) "The existence of Poole Harbour enables the clay quarry owners and miners to ship their clay . . . at a cheap rate, while it also enables coal to be imported cheaply into Poole. There are several potteries in and about Poole which work up the local deposits. These clays are of very fine quality . . .". The writer failed to mention that nearby Bournemouth was rapidly developing as a holiday resort and this could provide plenty of customers for the cheaper pottery wares, such as the motto wares that Aller Vale had pioneered, which could be bought as little trinkets for the tourist to take back as a memory of a pleasant holiday or a present for a friend.

Whether or not he read the article in the Pottery Gazette Collard decided to start his pottery in Poole. The company, Charles Collard and Co. Ltd, later to trade under the name of the Crown Dorset Art Pottery, was registered on 10th March, 1905 with a capital of 200 shares of £5 each. On 8th June the shares were allotted, Collard put up half the money, £500, and the Whiteway Wilkinsons the remainder, and the next day a £500 mortgage was taken out on the two houses which were to become the pottery.

Collard had bought number 21 and number 23 Green Road from John Norman and Mrs James respectively. Green Road leads down to the shore near the Quay in Poole; it was only partially built up at the time but the terraced houses opposite were in existence and nearer the sea was an old 'powder' house. Apart from private dwellings the road housed a boot maker, a tailor and a cartage contractor as well as the Poole Borough Infectious Hospital.

Numbers 21 and 23 were ordinary private dwellings and had

to be converted into a pottery. The total outlay including the mortgage must have been almost exactly £1,500 because the company's documents list the registration fee of £45 and preliminary expenses of £968. 1. 9d. which was for "the purchase of property at Poole, the erection of a pottery, printing, purchase of company books, seal and sundries".

The building and its workers

A long two-storied workshop was erected at the back of the property, behind the two houses; from the back windows of which one could look out over Poole harbour and a backwater which ran behind the building. This caused the pottery to be flooded several times in later years. The ground floor of this building was fitted out with potters' wheels for it was here that the pots were to be thrown and turned and the first floor was to be used for decorating.

The entrance to the pottery was marked by two very large wooden gates, which later bore the words 'Crown Dorset Art Pottery'; by the entrance there was a lodge, 23 Green Road, in which Samuel Main the caretaker lived. Also at the front of the property, presumably 21 Green Road, there were showrooms and a general office. Collard had his own small private office/workshop at the back in which he did a lot of decorating and carried out experiments with glazes etc.. Outside, at the back and to the side of number 21, drying sheds were erected and kilns built: there were two kilns, a box kiln and a round glaze one. Collard later proved himself quite capable of innovation in kiln design at Honiton and presumably the Dorset kilns were also built and designed to his specifications. Finally, in the middle of the central yard there was a pug mill which was the traditional method of getting clay into workable form. Whether all these changes and additions were made in 1905 is uncertain as their description is based on memories of pottery workers who joined the firm about 1912.

In the company records Collard is listed as 'manager' and titled 'Art Designer' which only partially sums up the work he did; he ran the business, designed the wares, produced most of the quality pots himself and instructed all the new workers personally. He lived initially at 'Tintagel', Ringwood Road,

Longfleet but did not stay there long; two years later he was living at 7 St Mary's Terrace, Union Road and he was to move twice more whilst he ran the pottery at Poole.

The secretary of the company initially was Alfred Chapple, an accountant in Newton Abbot, and not surprisingly some of the pottery workers also came from the Torquay area to work in the new pottery.

Sam Main sitting on Collard's left in the photograph of the Aller Vale pottery workers (plate 40) and his brother Jim (James) who is second from the left in the top row moved to Poole with Collard. Sam Main was a thrower, and an excellent one by all accounts, figuring prominently at the Arts and Crafts Exhibition held in Torquay in 1890. He made the move together with his pregnant wife and baby daughter. Perhaps because of this and also because Collard valued his services, he made him caretaker and gave him 23 Green Road in which to live. Mrs Main worked as a packer, packing the pottery which was soon travelling all over the country as the pottery got under way; it was a particular boast of her husband that not one piece she packed was ever broken in transit. Not long after they had settled in Mrs Main gave birth to a son, on 1st November, 1905; but obviously things did not go too smoothly or perhaps Mrs Main did not settle in Poole because a few years later she moved back to Torquay with the two children. Sam must have enjoyed it at Poole as he stayed on at the pottery until after Collard left and then returned to Torquay in 1918 to work for Longpark. In the meantime he visited his friends and family in Torquay regularly at weekends. Sam's brother Jim was a decorator, although his work was excellent he had a drink problem and on several occasions went tramping for a few months before returning to work at the pottery again. This type of behaviour was not that uncommon among pottery workers of that period.

William Ayling and his brother Fred were two local Poole men who came to work at the pottery. They lived in nearby Emerson Road and worked at the Art Pottery, as it was known locally, for many years until its closure. Fred also became a thrower, presumably trained by Sam Main, he was a "steady country kind of a man" whom the girls nicknamed 'Marmaduke' or 'Marmy' for some reason now forgotten.

The pottery was 'adopted' by the Way family who lived at 67 Green Road. William the father worked on the clay and operated the pug mill. He had four sons who worked at the pottery, Fredrick, Albert, Thomas and Ronald. Fred, the eldest, born in 1890 and therefore fifteen by the time the pottery opened, worked the kilns. The next son Bert was a turner and can be seen as a lad helping to produce the moulded grotesque cats in plate 44, he is the second from the right. Of the other two brothers little is known except that Tom was a handler, which means that he made and fixed the handles on teapots, cups, etc.. All the brothers worked in potteries all their lives, moving on to the other Poole pottery, Carter, Stabler and Adams when the Crown Dorset Art Pottery closed, where Fred was promoted from the kilns and put in charge of the paintresses.

The processes

The process of producing pottery at Green Road was much the same as Collard had learnt at Aller Vale; all the pottery was entirely handmade, machinery played a very minor role. It took a fortnight to prepare the clay, that is to remove all foreign particles and get it to a suitable state of plasticity. When the local red clay arrived at the pottery it was put into a plunger with water, worked into a liquid state, then passed through very fine lawn sieves and run on to large clay beds. Being heavier than the water it was mixed with, it settled at the bottom, and each day any water on the top was run off until the clay was sufficiently solid for the sun or wind to dry it so that it could be taken out in square lumps.

Having been cleaned the clay had to be brought to the state of maximum plasticity before being worked, this was done in the pug mill. This is described by P. Brears in 'The English Country Pottery' in which he says the traditional pug mill, driven by horse, fell out of use around 1900, but Collard was still using one at his pottery in Honiton up to the 1930s. The pug mill consisted of a wooden tub through the centre of which ran a heavy iron spindle turned by means of a long beam hauled round by a horse, see plate 67. A number of knives protruded horizontally from the central spindle, set at a slight angle so that the clay would be slowly sliced and pressed downwards to issue as a long strip of uniform clay from the base of the mill. The clay was then stored in the cellar and kept moistened with water until required.

It took nine different processes to turn the clay into the finished product. These were, throwing, turning, dipping in coloured slip, fixing the handles, scratching the mottoes, painting, firing in the biscuit kiln, glazing and, finally, firing in the glaze kiln.

On the ground floor of the workshop Sam Main started the process on his potter's wheel, which was worked by foot, see plate 43. He could throw six dozen teapots in half an hour, so a contemporary article tells us. The clay, which had previously been weighed to the required quantity by a lad, "grew beneath his touch with wonderful celerity into form and shape". The height and breadth of the pot were measured with a gauge to ensure a degree of uniformity and it was normal to make a gross of a particular shape at one time.

The shaped clay was then put on planks which were carried outside to the drying sheds and left on shelves there to partially dry. The next step, turning, was carried out by Bert Way, if required. All those items that needed to be symmetrical, such as cups, were put on to a lathe and all superfluous clay was removed leaving a smooth finish.

The third stage was to fit the handles and spouts, this was done by Tom Way and later by Rhoda Stephens. Almost everyone in the pottery was paid piece rate, as was the custom in those days, except presumably the boys who did the odd jobs around the pottery. One such job was to carry the planks with the pots on them on their shoulder to and from the drying sheds. When she needed a fresh load of pots Miss Stephens would ask one of the boys to fetch them, "but being boys they were not always around when they were needed", so one day she decided to fetch them herself. She regretted this when she found she could get no further than halfway up the stairs; the plank was so heavy and it was difficult to balance on the shoulder. Fortunately just when she thought she would drop the lot Mr Collard came to her rescue.

After that Rhoda Stephens realised the limitations of her strength and stuck to putting on the handles. Most of these were formed in a mould and then fixed to the body with slurry. When it was dry the excess slurry was cleaned off with a tool similar to a pen, this process was called fettling. The pots were then dipped into a coloured slurry, or slip, and put back in the drying shed before the decorating process began. It is unusual to find pieces of Crown Dorset Art Pottery which have been dipped totally in slip, the exception being cups and occasionally sugar bowls. Normally the slip covers the external surface of the piece only excluding handles, spouts and lids which are left in the natural state.

In the first years of the pottery the decorating was done by local Board School boys, trained at the Technical School, who had obtained their certificate of employment. This followed the pattern at Aller Vale where only men and boys were employed. Later however, after about 1911, this practice seems to have changed and girls in their teens were employed for decorating and motto scratching. Collard liked to employ young people, trying to help them get on in life perhaps, as he had himself at Aller Vale. At the age of fourteen the Board School lads received a shilling a day, this was for working from eight in the morning to six at night and on Saturdays till two o'clock. However the work was varied and an individual could develop his artistic abilities in a friendly, happy atmosphere, Collard being more of a father figure than an employer much of the time.

After the initial period none of the designs were copied from other potteries, and they were all drawn freehand. The Crown Dorset Art Pottery claimed to be above all things absolutely original in its designs, neither was the same pattern painted by the same employee year in and year out, as was the case in some potteries. The decoration was constantly changing, most of it originated by Collard himself, although presumably there was nothing to stop the boys experimenting on designs themselves as they were not told specifically what design to paint on each piece. What normally happened was that Collard would be permanently experimenting with new colours, glazes and designs and would produce one or two pots of a new type, which he would then leave with the decorators for them to study, copy and develop. The coloured bands round the ware were put on using a wheel, "the youth employed in this department showing so true an eye, cunning a hand, and complete command of his work that it is a pleasure to watch" according to a contemporary article. The final part of the decoration was the motto or idiom. Again the workers had complete freedom over the choice of words and these were scratched into the red clay, through the slip, with a sharp pointed steel tool, often an old nail!

After this the ware was fired. It took a week to fill the kiln with pottery, the items were carefully stacked on fireproof shelves and the doorway was bricked up nine inches thick, mortared so that no air could get through; then the kiln was fired for twenty-four hours. This produced biscuit-ware pottery of the texture of flower-pots with a rather powdery looking decoration. Each piece was then dipped into a bath of carefully mixed glaze. Unlike many potters, who bought such substances from the potters' merchants, Collard continued with the arts and crafts traditions learned at Aller Vale and made all his own glazes and paints either himself or under his direct supervision. The glazes were very often tinted in various shades, usually ranging from yellow to green, and were particularly bright and hard thus enhancing the colours. The paints also were very attractive, the colours being particularly clear and bright. Some, especially the blues and yellows, had a transparent quality. A dark green with a yellowish tinge and an attractive browny orange were two other typical Dorset colours, seen particularly on the cottage ware.

All these paints and glazes were developed by Collard personally, and he would test them himself on a few pieces before passing them over to his staff for use. Whilst they were in the experimental stage, however, his staff were requested to leave them well alone!

Chapter 5

Soft Focus

Crown Dorset Ware

Although Collard had worked at several South Devon potteries in the preceding years, they had all mainly used local red clay to produce broadly similar wares. Collard continued in this manner at Dorset. By this period sadly the Torquay potteries were concentrating on the cheaper tourist end of the market and Collard was to some extent forced to do likewise. Snowdon Ward in the Art Journal of 1900, in an article on Aller Vale and Watcombe potteries, said "from the stock in the showroom I selected two pieces as being the most individual, and was informed that they were the last of their kind, and would never be repeated because the public would not pay for the work involved". This was typical of the swing away from the arts and crafts movement at the beginning of this century, back again towards mass production. So at Dorset, despite some fine and distinctive pieces, Collard mainly concentrated on small items often with scratched mottoes, or idioms, as at Torquay, but mainly in Dorset dialect. Some examples of these idioms are given in appendix III. Typical tourist pieces of this period were a variety of small vases, jugs of all sizes, beakers, match strikers, etc..

Early Aller Vale Type Wares

Many of the early patterns used at the pottery at Poole were also inspired by Collard's experiences at Aller Vale and Longpark. Two well known Torquay patterns used were black cockerels and the scandy pattern, usually with mottoes. These pieces were marked with the codes originated at Aller Vale, i.e. N1 for scandy and N2 for cockerels. (Strictly speaking the Aller Vale code for a black cockerel was N3, a coloured cockerel was N2.) The other number scratched on the base represents the shape of the item, which again usually bears some similarity to the Aller Vale shape numbers during this early period at Poole.

A popular decoration on small vases, during the first year or two, was the K2 pattern. K2, as the reader will recall, is the code for flowers painted on a green ground, wild roses and daffodils being the most common choice; these are natural representations and very well painted on the whole, which suggests that Collard painted a lot of these himself, unlike some of the scandy patterns which are decidedly crude. Again Collard's memory for the Aller Vale pattern codes seems to be poor because one piece, daffodils on a brown ground, not on a green ground, is also marked K2.

He also produced some large pieces decorated with scrolls, see plate 10; these again were painted in many colours such as white, yellow, pale and mid blues, green, beige and red-brown. A characteristic of Collard's style of scroll painting can be seen in plate 10, namely the 'crown', in this case painted in white, used as a device from which new leafy stems flow. Other versions of this device can be seen in plates 7 and 16. A broad blue band with a thin yellow band next to it is very common at the neck or base of the piece, as it is on similar wares produced at the South Devon potteries, notably Hart and Moist, see plate 8. The A1 or Persian pattern was used at Poole, indeed Collard continued to use and develop this pattern all his life. At this time it was characterised particularly by long strap leaves often rising from the base and by the extremely large seed head flower that can be seen in plate 45. This design still appears to have been in vogue, and the interest in old Persian and Turkish pottery was still very much alive, an exhibition of such pottery being held at the Burlington Fine Art Club in 1907 under the name 'Faience of Persia'. Another pattern used at Poole was a variation of the rare Aller Vale D1 pattern; this consists of a stylised flower in white, yellow and pale blue on a mid-blue ground, together with dark green leaves and some red-brown circles in the decoration. The petals of the Dorset version were usually pale blue whereas the

Aller Vale ones were cream. This design proved quite popular and remained in use for some years.

He also started to develop his own patterns. One of the first, which is quite common and therefore must have been fairly popular, is that of a stylised rose almost in the art nouveau style (plate 46). This must have been a fairly simple pattern to paint, an advantage for decorators who were still learning the art. The colours used are nearly always dusky-pink roses with black thorny stems on a cream ground, together with broad bands of dark green and/or mauvy purple. Variations on this theme were later used by the Longpark Pottery around 1910 and after the First World War by Lemon and Crute also of Torquay.

In common with other potteries Collard adopted the popular iris design illustrated in plate 11. This was used and probably developed at Watcombe in 1903 and several potteries used the design in exactly the same form. Pountney's of Bristol were advertising it as late as 1907 on their china, by which time Watcombe was beginning to phase it out. Possibly the design came to Dorset with Jim Main as he is thought to have worked at Watcombe at about this time, but pencil sketches by Collard of this design exist on Crown Dorset notepaper.

Early Marks

All of these early pieces have flat bases often with wire marks visible crossing over each other in arcs where the bases were removed from the potter's wheel. The bases are usually glazed though some have unglazed patches; the glaze itself is fairly thin in comparison with pieces produced a few years later. Often three small circular white areas arranged in a triangle can be seen, these are the stilt marks and kept the piece from sticking to the shelf in the kiln. The clay is nearly always a very reddy brown, quite a distinctive colour, and the pieces are usually marked either COLLARD POOLE DORSET impressed from a stamp or 'Poole' scratched in handwriting. See marks 11 to 14. Virtually all the early pieces were decorated in slip but gradually this was replaced by pigment decoration. The only exception to this in the above mentioned patterns is the iris design which is slightly later than the others and was painted in pigments rather than slip.

Grotesque Animals

The pottery also made a series of grotesque animals. Such animals became fashionable around 1900 and were made by most of the Devon potteries. Aller Vale for instance made a series which included crying and laughing dogs, winking cats, frogs, pigs, owls, etc.. At Dorset Collard is known to have produced cats and frogs. These animals were moulded, as can be seen from plate 44 where they are producing two different shapes of cat, one of which appears to be identical to a popular Aller Vale cat. The Dorset cats were sometimes painted black and had a red ribbon tied round their neck. As late as 1915 the notepaper of the Crown Dorset Art Pottery advertised "quaint shapes in plain coloured glazes" together with a picture of what appears to be either a frog or a bulldog. This is reproduced in plate 51.

Developments in the years after 1906

Soon new shapes were developed which were practically unique to the Crown Dorset Art Pottery. Two of the most distinctive were the 'flip over lip' and the 'wavy top'. An example of the first can be seen in plate 11 where it appears on a large vase; it was also used on small dishes. A similar shape is very occasionally seen on Hart and Moist pieces of about the same period. The 'wavy top' design was used on many different types of vases and bowls but is shown in plate 14 on one of the most typical Dorset shapes.

A new series of numbers came into use after the first year or so. The old Aller Vale pattern numbers were dropped and replaced by the '400 series', so called because all the pieces seen to date bear numbers between 400 and 499. It is not known what these numbers stood for but some are much more common than others, 463 is the most frequently seen and appears on all manner of pieces not connected in any way in terms of shape or pattern, therefore it seems most likely that it denoted a particular outlet. This number, 463, is also found on most Mosanic Pottery pieces, see page 73. The number in the '400 series' is followed by a second number denoting the shape of the pot. These shape numbers range from 1 up to at least 160 but most of the first fifty numbers are the common shapes that were popular throughout the years.

Just after the introduction of the '400 series' the glaze and paints used changed. Many of the pieces made between 1908 and 1912, including most of the '400 series', have a particularly bright hard gloss glaze and some of the colours are particularly fine, clear colours, in particular the dark blues, greens and orange-yellow. Very little slipware was produced after the first couple of years. The clay of this period tends to be more brown in appearance than the earlier distinctive reddy brown clay, this is due in part to the colouring carried in the heavy glaze which is often tinted with green.

A design that was used during this period and which is unique to the pottery is one which is fairly simple to draw but more difficult to describe, see plate 47. This was obviously an ideal pattern for young people learning the decorator's art. Sometimes the 'apple' shaped blobs are interspersed with three dots arranged in a triangle, these dots were later used as part of the decoration at Honiton and also at the Carter, Stabler and Adams pottery at Poole. Designs that were much more demanding on the decorator were a series of rustic and period figures. Sometimes these figures are outlined in black and sometimes they are sgraffito as in plate 48. Similar figures were also stamped Mosanic Pottery, these are discussed on page 74. This type of decoration was particularly used on tobacco jars where the head and shoulders of a 'character' smoking a pipe was depicted. One particular rather sad looking Irish character holds his pipe upside down in his mouth while the motto on the reverse says:

> "Faith now! a poipe is gude
> If theres nowt in it tu smoke"

The backgrounds were always painted but often the outline of the characters was incised so that they stood out. The background on the pieces showing the head and shoulders of a character was usually the same and can perhaps just be seen in plate 48, it consists of dark lines painted vertically and horizontally to give the effect of stonework and a square window is almost always painted on the left hand side of the figure; the whole gives the impression of a castle or perhaps a prison cell! The figures are usually very cleverly drawn, just a few incised lines portray the emotion in the face of the character, showing the work of a competent decorator.

Cottage Ware

By this time, 1908 onwards, the Torquay style patterns, such as the scandy and cockerel, had been dropped on the run of the mill pieces and Crown Dorset had developed its own distinctive style of 'soft focus' cottages and windmills, see plates 13 and 49. These were painted in pigment colours under a thick glaze that made the colours run slightly giving the blurred effect that became the hallmark of the 'Art Pottery'.

It is thought that the production of pieces bearing cottages and windmills at Dorset predates most of the Torquay ware bearing similar designs. The cottage that became popular on Watcombe Motto Ware, and that many other South Devon potteries were to copy, dates from around the First World War. However a few earlier pieces with cottages marked Brewer Longpark allegedly exist. Pountney's of Bristol also followed the vogue for cottages and produced pieces with cottages almost identical to Crown Dorset but on white clay. Windmills were not popular as a style of decoration at Torquay until the 'sunset scene' was developed at Aller Vale in 1908, this consisted of "landscapes, water scenes, windmills and other buildings in the Dutch style with sunset effects".

The first examples of cottage ware produced at Dorset were large pieces either stamped COLLARD POOLE DORSET or scratched 'Poole' or 'Collard, Poole', these are obviously done by a very competent decorator. Also in the early period (1905-1907) smaller pieces were made with a coloured ground, such as dark blue or green, on which a panel with a cottage was painted in such a way as to give the effect of a pot covered in dark blue or green paper which had been torn away to reveal part of the countryside, see plate 12.

Soon, however, small items with either a cottage or windmill as decoration, and carrying mottoes in Dorset dialect, were being produced in quantity for the tourist and cheaper end of the market. The cottage was the more popular and consisted of a cottage, often with a thatched roof, surrounded by trees with a rather vague pathway leading to it across a grassy field. Rather obviously the cottages were replaced by windmills on tall thin vases which lent themselves to that shape of decoration. Sometimes small pieces have neither a cottage nor a windmill but simply a countryside scene of a winding road through fields and trees, these pieces are usually early and bear the mark COLLARD POOLE DORSET. Very occasionally the decoration is composed solely of trees with the emphasis being on their long straight trunks, rather reminiscent of later art deco patterns, but the colours are the typical dark Dorset yellowy greens.

The 'soft focus' effect was caused by over firing or by the use of too soft a glaze, perhaps this was an accident at first but it obviously proved popular with the public. Apart from the 'arty' look it gave the piece it also helped to hide poorish painting which could be an advantage on occasions! Thus a degree of running of the paints and glazes was aimed for, but this must have been rather tricky to judge correctly and sometimes the effect was overdone. This is not surprising as Collard was always experimenting with different paints and glazes which must have made the job of the kiln man, Fred Way, a difficult one. In the event of excess running of the colours the pieces were sold off as seconds. Collard would tell his assistants to keep those items back in case the gypsies, or higglers as they were known locally, came round. A basket of seconds would be sold to the gypsies for five shillings, Effie Knight a pottery worker recalled; she thought that this was far too cheap as they then went round the houses selling them for much more. Therefore some of the poor pieces that can be found today were probably not sold by the pottery but were seconds which most potteries would have destroyed.

Mottoes

Often cottages and windmills would be produced in pairs, so it was possible to buy a pair of vases or oil jugs, one bearing a cottage, the other a windmill, with complimentary mottoes that could be read from one piece to the other. Two such mottoes are listed number 3 in appendix III.

Some of the small items bear messages rather than mottoes, and were probably meant to be sent to distant friends or relatives as a present cum postcard, much as Collard sent the inkwell to

his wife many years before. Examples of these messages are:
"Come an' zee us in the zummer" a quotation from William Barnes,
"Where be you now, dear?" a quotation from Thomas Hardy,
"In friendship's name", etc..
These messages appear on useful items such as small jugs, vases and cream bowls. Sometimes after about 1912 a boat replaced the cottage or windmill as decoration.

Larger pieces, however, had greater scope for mottoes or quotations and some ran to four lines or more. William Barnes the Dorset poet was the most popular source of these. He was born in 1801 and died in 1886 and wrote his poetry on nature and the rural way of life in Dorset dialect; this made his work a first class source of ideas for the pottery. The first verse of his poem "Praise O Do'set", which follows, provided at least three different quotes.

We Do'set though we mid be hwomely,
Be'nt asheäm'd to own our pleäce;
An' we've zome women not uncomely;
Nor asheäm'd to show their feäce:
We've a mead or two wo'th mowèn,
We've an ox or two wo'th showèn,
In the village,
At the tillage,
Come along an' you shall vind
That Do'set men don't sheäme their kind.
Friend an' wife,
Fathers, mothers, sisters, brothers,
Happy, happy, be their life!
Vor Do'set dear,
Then gie woone cheer;
D'ye hear? Woone cheer.

Thomas Hardy was also quoted, and he produced a special series of mottoes for the pottery drawn from his Wessex novels which were used on a range of pottery known as 'Hardy Ware'. One jar in this series represents the story of Gabriel Oak and bears the motto:

"To his scornful Love comes Gabriel Oak
And asks to be one of her Shepherd Folk."

Other examples of the mottoes used are given in appendix III.

The style of writing in which the mottoes were scratched is quite distinctive, and a piece could be recognised by this alone if not marked because the letter formations are quite different from those on the Torquay pots with which the Dorset pottery might be confused. Some typical letter formations are given in appendix IV, it must be remembered however, that many different hands scratched the mottoes, so there are variations in some of the letter formations.

Puzzle Jugs

Another line that proved very popular was the puzzle jug. This was a steady seller at Aller Vale and Longpark at the beginning of the century with the scandy pattern or black cockerel as decoration, and has of course been produced by potteries on and off for a long time. Collard took the idea, adapted it, and produced some very distinctive puzzle jugs, noted primarily for the length of the jug's neck and for the unusual holes in the neck. An example can be seen second from the right in the bottom row of plate 52. The bulbous part only of the jug is covered in slip and this invariably bears a cottage as decoration and the standard puzzle jug motto, see motto 2 appendix III. A large area of the neck is cut away with distinctive Dorset holes which also appear later on their pot-pourri vases. There are usually four large circular holes, each of which is surrounded by a series of smaller ones.

Later Marks

By the time that the production of cottages and windmills was in full swing the numbering system had changed again, so a mark such as 4 36 R may be seen scratched, or very occasionally painted in black, on the base. 36 is the shape number and remains unchanged from the previous system and 4 represents the height of the piece measured in inches. The earlier system did not specify the size of the piece and because small 3 inch pieces could be made in the same shape as 8 inch pieces this was obviously a disadvantage from the point of view of reordering. Usually the height in inches appears before the shape number but this is not always so, it is sometimes reversed. The height measurement is approximate to say the least! The letter is nearly always R and represents, it is thought, 'regular'. Thus the regular decoration for shape 5, a tall thin vase, was a windmill, any abnormal or different decoration on this shape would bear a different letter. For a small sugar bowl, shape 33, a cottage was regular. To add to the confusion these regular patterns obviously changed over the years, so what might have been regular in 1910 was not so in 1915. Other letters appear sporadically; E appears quite regularly on the Aller Vale DI pattern discussed on page 60 and H on the pattern of a chain of Dutch (?) walking figures. Several other letters can be found but they do not appear to have been used consistently and quite often the letter is omitted from the numbering system, so that a piece may merely be marked 36/4. One of the pottery workers recollected that each decorator had a separate letter for their work; if this was so then R must represent the work of the general painting room as opposed to that of more skilled decorators who had their own letters. This theory however seems unlikely as decorators never had their own marks at any other pottery at which Collard worked.

In addition to the changes in the code the pottery mark also changed at about the same time. The scratched mark 'Poole' was replaced by a scratched 'Dorset' normally in lower case letters. This mark is invariably found on the small pieces decorated with cottages and windmills, in the instances where these pieces are marked which is only about fifty per cent of the time. A new impressed mark with the words 'Crown Dorset' written around a picture of a crown, see mark 17 in appendix I, was also introduced and used mainly on the better quality items. These marks obviously reflected the change in the name of the pottery to the Crown Dorset Art Pottery which must have occurred in 1910 or earlier.

Handle Shapes

There are about half a dozen different styles of handles found on pieces made at the pottery, but two are much more common than the others and it may be possible to identify a piece of pottery by either of these handles when the piece is not marked, as they seem to be almost unique to the pottery. The first was used as soon as the Art Pottery had developed its own style, and therefore appears on middle period pottery (1908-12) mainly, usually those with a high gloss glaze and of good quality. The handle is fairly substantial and the shape of its cross section and of its terminals, both of which are moulded, is indicated in appendix IV. The other handle shape which was widely used is found on slightly later pieces, often cottage ware, and on the whole is not of such good quality, athough still quite attractive. As can be seen from appendix IV, the cross section is rectangular and the terminal is shaped rather like an inverted fleur de lys, but usually only the bottom end of the handle is shaped in this way.

Green Ware Pottery

A small amount of green ware was produced at an early stage and marked COLLARD POOLE DORSET. Some of these pieces bear a strong resemblance to the Aller Vale M1 pattern, that is a piece covered in a plain translucent green glaze. An interesting example which has strong Aller Vale connections is illustrated in plate 50. The jug was first turned to give a ribbed effect and dipped into a white slip which was allowed to run down and cover most of the body in an 'arty' fashion. The jug was then coated all over with a green irridescent glaze which gave the exposed red clay a dark brown lustrous appearance.

This ware was developed at a later stage into a cheap run of the mill line which was of poorer quality and such refinements as decorative handle terminals were normally omitted, the pieces were however made in the normal Crown Dorset shapes. A popular decoration on this ware was the coat of arms of a town, such as Leicester or Nottingham, scratched through the glaze and slip. Occasionally pictures were painted in various colours under the glaze, but this is not very effective because much of the colour is masked by the green glaze.

The base of the later type of green ware is nearly always recessed and is usually, but not always glazed. Sometimes no marks at all appear on the base, and it is rare to find a piece marked 'Dorset' or stamped Crown Dorset possibly because Collard considered this bread and butter ware not a credit to the pottery. Some pieces however bear the impressed mark

MOSANIC POTTERY, see page 73. The coding series is more commonly found on the base, in particular a scratched 463 followed by a shape number.

Another vase with a plain glaze but of better quality than the cheaper green wares is depicted in plate 50. Probably made around 1910 it was again coated in white slip before a rather attractive sea-green glaze with blue flecks was applied.

All manner of different patterns were produced as Collard tried to find the designs that appealed most to the public. One rather skilful one was a moonlight scene of a sailing boat depicted simply in black, white and yellow on a dark green-blue background. Moonlight scenes very similar to this became the stock in trade in the 1920s and 1930s of the Barton Pottery, Torquay.

Beach Scenes

Just after the introduction of the code marks giving the height in inches and bearing the letter R, a better quality tourist line was introduced of beach scenes, usually depicting a lone child on a beach. Very often larger pieces were produced in pairs. For instance one vase would show a little girl, with her back to the viewer, looking out to sea, she would be dressed typically for the period with a large straw hat or bonnet. The other vase would show a little boy, in the same pose, probably wearing a sailor suit, on a ground of either pale or mid-blue which represented the sea and sky. Smaller items were made with similar designs, sometimes on a brown ground to represent the beach with the sea painted in blue, rather than on a blue ground with the sand painted in yellow. These pieces often bear the name of the seaside town in which they were sold, such as Eastbourne or Cowes, together with a standard motto such as 'Contentment is a constant feast' (one of the most popular quotations from Barnes), and were clearly meant as holiday mementoes. It is interesting to note that none of the decorators interviewed remembered seeing or decorating these pieces and, as they were produced in quite large numbers, this tends to suggest, together with the skill in painting, that this type of decoration was done by Collard or by his top decorator. The outline of the child is painted simply in dark brown and then blocked in with different colours, this simple treatment is very effective as can be seen in plate 14.

This design was one of the first to be used on the pot-pourri vases that became such a hallmark of the pottery in its later years. Initially the pot-pourri vases were of good quality and were made to cash in on the interest in gardening and the outdoor life that was prevalent amongst the middle classes at the beginning of this century. The making of pot-pourri seems to have become almost a craze at this period and in 1910 such a well known figure as Gertrude Jeykell wrote an article in Country Life on how pot-pourri should be made. The Crown Dorset pot-pourri vases are very distinctive being mushroom shaped with a large central hole in the top surrounded by a series of smaller holes. The rose pattern, described below, is another example of a pattern used on the early pot-pourri vases and is illustrated in plate 46.

Rose Pattern

Unlike the beach scenes which were obviously original the rose pattern was adapted by Collard from his favourite sixteenth century Turkish pottery, and is of a stylised sgraffito rose, see plate 46. Some have a rose and trailing leaves in a dark blue glaze on an unglazed rough cream slip which gives the impression of stoneware; they are nevertheless made of the standard brown clay used by the pottery. These pieces are most effective and distinctive, but perhaps were not popular at the time, or perhaps the technique for achieving this was too difficult or costly, as not that many seem to exist today. The rose pattern is the only one to have been seen combined with this technique and the standard of decoration is very high on these pieces and they must have been done by Collard himself.

The rose pattern was also used on totally glazed ware. In this case more colours were used, so that the roses might be dark blue and reddy brown together with green leaves on a cream ground. Occasionally the centre of the rose is orange-brown surrounded by deep mahogany coloured petals with turquoise bands at the top and base of the piece.

Collard took this pattern with him to Honiton and it

developed into the popular Jacobean pattern. It is thought that the rose pattern was used at Crown Dorset from 1910 onwards for several years and, as has been already mentioned, it was mainly used on pot-pourri vases upon which it was particularly suitable.

Yet another design found on pot-pourri vases is that of Dutch (?) men and women walking round the pot forming a chain by holding hands. Usually two men and two women fit the circumference of the vase, the men wear top hats and smoke pipes, the women wear bonnets and shawls, all of course wear clogs. The outlines are incised and are blocked in mainly with different shades of blue but also with some green, yellow and brown.

Later on, around the time of the First World War, the pot-pourri vases became very cheap and poor looking, and may have even been made to contract for a firm manufacturing pot-pourri as these late ones are rarely marked. A series of six different shapes were regularly produced and decorated for instance in a dark green with a band bearing a geometric design painted in black around the vase. The only mark on the base is the shape number 1 to 6. In addition unglazed pot-pourri vases were made which were impregnated with perfume, these are discussed in more detail on page 86 together with other types of perfume pottery that were made both by Collard and his successors.

Finally it must be mentioned that Collard did produce one or two pieces made of white clay other than moulded pieces such as the grotesques and the little scent bottles mentioned later. For example a pair of vases decorated in the Persian A1 pattern were made of white clay. They are marked on the base with the Crown Dorset mark number 17 and incised 8-159-P, in other words eight inch vases of shape 159, from this information and from the style it would appear that they were made around 1914. One of these vases is shown in plate 45.

Mosanic Pottery

Some pottery produced by Collard at Green Road, from about 1908 onwards, bears the impressed mark MOSANIC POTTERY. Mosanic is the trade mark of Max Emanuel and Co.

a London firm of china and glass importers. Most of the china bearing the mark Mosanic was made by Porzellannfabrik Mitterteich of Bavaria which was acquired by Max Emanuel in 1895. The china produced bore the backstamp of Mosanic and was mainly souvenir ware such as pink tinted ribbon plates with transfer printed pictures, and model buildings. Other pieces bearing a black painted Mosanic mark are French in origin and are made of a pink-beige colour clay and are models of pieces such as continental clogs decorated in bright blues, yellows, greens and reds and moulded cats slipped in bright yellow with glass eyes.

The Mosanic ware produced by Collard, however, has the impressed mark MOSANIC POTTERY, see appendix I, and not simply the word Mosanic, therefore no confusion should exist between the wares of the different producers, especially as the pieces made at Green Road are all typical of the pottery's normal style and are made of red clay. These pieces were made under contract for Max Emanuel and Co.. and nearly all bear the number 463 together with a shape number on the base. The number 463 is the most common number in the 400 series to be found on COLLARD POOLE DORSET pieces, the only difference being that on COLLARD POOLE DORSET ware the number is incised and on MOSANIC POTTERY it is impressed, together with the shape number, in small, neat, slightly forward slanting numbers that are not always easy to read because of their size. This gives weight to the theory that the 400 series was used to identify pottery passing through different retail outlets, and that 463 was the code for Max Emanuel and Co.. The Mosanic Pottery pieces are later than those marked COLLARD POOLE DORSET bearing the scratched mark 463, presumably Collard did not use the Mosanic stamp initially for pieces intended for this outlet. The shape numbers appearing on Mosanic Pottery accord with the Dorset shapes as far as can be tested and Collard produced some very distinctive shapes at Dorset. There is no doubt that the pieces marked Mosanic Pottery were produced at Green Road.

Some pieces bearing the Mosanic Pottery backstamp are very ordinary such as a vinegar bottle in brown clay with a white slip covered in green glaze, with the incised name and coat of arms of the city of Nottingham. Other pieces of Mosanic Pottery are highly decorated and include a large 'flip over lip' vase identical in shape to the one marked COLLARD POOLE DORSET in plate 11 but on this occasion decorated with a 'soft focus' windmill. Mosanic 'soft focus' cottages also exist. Some vases were decorated with men in seventeenth century costume (possibly roundheads), they are very similar to the drinking man marked COLLARD POOLE DORSET illustrated in plate 48, except for the fact that the Mosanic Pottery pieces usually show the whole figure set against a typical countryside background very similar to that on cottage ware. Other period figures exist such as a girl in a tunic playing with a diabolo. A rather strange rustic character appears both on a piece marked MOSANIC POTTERY and on a piece with a scratched 463 code, he is attempting to lead a pig to market, without much success! In both examples he wears the same type of hat and cravat and has a pink jacket, the only difference being that in one case he carries a basket of eggs. The piece marked MOSANIC POTTERY is illustrated in plate 54. Some of these characters and historical figures are outlined in black and others are incised but all are filled in with typical Dorset colours predominately greens, browns and yellows. Other pieces in this series dispense with the character and depict the pig alone!

A different style of decoration is used on the tobacco jar in plate 47, the Dutch boy is outlined in brown slip and a very pale wash is applied to some areas so that his hat and bundle of sticks on his back appear pale pink, the smoke rising from his pipe yellow and his trousers and the trees in the background a pale green. Very little pottery marked Mosanic is motto ware, but there are some exceptions including a small Persian pattern bowl.

In later years Collard recalled that Max Emanuel were a very good firm to work for. They would send him a postcard requesting new samples from him; on receiving this he would work out some new ideas and take them up to London, staying over-night at a hotel at their expense. This resulted in good monthly orders for the pottery which suited Collard well as it kept production regular and steady and payment was made every month as promised. Unfortunately this excellent business arrangement must have come to an abrupt end with the outbreak of the First World War as Max Emanuel had strong German connections.

Dating Crown Dorset Wares

Although much of the dating of the pieces described in this chapter is not certain and is to some extent guesswork, some definite information can be gleaned from articles, etc.. For instance it is known that Collard displayed a case of Crown Dorset ware at Turin in 1911; this is discussed in more detail in the next chapter but the ware included "some quaint figures and a number of motto jugs, etc.".

An article on the pottery written in the same year describes the designs then current: "cottages, windmills, conventional patterns, Dutch figures, tiny maidens; in fact a marvellous variety of novel and original ideas". The same writer describes the style of decoration: "Beside the solid colours usually seen in decorative pottery there is underglaze painting which produces lovely clear colourings, and a species of what — for lack of a better name — I may perhaps be permitted to call outline work in which the design is indicated in a light graceful style extremely fascinating instead of being blocked in by solid colour". The pieces made were: "all manner of artistic, useful and ornamental articles, teapots, hot-water jugs, candlesticks, vases of diverse shapes, tobacco jars, artistic flower pots, cream jugs, sugar basins, etc.". From the above descriptions it seems clear that some of the ware described was Mosanic pottery. The tobacco jar decorated with a Dutch boy outlined in slip and very delicately 'washed' fits this description perfectly.

In addition headed notepaper produced some time between 1911 and 1914 bore the picture, reproduced in plate 51, of some examples of the pottery produced at that time. Apart from the inevitable cottages, windmills and boats, this includes a piece in the ever popular A1 pattern as well as two magnificent vases, one decorated with a wading bird and the other (as can just be seen) with a mythical beast amongst scrolls. Finally, not to be forgotten, there is a little grotesque.

The most detailed guide to dating the later wares however is an advertisement, see plate 52, which Collard placed in the Pottery Gazette and which appeared every month for the last six months of 1913. It is interesting not only because it informs us that he had a London agent, Mr H. Britain, but it shows patterns which would otherwise be unknown today. The three pieces in the left corner show a remarkable similarity to Barnstaple wares with their plain glaze and snaking handles. The three pieces on the right of the top row anticipate the work he was to produce at Honiton, especially the shape of the candlestick on the left and the decoration of small posies and three dots which is also similar to ware produced slightly later at Carter, Stabler and Adams pottery in Poole. There is also a whole range of 'experimental' pottery which has a decidedly art deco look with its stylised designs and angular shapes. Some pieces in this range were not glazed and some were made of a yellowish clay. This type of pottery is very rarely found and was presumably not popular at the time and therefore did not remain in production long. One of the pottery workers remembers that when she joined the pottery in 1912 Collard was experimenting with new designs to replace the old, soon to be outdated, cottages and windmills. Presumably these designs fell into this category.

Chapter 6

Commissions and Exhibitions

Local and International Recognition

The pottery proved to be very successful and established itself within a few years. A writer in 1911 said that "each year this Dorset Art Pottery is extended to meet the increasing demands for its ware; each year, therefore, more employees are needed and more work is offered". Certainly by 1912 the pottery was a thriving concern as can be seen from the capital invested in the business which had increased fourfold to £4,000 by that year. Collard seems to have had plenty of business sense as well as artistic ability, he soon established bread and butter lines whilst also making high quality pieces himself whenever he could. He had built up a strong export trade and regular foreign orders were received. Pottery workers can remember working overtime to complete and pack a large order for Buenos Aires. Orders were also received from places as far flung as Hong Kong, Norway, Australia and Constantinople.

One of his major successes in terms of advertising came when the pottery was awarded the contract by Poole Council to produce coronation mugs in 1911. The Council were unanimously in favour of the purchase of mugs that were to be given to the children in the area to commemorate the occasion, and had made quite a few enquiries to different potteries concerning style and price. The matter was decided at a Council meeting at the Guildhall where quite a few specimen mugs were available for consideration. Councillors Norrish and Hunt were particularly concerned that the mugs purchased should be

British and passed a motion to that effect. Collard's sample was well liked, the cost was to be £101. 10. 0d for 7000 mugs, just about 3½d each. The mug bore the heads of the King and Queen and on the back an inscription which could be changed to meet the Council's needs. In addition, and perhaps this clinched the contract, Collard guaranteed to complete the order within a month. This must have been a relief to the Council because, like most committees, they had left things to the last minute and the meeting at which the decision was made was held on 27th April and the coronation was to take place on 22nd June. Alderman Carter was particularly keen that Collard's mug be chosen because it was made in Poole, thus supporting home industries, and also it was more ornamental than the others and therefore of better value!

Apart from the mugs the Council spent £180 on decorations and illuminations for Poole Park, £90 was spent on a sports programme, £110 on dinner and £210 on tea. This lavish expenditure was made because the Council wished to do things properly and "not to do the thing 'scaly' ".

The lead from Poole Council was taken up by Lytchett Matravers who had an identical mug made for their festivities. Three coronation mugs appear to have been made in total. The first for Poole bearing the heads of the King and Queen, the heads were moulded in red clay and applied to the body of the mug set over a rose, with a thistle and shamrock on either side, see plate 15. The inscription on the back reads "Borough of Poole To Commemorate the Coronation of their Majesties King George V and Queen Mary 22nd June 1911. I. D. Ballard Mayor". The mug for Lytchett Matravers was identical apart from the inscription and a third mug was made for Poole with the heads of the King and Queen replaced by slip decoration with G. V. R. in the centre. It is not surprising as countless of these mugs were made in a month that the quality is not always as good as one might have hoped, one thing is certain there must have been plenty of overtime at the pottery in May 1911! These mugs are very rarely marked in any way on the base.

The pottery made items to special order in addition to its normal production. For instance a series of jugs were made for

Sauls, a local chemist, in a green and black design with the words 'Sauls' and the mixture the jug was to advertise such as 'quinine tonic' written in fancy lettering on the side. Presumably these jugs were made to decorate the shop rather than for any practical use. One particular order that Collard was very pleased to get according to a pottery worker was that for Hunt's cider. These pieces, presumably meant for use in public houses, bore the verse:

> "The apples of Devon make cider so fine
> Try HUNTS DEVON CIDER, it's better than wine."

Perhaps Collard felt it was one up on his old colleagues in Torquay that he should get this order rather than they! On a different scale anybody could go to the pottery and have individual pieces made. A doctor, for instance, asked for a teaset to be made for his children with their names and a little verse of their choice on the cups.

The company's greatest success artistically came in 1910 when it was awarded a Gold Medal at the International Brussels Exhibition. This must have been a major achievement for a small firm, certainly Collard prized the award as he mentioned it on the company's letter headings at Dorset and subsequently many years later at Honiton. Strangely enough, however, Collard's name does not appear in the catalogues of the exhibition nor in the list of prize winners published in the Times. Nevertheless the Gold Medal is in existence today and therefore there can be no doubt of his presence at the exhibition. Sadly most of the documentation in the British Museum relating to this and the subsequent Turin Exhibition was destroyed during the Second World War, therefore little is known about his exhibits.

Previous international exhibitions had been held but the British contributions had been disappointing, as a result 'all the stops were pulled out' for this major event. The Board of Trade set up a new department, the Exhibition Branch and, as a result of this, a strong co-ordinating committee under the chairmanship of the Earl of Lytton was formed. The Prince of Wales (King George V, by the time the exhibition was held) made an appeal to the nation's manufacturers for a special effort to show the rest of Europe what Britain could achieve.

The exhibition was a splendid affair with the buildings erected on the outskirts of Brussels close to the beautiful Bois de la Cambre; an electric tram service ran from the centre of Brussels to the entrance of the exhibition. It opened in July but on 14th August disaster struck. A fire broke out in the Belgian section and totally destroyed the British hall and caused severe damage to the French and Italian sections. Heroic efforts were made to salvage the situation and after public appeals nearly all the original exhibitors and some new ones took part in the reconstituted British section which reopened in the Salles des Fetes on 15th September. There seems little doubt that Collard was one of the new exhibitors who in a rush of patriotic fervour answered the nation's call for assistance.

In the following year 1911, Collard won another Gold Medal at the Turin Exhibition for a display of a single showcase containing amongst other things rustic figures and puzzle jugs. This exhibition was held in the Valentino Park on the outskirts of Turin alongside the river Po, and once more the British section, under the guidance of the Board of Trade, seems to have been large and imposing. Again due to the lack of contemporary catalogues little is known about Collard's exhibits, but they obviously created a favourable impression on the international jury for the award to be given to such a small company for such relatively unpretentious pottery.

These two events appear to be the only ones of this type that Collard ever exhibited at. Even later on, when at Honiton, he took part in none of the well-known national exhibitions such as the Ideal Home Exhibition at which many of the potteries exhibited. He preferred to keep his staff at the pottery which had a full order book, so he had no need to exhibit to advertise his wares.

Vor Do'set dear

Chapter 7

The Later Years

Recollections of the Art Pottery Girls

By 1912, the heyday of the pottery, there were about twenty-five workers. The men worked on the ground floor of the workshop, whilst upstairs about fifteen girls were employed fixing the handles and decorating the pots. They were all local girls in their early teens, employed around this period and trained personally by Collard, most of them stayed until they got married early in the 1920s or until the pottery closed a few years later.

One of them, Miss Stephens as she then was, remembered Collard with these words "Well I can honestly say I have never met a more gentlemanly man than Mr Collard, he was one of the kindest and best employers ever anybody knew". Rhoda Stephens lived opposite the pottery, her father was a baker, and when she was twelve she developed epilepsy. Because of this she could not get a job and when she saw Collard advertising in the paper for girls to work at the pottery she made up her mind to go and see him. When she told him that she was an epileptic she expected that the interview would end but he said "that makes no difference, if ever you feel unwell go on home you don't have to tell anybody".

Collard was very keen that they should be well trained and paid for them to go to art school with varying degrees of success. Nellie Lambert remembered that it was compulsory to go two afternoons a week to the school which was above the old free library in Poole. For her it must have been a success because she became a decorator in her own right with her own room and, apart from other things, painted the samples of pottery that were sent abroad. Effie Knight, on the other hand, was not so lucky and her classes were in the evening. Being a typical youngster she was not too pleased at losing two evenings a week and after a while she told Mr Collard "that she couldn't get on with it". "That's alright he said it's not your fault you've tried your best."

The hours of work had been reduced by half an hour to 8.30 am to 6 pm by this time and on Miss Knight's suggestion they were changed again to 8 am to 5.30 pm. She was obviously keen to stop work early to go out with her young man and she could remember a song the young men used to sing outside the pottery whilst waiting for their girls:

> "Pottery girls, pottery girls,
> High legged boots and their hair all in curls,
> Eyes like violets, teeth like pearls,
> None to compare to the Art Pottery girls."

The young girls were paid a fixed rate and Effie Knight could remember walking down Green Road with Mr Collard when he said "How old are you now?" She said quickly "I've got a birthday coming up, I'll be sixteen. I think I could have a rise, don't you?" Whether this was the purpose of his question or not he ended up saying "I'll give you an extra 6d a week, but don't tell the others will you? After a couple of weeks you can go on piecework".

All the older girls scratching the mottoes and painting the cottages and windmills, etc. were paid piecerate. The rate seems to have been ½d per dozen of the brief mottoes or if they were longer 12 lines for ½d, and the rate for painting cottages, windmills or boats was 2½d per dozen. There was often overtime available, if required, for a couple of hours in the evening if a large rush order was being processed; in addition work could be taken home, such as plaiting the raffia for the pot-pourri vases, the rate of pay for this was 6d for 25 yards and some of the girls were quite keen to earn an extra 6d a week by plaiting 25 yards in the evenings. They also used to take it home for their mothers to do!

The holes in the pot-pourri vases and in the puzzle jugs were made by the handler with a pen with a detachable nib. The nib was put into the holder, writing end first, leaving the half round end outwards for making the holes in the dry clay. Before a girl qualified to make the holes in the puzzle jugs she had to work out the puzzle in the jug!

Most of the girls were not trained to any degree but were quite capable of producing the routine motto ware that was the bread and butter of the business during the earlier years and decorating the pot-pourri vases later on. Nearly all the more elaborate decorating was done by Collard himself, therefore there was little skilled decorating done at Crown Dorset after he left. "He would paint a board full of pots in no time" Effie Knight remembered. She watched him paint pictures on two vases, one a landscape with a windmill the other of boats on a river, when she said to him that she wished she could paint so well he modestly replied "this is what time has done". She also remembered watching him decorate a pair of six inch vases with storks and then buying them as a present for her mother when he said they were not part of a special order.

Although life inside the pottery went on quite happily the elements outside were less than kind; because of the position of the pottery it was liable to be flooded, a constant hazard in that part of Poole. Fred Way, who lived in nearby Stanley Street, recalled that as a child he would be sent to collect sand from the beaches in order to make sandbags. To keep the water out these would be put against the front door of his house which opened directly onto the street; and at the first sign of flooding all the furniture would be moved upstairs. On one occasion Collard found the flooding so bad when he arrived at the pottery early in the morning that a sailing boat had been swept through the pottery gates and gone aground in the pottery yard. It may seem difficult to imagine such flooding looking at the site today but at that time the back-water of the harbour ran behind the pottery. This part of the harbour was filled in during the second half of the 1920s and a gas works was built on the site.

In 1912 Collard was living at 73 Bridge Road and on 20th June that year he married Emily after a courtship which had lasted ten years. They were married in London at the Chapel of Ease, St Mary le Park, Battersea, as by now Emily was living in London with her sister and was working with a court dressmaker. A year or so later they moved into a newly-built house, St Martins in Garland Road, Poole, where their only child, Joan, was born. Effie Knight remembered the house well because when Collard was planning to work late at the pottery he would send her up to the house with a message to that effect for his wife.

Just after the beginning of the First World War there was a fire at the pottery. Rhoda Stephens remembered waking up one night and looking out of her bedroom window at the pottery opposite to see the whole of the roof of the workshop alight. The next day when the girls arrived for work Collard sent them home saying that he would not need them for a few days, but the boys and men had to set to work cleaning up the mess. The fire does not appear to have done much damage to the structure of the buildings, although obviously the roof was destroyed, as none of the workers could remember production being held up for long. However it can not have been that minor because most of the workers lost possessions, especially the girls who worked on the first floor of the workshop. Collard made sure that none of the girls suffered financially as a result of the fire and asked them all whether they had lost anything; "Oh no, only an overall and that doesn't matter" replied Rhoda Stephens. "Oh yes it does" Collard retorted "are you sure you didn't loose anything else?"

Pottery fires seem to have been quite a common occurrence judging from the number reported in the Pottery Gazette around that period, which seems hardly surprising. It is believed that there was a second fire in the early 1920s at the Dorset Art Pottery after Collard had left and it was owned by Paine.

The First World War severely affected the pottery as it did all other potteries and, indeed, most businesses. The girls who were over eighteen were called up to work in munitions factories; most of the men at the Art Pottery were too old to be called up and the boys too young, so they remained but obviously not a lot of quality pieces were produced, and of course all the lucrative foreign orders were lost. Collard seems to have anticipated the problems that the war would bring; having tried unsuccessfully to raise more capital in August of 1915 to tide the business over the wartime years, he wisely sold the business to George Paine. Perhaps in a way he was relieved to do so because he had never considered Poole to be a healthy environment and now with a young child this consideration was more important. On the other hand it must have been a terrible wrench to sell the business that he had put all his effort and imagination into for the preceding ten years; he had worked and saved very hard to be in a position to run his own pottery and it must have been a very sad day when he sold it. The company Charles Collard and Co. Ltd was formally dissolved on 14th December, 1917 but by then Collard had been living for some little while at Ilminster, Somerset.

Crown Dorset after Collard

The story of the last years of the Crown Dorset Art Pottery appears to be one of difficulty and decline. Early in 1920 Paine sold the business to a company, the Dorset Art Pottery Ltd, which was set up to acquire the business and in which Paine, although a director, held only one share. It is interesting to note that he tried to register the company as the *Crown* Dorset Art Pottery Ltd but permission appears to have been refused by the Registrar of Companies. Most of the finance for the company was put up by Charles Paris, a merchant navy officer, who took little active part in the business.

From an advertisement in the Pottery Gazette of October, 1922 it seems that during the early 1920s production continued much as before with traditional glazed-ware pieces decorated with cottages or ships and their "famous handmade Dorset perfumed pottery" but with the addition of a new line called Wessex ware. The latter was decorated in black with raised coloured flowers arranged in a garland and was similar to the design produced at the Honiton Pottery at about the same time, but at Honiton the design was not raised but painted in the usual way, see plate 58. This ware should not be confused with the products of the Wessex Perfumery and Potteries mentioned on page 87.

The venture however did not prove a success and a liquidator was appointed in February 1925 and the company was finally wound up in January 1927. Many of Collard's ex-employees had stayed at the pottery during its declining years although they found the atmosphere somewhat changed. Paine spent all his time in the office and took no part in the making of the pottery and the regime appears to have become more restrictive. When the company went into liquidation it is believed that the business was sold to a Mr Walker who traded as The British Perfume Company. As the name of the business implies it appears to have concentrated more on the perfumes than on the pottery in which they were contained. However all the pottery containers used were of shapes originated by Collard, and the contents ranged from Florida Water and Opoponax to the more prosaic Lavender Water. This venture obviously also soon foundered as there is no reference to it in the Kelly's Directory for 1926, so both Mr Paine and Mr Walker must have given up during 1925. When the works finally closed many of the employees moved to the nearby pottery of Carter, Stabler and Adams, as indeed did Mr Paine.

Gradually over the last years of its life the business changed from producing pottery to marketing perfumes and pot-pourri in fancy containers. This change started while Collard was at the pottery, it was only a short step from producing some of the beautifully decorated pot-pourri vases of the earlier period to mass producing an inferior version for a perfume company at Corfe Mullen to fill with dried lavender or violets. These vases were glazed initially but gradually more and more of them were produced in the biscuit state painted in pale blue and white with flowers such as the lily of the valley. In addition, little containers for perfume were made, these were moulded in two sections and made of white clay. Different shapes were made with a basket weave texture on the outside and another container was made in the shape of a fir cone and covered with a yellow-brown glaze. Both of these type wares bear the Crown Dorset mark 17, in appendix I which would seem to imply that they were made during Collard's period. For some time companies had been making Bournemouth pine perfume from the local pine trees and marketing it as for instance "a delightful souvenir of sunny Boscombe" and it seems that this must have been the purpose of the pottery cones. It is interesting to note that the South Devon potteries made similar items between the two World Wars, namely little conical pots usually decorated with violets to be filled with that perfume. In Paine's day the perfume essences and glycerine were kept in the house that had previously been the offices; these essences, lavender, carnation or violet, were syringed into the terracotta pottery on the premises.

The change to this type of ware had evidently started by July 1913 as can be seen from the advertisement in the Pottery Gazette, reproduced in plate 52, which advertised perfumed terracotta, this presumably refers to impregnated pottery. Little discs about the size of a 50p piece were made some with lilac and some with rose written on them and smelling of that perfume, they were used for keeping linen fresh and were called scented sachet blocks. Penny perfume bricks were also manufactured; these were the size of a tablet of soap and were used for rubbing one's hands on to make them smell pleasant. The perfume bricks were still being made when the pottery closed down because a young girl, who had hoped to go and work there when she left school, remembered buying two as a present for her mother out of her pocket money at a closing down sale of the pottery. These perfume bricks were also made by Collard when he first started at the Honiton Pottery a few years later.

After the pottery closed there were plans to use the site for a soda factory but these did not materialise and the premises were left empty for many years. Just before the Second World War numbers 21 and 23 Green Road were demolished and six houses were built set back from the road; these are known as Green Close and behind them the two storied pottery workshop still stands and is used today for light industrial purposes.

Wessex Pottery

Around 1915 a firm called the Wessex Perfumery and Potteries was formed with premises in the High Street, Poole and works in Old Wareham Road, Parkstone. Some of the wares of this pottery bear a strong resemblance to those of the Crown Dorset Pottery, therefore it seems likely that when Collard left Green Road some of his employees joined this new venture. Prior to this it is believed that Collard rented this business a room at the Crown Dorset works for the production of perfume. Pieces from this pottery were made in white or orange-beige clay and are incised 'Wessex Poole' on the base. Crown Dorset patterns, shapes and mottoes were used and, in some instances, the handwriting appears to be identical also. Not surprisingly, considering the name of the pottery, much of the ware was perfume orientated, and remarkably vessels for holding perfume were sometimes decorated in the Scandy pattern, a pattern which had not been used at Crown Dorset after the first few years.

Chapter 8

Marking Time

The years at Ilminster

On leaving Poole, Collard moved his family to Ilminster, Somerset where he bought Acacia House, Station Road a large old detached house on the Exeter to London road. They lived here between 1916 and 1918, but why they chose to settle here is not known. It is possible that Collard intended to acquire the Donyatt Pottery, a famous old pottery which had been producing slipware for several centuries, which was sited a couple of miles outside the town. By this time the pottery mainly produced domestic terracotta although a little art ware was still being produced.

It would appear that Collard did not have a full scale commercial pottery during this period, although he did have business cards printed and must therefore have been carrying out some sort of pottery business. He produced some fine pieces which were fired in the garden in a small kiln which he built himself. One such piece is the magnificent covered urn, shown in plate 16, which was made by Collard for his wife Emily and which bears her monogram on the lid. It is made of a pinkish-white clay and is incised on the base 'C. Collard 1916' in lower case. Although the decoration is strongly reminiscent of his previous work, (note the similarity of the mythical beast to that decorating the Longpark jardiniere illustrated in plate 9), the paints and glazes used are similar to those which he was to use later at Honiton. The paint was applied after the urn had been glazed and not before as had been his practice prior to this.

One of the characteristics of most of Collard's scroll decoration can particularly be seen on this urn. This is the 'three leaf' formation that almost resembles an inverted crown which can be seen immediately over the beast's tail to the right of the wing. This device is used to develop a series of scrolls from a single stem and can be seen on Collard's work at Crown Dorset and can also be seen on some Aller Vale pieces. Collard used this design of a mythical sea creature amongst scrolls again at Honiton on one or two large items.

Collard also decorated bone china, probably for the only time in his life, whilst he was at Ilminster. For example he decorated a tea service with a beautiful version of the Persian A1 pattern. Presumably his work during this period was only for his interest and as presents for his family and friends as so very little of it exists. If he had had a particular purpose in moving to Ilminster it would not appear to have been fulfilled, and his stay was only a brief one.

PART III
HONITON

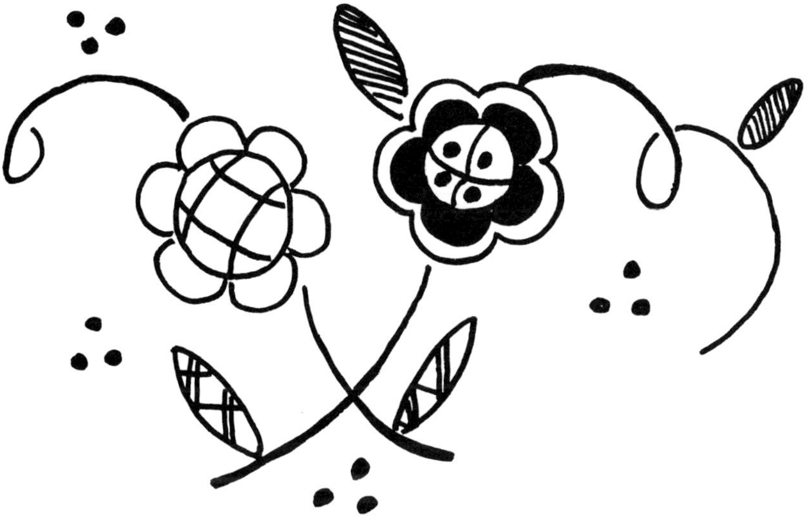

Chapter 9

A New Pottery Evolves

Honiton during the 1920s

When it was obvious that the war was drawing to its end Collard started to look around for another pottery. He heard of a small firm for sale in Staffordshire and went by train to the Midlands to see it. However when he got off the train the area was covered in a dense blanket of smog and Collard, a great lover of the countryside, decided that he had seen enough of Staffordshire and quickly turned around and caught the next train back to Somerset without stopping to view the pottery! Soon after this he embarked on a shorter and more successful journey by bicycle to look at another pottery for sale, this time at Honiton in Devon. Collard realised at once that this one had great potential and was just the opportunity he was looking for. The facilities at the pottery were very basic, this was quite an advantage as his funds must have dwindled during the previous three years and only half of the capital invested in the Crown Dorset pottery had been his. It also had the advantage of a good clay soil which would provide the raw material for his product without going to the expense of buying it in from a clay merchant. Additionally the pottery had a good frontage onto Honiton High Street which was then on the main tourist route from London to the South West, and thus thousands of potential customers would pass the door of the pottery every year.

Honiton Pottery before Collard

Collard is believed to have bought the business from Foster and Hunt who had run it for some years; exactly how long is not known because the directories and rate records of the area for that period were rather poor and erratic in their coverage and Foster and Hunt are not mentioned in them. Probably because of wartime conditions the business seems barely to have been functioning by 1918. The pottery Foster and Hunt produced was the typical Torquay type ware of the period, for instance cottages and boats in slip on a cream ground with mottoes scratched through the slip to show the dark local clay. The majority of these pieces were unmarked and may be attributed in error to Longpark of the Brewer period (prior to 1903). Occasionally more imaginative pieces were produced such as a vase with a royal blue slip with sgraffito decoration of a butterfly, flowers and leaves which anticipated the styles of the 1920s. Some of the pieces were marked on the base with the scratched mark F. H. HONITON in capital letters. These pieces are not very common and probably represented only part of their production, the bread and butter lines being baking dishes, bread containers, etc.. However there is some doubt about the ownership of the pottery during this period as at least one piece exists with the incised mark Frisk and Hunt, Honiton.

Prior to this rather doubtful period the pottery was run for many years by James Webber, who originally operated on a different site in Honiton moving his business to the present site of the pottery in 1881. In that year, 1881, John Phillips the owner of Aller Vale referred to the work of James Webber in a talk given to the Devonshire Association. In the course of which he said that Webber produced ware in the same style as Brannam of Barnstaple, namely highly decorated and quaint pottery. This was probably a minor part of the pottery's activities, the major part being the traditional cooking items, flower pots, etc..

The first years of Collard's ownership

Despite the fact that pottery of reasonable quality had been produced on the site for many years the buildings were very primitive and Collard's first job on acquiring the site was to bring the facilities up to date. During this period and the first few months of production Collard cycled from Ilminster to Honiton and back every day, a round journey of thirty-two miles. This was quite a journey on top of a hard day's work for a man of forty-four but Collard, who was an active man all his life, probably did not find it too onerous. After a few months he got the chance to rent the flat on the top floor of Manor House at the other end of the High Street to the pottery and his family moved there from Ilminster. Manor House is now a listed building, during the Collards' occupancy the ground floor was used for offices and the first floor was occupied by the Conservative Club.

When Collard bought the business the water, of which a pottery requires a great deal, had to be fetched from a nearby stream in buckets; there were no toilets for the workers and lighting was by oil lamps. This soon changed and water and gas were laid on. It was because he had gas installed that Collard first met the man who was to fire the kilns through virtually all of the pottery's life under his ownership. Bert Nott, affectionately known as Potty by his friends, had got a job in 1918 just after the war with the gas company and helped to install the gas pipes at the pottery; Collard obviously took a liking to him and offered him a job and although Bert Nott had no experience of pottery work he accepted. Another worker at the pottery in its early days was an old chap called Mike who had worked with Foster and Hunt as a pot turner, he worked as a decorator for Collard but found it difficult to fit in because he had been used to being in charge and had developed his own eccentricities.

In August 1919 Frederick Phelps came down from Ilminster to join the new pottery giving up his job as driver for the George Hotel, Ilminster, which was presumably where he first met Collard. The following month his wife moved down to join him and they lived in what was then known as Belmont Terrace. It is interesting to note that the sixteen mile journey from Ilminster to Honiton with the furniture took all day with breaks for lunch and tea and that Mrs Phelps did not go back to Ilminster for over fifty years. This is rather in contrast to Collard's speedy bicycle journeys. Mrs Phelps worked at the pottery packing and making raffia tassels. Initially the production was very similar to that of the Crown Dorset Art Pottery in its later years under Collard's ownership and included perfume pottery. Little Devon Violets perfume pots were made, around the narrow neck of which a loop of raffia with a tassel was fixed. Mrs Phelps made these by brushing the raffia with a wire brush for which she was paid 6d for 144. She also packed the pottery into round barrels and had the misfortune on one occasion to pack her ring along with the pottery. In what part of the world it ended up or whether it was ever found is not known. Probably it was thrown away with the packing; certainly she never saw it again.

Her husband packed and fired the kilns as part of his job. Initially this was done once a week at night and Frederick Phelps was glad of this extra work even though it meant missing a night's sleep because he received an extra 10/- a week for it. The kiln used was the old one that was in use in Foster and Hunt's day and was of course coal fired; it took three men to fire the kiln, Frederick Phelps, Collard and Bert Nott. Unfortunately Phelps contracted lead poisoning in 1922 and moved to Monkton to become a kennel huntsman for the Otter Vale Beagles where he remained for fifteen years. Collard may have used lead glazes during his first couple of years at the pottery but once the business got underway as explained later he changed to leadless glazes.

In all about a dozen people were employed at the pottery during the first few years: a thrower, a turner, a fireman, a plaster cast man and about half a dozen girl decorators. As he had done in his later years at Crown Dorset he employed only females to decorate and liked wherever possible to employ school leavers and train them himself. Among the decorators employed during this period were Mabel Rattenbury and the two Cowling sisters, Queenie and Gwen.

The first thrower that Collard employed at Honiton was Freddie Jeanes who was, by all accounts, a real character. He came from Poole originally and therefore may have first met Collard there and most probably worked at the Crown Dorset Art Pottery. Freddie joined the pottery at the start and was one of the traditional 'tramping' pottery workers who would wander off for a few months and then return to throw some more pots. He must have been an exceptionally good thrower because Collard put up with this and his drunken ways. Apparently he thought nothing of drinking a gallon of cider and was only fit to work three days a week, but in that time he produced more than most people could in five days. An early example of his work at Honiton which bears his name can be seen in the local museum.

This rather strange pot is well thrown but the unusual black matt decoration is extremely crude and not a credit to the decorator, who may have been Freddie himself! He can be seen at work in plate 53, where it can clearly be understood why he was given the nickname of the 'walrus'. He was also known as Captain Jeanes and may have been a seafaring man, being born in Poole. He stayed in lodgings with Mrs Campion who used to take in 'waifs and strays', and as old age crept on he gradually settled down in Honiton and gave up tramping. When the kilns were being fired Freddie would go up to the pottery and sit by them all night to keep warm.

Innovations to the processes

After the first year or so Collard, who was always experimenting, made changes to the processes that were to remain in effect until he retired after the Second World War and which gave pottery from Honiton its individual stamp. The first change was hardly a major one and was made very early on by necessity. The local red clay which was used initially proved to be less than satisfactory, it was too strong and blistered during firing. Blisters like 'duck eggs' appeared, usually on the bottom of the pot making the piece wobbly, this happened particularly if the body was thrown too thickly. This effect can be seen in plate 55. To remedy this, white china clay from Cornwall was used to mix with the local clay to 'weaken' it. Usually one quarter of the mixture was white clay but the exact proportion depended on the quality of the local red clay. This mixture gives the pots the unusual appearance of being made of beige coloured clay. The pottery had its own bed of clay which was used but Collard would also get clay from all round Honiton from building sites and such like, therefore constant judgement was needed as to the quantity of white clay necessary to form the right mixture. If too much white clay was used the pot would craze and the glaze would peel. The glaze would also peel if the leather dry pots were dipped in the slip when too dry and so this had to be carefully watched as well.

The second innovation to the processes, a major one, was to the glazes. Collard developed a white leadless glaze that was applied before decoration; normally pieces are decorated and then covered in a transparent glaze. In the early part of the twentieth century there was a great outcry and much agitation in Parliament concerning the dangers of lead glazes that resulted in lead poisoning in some pottery workers. As early as 1886 a German chemist, Hermann Seger, published a paper suggesting formulae for possible leadless glazes; his ideas were taken up by the English ceramic chemist J. W. Mellor and in 1912 he suggested a formula for a leadless glaze to be fired at high temperatures. This glaze, however, was criticised as being unsuitable for underglaze colours, causing the blues to flow. It was also criticised because it tended to drain off sloping surfaces and became full of bubbles where the glaze accumulated thickly. Art potteries were among the first to use leadless glazes; the mass production factories in Staffordshire were more reluctant to adopt such glazes on account of the cost. The advantage of lead in a glaze was that it produced greater fusability and when applied to a clay body firing could take place at a lower temperature.

Collard was one of many potters during this period to use leadless glazes. It is not known for certain when he first began to use these but, knowing his regard for his workers, he would have done it at the first practicable opportunity. Certainly the white glaze that he developed around 1922 was leadless and was applied before the painted decoration; once developed, this technique was used on nearly all the ware produced at Honiton during Collard's time there. The process consisted of dipping the pot in slip, firing, dipping the pot in glaze, painting and finally firing once more. This method is similar to one used at the Carter, Stabler and Adams pottery at Poole, which may account for the similarity which some people consider exists between the two firms' pottery. This glaze produced a matt surface; if, however, the pieces were fired to a greater extent the surface became shiny and the colours of the paints began to run, see plate 17. Some pieces can be found where one side has a matt finish and the other side which was nearer the fire is quite glossy and the colours are fuzzy looking. This over firing is of course the technique he used at Green Road to produce the soft focus cottages and again at Honiton a slight 'fuzzing' of the colours was aimed for on some pieces.

The final innovation was in the manner of firing the kilns.

The kilns took two days to fire initially and the biscuit and gloss pottery were fired separately as was the custom. Collard had the idea that both types of pottery could be fired together, this would of course cut the firing time and save money. With this in mind he climbed inside the old kiln and removed bricks to make four new flues, eight in total, so that the kiln got very hot. This proved successful and allowed the soft pottery that was to become biscuit to be fired at the top of the kiln, which was the hottest part, and the biscuit ware which had been glazed and decorated to be fired at the same time in the lower part of the kiln.

Bert Nott the fireman described the process as follows. The kiln would be bricked up on Friday afternoon and Nott would go back to the pottery at half past nine in the evening to light up one fire with the ashes of the last kiln. Then at about five o'clock in the morning he returned to get the other three fires going and by six o'clock that evening the firing finished and Nott would return once more at nine o'clock on Saturday evening to rake it out. Not only did this system save money but the fireman did not have to lose a night's sleep. During firing the fires were stoked at precise ½ hour intervals. The kiln was fired when full once a week, if it was not ready for firing on Friday and could not be bricked up until the next day it would not be cool enough to unpack on Monday morning. Therefore it was important that the volume of production was kept up and sometimes late on a Friday morning Collard would go round to the decorators to say "Bert Nott wants those pots by two o'clock!" Then there would be a rush to get them decorated in time and the girls would choose the simplest decoration which was the pattern called 'bands' which consisted of just a few coloured lines round the pots in green, orange and brown. This method of firing the kilns seems to have caused considerable amazement and people came down from the Potteries to see the process unable to believe that both types of pottery could be fired together and in so short a time. The process was not, however, unique to the Honiton Pottery, similar ones were in use at about the same time at Carter, Stabler and Adams and at the Torquay Pottery Co. Ltd. A picture of the kiln during firing can be seen in plate 56; apparently so high was the temperature that flames could be seen rising from the top of the kiln between 5 and 6 o'clock in the evening. The coal for the kiln was delivered by lorry from Radstock collieries and Collard was most insistent that it should be well covered during the journey so that it arrived dry; if the coal was wet the desired temperature could not be reached.

Bert Nott's job became much more skilled with this altered kiln because the horseshoes (thermoscope bars) would bend so very quickly that he had to keep a close eye on them. Collard was a very fair man and if anything went wrong in the firing of the pots and the horseshoes were correctly formed then Nott obviously could not be blamed. Very occasionally a whole kiln load of pottery was ruined, this was of course a financial disaster as a whole week's production was lost. Sometimes some of the pots were spoiled in firing possibly because one of Collard's many experimental glazes had not worked as well in practice as on the test pieces.

In 1925 Collard experimented with oil fired kilns which appear to have been designed and installed by Lord Somers. The system, based on the gravity feed principle, consisted of four kilns with flues one into another, one kiln could be used for glaze, the second for biscuit, etc.. A letter from Lord Somers written at the Turf Club exists in which he expresses his pleasure that Collard obtained good commercial results from the system; this was because, as he goes on to say, "I am hoping that the system will interest Mr Richardson and that he will recommend the system to the Potteries". After the initial good results the oil kilns were not used and the Honiton Pottery returned to its old coal fired kilns, the oil kilns remained in place, however, until the pottery was sold, one having been adapted for use with coal. The reasons for their fall from favour seem to be several: firstly they got too hot over the fire brick, secondly there were noisy and crude and thirdly some thought that they did not give the sheen to the pots that was achieved by firing with coal, a criticism that could also be levelled against electric kilns.

Collard and his family

After a time Collard moved his family from Manor House Flat in the High Street, which was quite a walk from the pottery, to Westcott House near the station. This house had the great advantage of a footpath which led from the station to the back of the pottery, it was convenient for Collard to use the back entrance as he obviously got dirty at work. It was also much nearer the pottery than the previous house which was a great advantage as Collard spent most of his time there. He could be found at the pottery on Saturday afternoons and he used to go there on Sunday mornings before church to watch the pottery and make sure that it was in the correct condition. In the hot weather pots made on Thursday and Friday needed turning by Sunday otherwise they would dry out on top to too great an extent, so the pots had to be turned in order to even the drying process and to slow it down. Therefore when, a few years later in 1927, the house next to the pottery, known as Kingswood, suddenly came on the market Collard was eager to buy it, which he did, to cut out the journey completely.

Once Collard had moved next door to the pottery it could be said that it never closed, if a charabanc of visitors arrived unexpectedly on a Sunday they would be shown round and his daughter who was now fourteen would help to do this. The courtyard between the house and the business was brightened up by the addition of roundels and tiles made by Collard in a spare moment which were cemented to the exterior walls; in addition shelves were erected outside on which the pots for sale stood in the summer so that the whole place had rather a festive, continental atmosphere. Some of the roundels, rather the worse for the action of the weather, can be seen today and inside the pottery building there is still a plaque bearing Collard's coat of arms made of clay.

Collard had scrimped and saved to send his daughter to a small private school nearby. Although the pottery was a success it was quite a struggle to get the business well established financially during the ten years after the First World War. This was firstly because Collard had made so many capital improvements when he purchased the pottery and secondly because it was growing steadily during these years more cash was needed to sustain the business. This had to be supplied largely from past profits because the Honiton Pottery was not run as a company as Crown Dorset had been. Collard was the sole proprietor until his daughter became a partner in the business in the 1930s. He obviously preferred being entirely his own master unlike the situation at Crown Dorset where the other directors changed on a number of occasions as different people put money into the business, thus the financial set up at Honiton obviously had advantages although it made expansion difficult. Nevertheless the business did expand and by the late 1920s the staff employed had grown to around thirty at which number it remained throughout the 1930s, and that decade proved to be a very successful and prosperous one for the pottery.

Sadly Emily Collard died in her early forties before the business became a success. Although she had not played a large active part in the running of the pottery she had kept the books and had been a great support to her husband putting up with a certain amount of hardship which was inevitable in running one's own pottery during the early years of this century. They had been a very close family and her death came as a great blow to Collard and his daughter.

Chapter 10

The Jacobean and Stuart Periods

Designs and styles

The pottery produced initially by Collard at Honiton was very similar to some of the later Crown Dorset wares. The first type produced was unglazed perfume pottery made from the local red clay, such as the piece that can be seen in Honiton Museum decorated in pale blue with white lilies of the valley. Other pieces of perfume pottery were made such as tablets the size and shape of an oval bar of soap which were impregnated with Devon violets and when rubbed on the hands left them smelling sweet. Some of these were given away as a sales gimmick to help the business get started. In addition to these perfume pots, with raffia handles and tassels, were made for lavender water, Devon violets, etc..

Once this production was underway Collard began to train his staff to produce typical Torquay type motto ware decorated with cockerels, cottages or windmills. They differed from their Torquay counterparts in that the design was usually outlined in brown slip rather than being incised. The colours used were also quite different to those Collard had made and used at Dorset, the greens have much more blue in them than the rather yellow Dorset greens. Very often two cottages appear, the left hand one having a blue roof; this colour, a petrol blue, usually appears again on a band around the top edge of the pot. The trees are painted a dull mustard yellow to give them an autumnal effect.

One line mottoes were nearly always used including some previously used at Dorset such as 'Elp yersel tu th' cream', and 'Remembered joys are never past'. These pieces were produced in the local red clay which appears deeper in colour than the Dorset clay, almost a chocolate colour with small black flecks in it. This clay however proved rather unsatisfactory as it caused blistering on some pieces; therefore Collard produced some in white clay instead. Though some of this ware is pleasant enough it was not marked and may be mistaken by collectors for the products of Torquay potteries. Examples of this type of ware can be seen in plate 58 which is a reproduction of an advertisement in the Pottery Gazette of October 1921, the same photograph was used in an advertising leaflet. The other design featured in this plate is simply one of four petalled flowers outlined in white slip and linked to each other by a chain of dots in slip, the petals of the flowers have been blocked in with colour. In this instance all the flowers appear dark and the main ground light, but other colour combinations exist such as a dark blue ground with sand coloured flower petals. This pattern was in production at Honiton prior to Collard's acquisition of the pottery, thus some pieces are marked 'F.H.Honiton'. The shapes of the pieces shown in this advertisement are very similar to the later Crown Dorset shapes and bear hardly any resemblance to the much more common Honiton shapes developed a couple of years later and shown in the 1930s catalogue illustrated in plates 70 to 82. The early advertising leaflet lists wholesale prices for the pots, the covered flower holder number five was the most expensive costing 3/6d, this compares with a wage of, say, 7/6d a week for a fourteen year old pottery worker.

Whilst the pottery was producing the type of ware shown in plate 58 it traded under the name of the Honiton Art Potteries. However Collard was not happy with this production and was looking around for new ideas to suit the new market that was developing as life returned to normal after the First World War. He felt that the Torquay type ware was 'played out' and if his new venture was to succeed it must offer a new image and a new style of pottery. This assumption proved to be correct as witnessed by the number of Torquay potteries which closed in the inter-war years. The first changes he made were not very dramatic as can be seen from the small jug in plate 57. He was aiming at a simpler less decorated style to suit the current taste of the time, and, in keeping with this, he simplified the name of the business to the Honiton Pottery. The jug in plate 57 is covered in a beige-brown slip and decorated with simple sgraffito leaves and fruits in green and yellow under a light glaze and bearing the most popular sentiment of the time 'Lest we forget'. This shows that he had not entirely deserted motto ware yet, although he was keen to do so, and other similar pots exist bearing mottoes such as 'A good wife's price is beyond rubies'. These are made of a dark (by Honiton standards) red-brown clay, and were produced in the very early 1920s.

The New Honiton Style

Suddenly a considerable change took place and a whole range of new patterns and shapes were evolved, using the new white leadless glaze that Collard had developed. The pieces are noticeably larger than those made before either at Honiton or Dorset and are nearly all large jugs, vases or bowls. An advertisement first placed in the Pottery Gazette in February 1924, which is reproduced in plate 59, shows early examples of this new type of ware. Geometric and Celtic patterns obviously were a popular line during this period and the biscuit barrel shown in this plate is a very fine piece. Gradually the shapes were standardised so that by about 1925 a range of some fifty or sixty shapes existed. Around 1934 a catalogue was produced showing as many of the different styles of decoration as possible and all of the shapes available which by then numbered 106, this is reproduced in plates 70 to 82. These could be requested by the customer quoting the number which was painted in black on the base of the piece. The base of the piece was recessed, to give it a professional finish as Collard said, and the slip was wiped from the base exposing the clay, but the base was glazed. Stilt marks are not visible as stilts were only used on rare occasions, this was because the new glaze did not stick to the saggar so readily as the old one and in any case the glaze was wiped from the bottom rim to prevent the pot sticking. Virtually all of this type of ware was slipped inside as well as on the outside of the pot unlike the pottery Collard produced earlier at Crown Dorset and Aller Vale.

Once developed virtually all of the production was decorated overglaze. This nearly always gave the pottery a matt finish although firing to a greater extent produced a glossier finish. Despite this matt finish the pottery produced was not porous and tea-sets could be made quite satisfactorily in it. However Collard's successor Mr Hull had great difficulty achieving the same effect and had to cease production of tea-sets.

Jacobean Ware

One of the first and most popular patterns to be developed with this matt finish was the Jacobean, illustrated in plates 18 and 30; this pattern typifies the style of the Honiton Pottery during the inter-war years and helped to make the pottery famous. The Jacobean pattern is still linked in the public's mind today with the Honiton Pottery, just as cottage motto ware is with Torquay, and a version is still in production today at Honiton. The inspiration for this pattern may have been derived from some of the early Aller Vale barbotine ware (see plate 1) but more obviously came from the needlework of the Jacobean period and was in accord with the popular vogue for Tudor and Stuart styles in furniture, textile and house design in the 1920s and 1930s. The Jacobean pattern appears in infinite variations and it is unlikely that two identical pieces could be found unless painted as a pair. The arrangement of the flowers varies from piece to piece as do the fantastic flowers themselves; there are many different flower styles, each decorator presumably having her own favourites and personal style. The flowers are first outlined in paint and then blocked in with some of the vast array of coloured paints that Collard developed, and although each flower is different they always grow from the base of the design and sweep from right to left across the pot. Usually only two flowers are painted on vases and jugs on opposite sides, these are then linked with intertwining leaves. Usually a blue dotted line formed by brush strokes is found around the rim.

Dating Honiton Pottery

Production of the Jacobean pattern started very early on and remained popular throughout Collard's years at the pottery, therefore dating pieces can be quite difficult. In order to do so a number of factors need to be considered; the colour of the paints, the design of the border, the colour and degree of flecking in the slip, the degree of matt finish, the colour of the clay and the pottery mark. Each one of these factors will be dealt with in detail, it must be noted, however, that all factors should be taken together to date a piece as there are exceptions to every rule. All these points, with the possible exception of the first, hold good for dating all Honiton pottery regardless of pattern.

1. *Paint colours.* Early pieces of Jacobean ware have their flowers and leaves outlined most often in brown or gold-yellow, although grey or blue is occasionally used during this period. Late pieces, made in the 1930s, nearly always have the outline painted in green. On the whole the paints used to block in the pattern tend to orange and brown more often on early pieces, blues and greens tend to dominate on later pieces; this however must only be taken as a rough guide as a wide range of colours were available to the decorators the whole time. One colour that does not appear to have been developed until about 1926 and was not used extensively until the second half of the 1930s was a distinctive lustrous green paint, particularly associated with the Woodland pattern. This paint was made from copper and was black when applied to the pot but turned green on firing. The decoration on early pieces of Honiton pottery was often naive, but with time the decoration gradually became more polished.

2. *Borders.* Early pieces circa 1920-1928 very often have borders on the top section of the body consisting of small outlined rectangles. Later pieces made in the middle of the 1930s tend to have a border consisting of blue sweeping brush marks alternating with mustard yellow dots. Sgraffito pieces which usually date from 1930 onwards often have borders comprised solely of outlined circles filled with paint.

3. *The slip.* The slip is nearly always a neutral colour and on early pieces tends to be flecked, usually with purple or brown flecks and sometimes the surface of the slip is covered with small pinholes, this changes by the later half of the 1920s and the slip becomes plain in colour but often with a subtle tinting of green or brown. Some pieces of all periods have strongly coloured slips which form a major part of the decoration, see plate 22.

4. *Matt finish.* The degree of matt finish changed over the years, but within this there is quite a variation with one kiln load varying from the previous one. Pieces became more matt in appearance up to about 1930, thereafter the process was slightly reversed and some of the later pieces have quite glossy finishes.

5. *Colour of the clay.* The colour of the clay that can be seen on the base and sometimes on the inside of the pot varies considerably, this is because Collard got his clay from different sites and added different proportions of white clay to the local red clay. Initially the colour was especially variable. In the main between about 1920-1927 it appears as a pale grey-brown, but some quite reddish-beige and some yellow-beige clay also exists from this period. Then between 1927 and 1937 approximately the clay became paler and more consistent in colour, and may be described as a pale fawn, presumably this was because more white clay was used and the source of the red clay was more stable. In the last period of Collard's ownership the clay suddenly became much darker, perhaps as he perfected techniques he needed to add less white clay to the mixture, it is a deep (by Honiton's standards) red-brown. In addition on some of the late pieces the white slip is not wiped from the base. Very occasionally pots were made from white clay, these were experimental pieces and are nearly always late.

6. *Pottery mark.* Pots are nearly always marked on the base with an impressed stamp either HONITON ENGLAND or COLLARD HONITON ENGLAND in capital letters, see appendix I. HONITON ENGLAND was the first mark to be used and is found on pots made between 1920 and 1929, therefore it is found most often with grey-brown clay, with flecked and tinted slips and fairly matt glazes. The second mark, the small COLLARD HONITON ENGLAND probably overlapped the first mark slightly and was used therefore between 1927 and 1937. It was definitely still in use in 1937 because the commemorative coronation pieces have this mark and are made of very pale clay; by 1937 the glaze had become quite glossy but earlier pieces with the small COLLARD HONITON ENGLAND mark have a very matt

finish. The final mark, the large COLLARD HONITON ENGLAND, was used between 1935 and 1947 and is almost always found on pieces made of red-brown clay. The commemorative piece made in 1946 bears this mark. The dates of the pottery marks, just discussed, are drawn from comparison of different pieces of pottery and may not therefore be absolutely correct, it is definitely known however that the mark HONITON ENGLAND was not used between 1930 and 1947. Very occasionally on rather special pieces the word 'Honiton' is incised or painted in black. Usually the decorator's mark does not appear on the pottery, but again very occasionally on special pieces a signature or initials may be found, either painted or incised. Another very rare mark is simply MADE IN ENGLAND. This mark appears on pieces that one would expect to be stamped HONITON ENGLAND and was obviously used during the 1920s, probably the early 1920s as some pieces with this mark have a black shape number that does not tally with the numbers listed in the 1930s catalogue nor with the leaflet of 1920. For instance a shape which is in fact number 91 in the 1930s catalogue is marked number 6. on the base of a MADE IN ENGLAND piece, this little pot is decorated with a Celtic pattern similar to the biscuit barrel number 17 in plate 71. Finally a word of caution concerning the HONITON ENGLAND mark. It appears that this mark was revived for a short period immediately after Collard sold the business and thus thrown pieces (as opposed to pressed ware) made between 1947 and 1949 may bear this mark. Most of the pottery made during this period was of white clay and is therefore easy to distinguish, but a few pieces were made of the local red clay, they can usually be identified by their style which is slightly different from the earlier pieces bearing the HONITON ENGLAND mark which were made prior to 1930.

Other Patterns

A much rarer pattern than the Jacobean was known as the Stuart, surprisingly the name of this pattern has no historical connections, it is in fact named after Vera Stuart, the decorator who specialised in it, an example can be seen in plate 19. Another decorator who gave her name to a design was Beryl

Radford; known as the Beryl pattern it is in an Eastern style and is of a pheasant-like bird perched on a flowering tree.

A pattern that was popular during the 1920s was the de Morgan, see plate 20. This was named after a William de Morgan design which was itself based on an old Turkish one, so Isnik pottery was still providing an inspiration for new ideas for Collard and of course he continued to produce versions of his Persian pattern, these were usually painted by Jessie Banbury and later by Florrie Loving. The very best examples were of course painted by Collard himself, and a large covered vase, which is reproduced in plate 21, was one of which he was particularly proud. This was thrown by Collard himself and decorated by him in 1927 and stood for many years in the pottery showroom. Gradually the Persian pattern changed to incorporate the 'saz' pattern, and a distinctive 'seed head' flower, these designs had only rarely been used by Collard before at Crown Dorset or Aller Vale. The 'saz' pattern can be partly seen in plate 21 while the seed head can be seen in plate 64 where the Persian pattern is used to decorate the plate in the top right corner. This plate, decorated in pink, lilac, turquoise, royal blue and green, was made around 1940 and shows the considerable changes that had overtaken the Persian pattern by that time. In addition the borders of the Honiton Persian pattern pieces are nearly always decorated with a mass of swirls seen on the original Isnik pottery but used sparingly on pieces made at Aller Vale. He also used one or two Isnik shapes such as the two handled mug in plate 18, this shape had also been used at Aller.

Other links with the patterns of Aller Vale include the piece photographed in plate 22 of trailing leaves and birds on a blue ground. Although the decorating technique is much changed the pattern is noticeably the same as that of the jardiniere depicted in plate 32. Another link between the designs of the two potteries is that of a dolphin. In the Honiton pieces the dolphins appear many times in a running border as illustrated in plate 72, number 25. The outline of the dolphins was handpainted, as normal, and the blocked colour was applied with a small sponge cut in the shape of the dolphin, the same sponge method was also used when regular square blocks of colour were required in a border. This was the only concession that was made to mass production decorating techniques at Honiton. The sponge was also used in the production of a design used on fruit bowls which consisted of a bunch of grapes and other fruit; an example decorated by Florrie Loving is shown in plate 60. This time the sponge was not used as an aid to mass production but merely as a method of applying the paint to achieve a less solid effect, highlights were then applied with the brush.

The Jacobean and Persian patterns were by no means the only floral designs, one popular at the end of the 1920s, but apparently no longer in production by the time of the 1930s catalogue, was that of a rose with a butterfly on the reverse side, this design is shown in plate 23. Another design not shown in the catalogue but produced about 1930 uses the heads of moondaisies and can be seen in plate 65. Small posies of flowers were used to decorate smaller items, such as those on shapes 26 and 27 in plate 72, and individual sprigs of flowers were used on larger pieces. Other flower designs include cabbage roses, sweet peas and honesty (plate 75, number 60). Another floral design, introduced in the mid 1930s, was that of a broad band of flowers (sometimes the Jacobean pattern) between two broad bands of colour, usually a deep sea-green, two jugs in this style are seen in plate 73. These bands of colour were produced by dipping the bottom of the pot to ⅓ of its height in the green slip, removing it, wiping and cleaning the base and then repeating the process for the top ⅓ of the pot, thus leaving the middle free for decoration with flowers.

A whole range of designs were produced that were suitable for decorating small pieces, these encircled the piece in bands; some were based on triangles, some on arcs and others on circles. Three such designs are shown in plate 24, the teapot in which is decorated in a design that developed over the years from a Jacobean flower. Examples of this design during its early stages of development, a running band of a Jacobean flower, can be found on pieces marked HONITON ENGLAND. Gradually the design became simplified until on early pieces marked with the small COLLARD HONITON ENGLAND only the base line which is formed in two parts to give the curve of a petal betrays its floral origin. A few years later the two lines become one at the base and the design resembles a series of hills rather than a flower. By 1940 the design seems to have been modified again and once more bears some resemblance to a flower as can be seen from the lamp in plate 64. Occasionally running patterns were used on large vases ranging from the simplest, three solid bands of colour, to a much more complicated design of ships, sometimes Viking boats and sometimes Spanish galleons, illustrated in plate 72 on shape 34.

Design Developments in the 1930s

A design that was most successfully introduced in the 1930s was the Woodland Series, shown in plate 61. This consists of a dappled leaping stag and on the opposite side two stylised roses rather reminiscent of the rose Collard used at Crown Dorset, shown on the pot-pourri vase in plate 46. Many pieces were produced with this design and it is one of the most standardised of all of the Honiton patterns. The vast majority were painted in the semi-lustrous green that was one of the pottery's most distinctive and attractive colours and was of course particularly appropriate for this pattern. Sometimes however the design was painted in a whole range of colours and sometimes just in two contrasting colours such as bright yellow and blue. This design is one of quite a few produced at this period which incorporate the motif of three dots arranged in a triangle. It was first used at the Crown Dorset Pottery around 1912 as can be seen from plate 52 and Collard introduced it again years later on several different patterns; for instance a pattern of tiny recurring posies of flowers is interspersed with these three dots, this was popular just before the Second World War.

By the mid 1930s, having established a successful Honiton style which had been in production for some years, Collard began to look around once more for new ideas. One rare design developed just before the Second World War is shown in plate 25, it is different from most other Honiton pottery in so far as it is covered completely in colour and is reminiscent of Dutch pottery, for which it might easily be mistaken. Another complete change of style, on a rather special piece, is shown in plate 26. The lamp base is made entirely from pottery, the top and base being covered in a dull grey lustre paint to imitate metal. In this particular example Collard took his ideas from Chinese pottery and produced a very individual design, other styles of decoration on this shape lamp base are much more in keeping with normal Honiton flower patterns.

Some of the 1930s patterns were outlined in sgraffito rather than in paint and were decorated in the traditional method, underglaze, rather than overglaze. An example of this style of work can be seen in plate 27. Many of these art deco designs are geometric and in some cases the sgraffito work appears to have been drawn with a compass. The paints used are clear, autumnal colours, usually browns, yellows, and greens with the occasional addition of blue and black on a cream ground. The technique and type of colour used is very similar to the Aller Vale Q1 design from which it was probably derived and this similarity extends to the use of vertical strips to split the panels of decoration as can be seen in plate 35. Another type of ware that was painted before it was glazed, and which is reminiscent of Italian pottery, is shown in plate 28. This jug has a textured body and the effect was achieved by applying very thick slip to the body with a brush, it was then decorated with an incised pattern and painted before being given a dark glaze. (Sgraffito work at Honiton was done, just as at Aller Vale, with a nail rather than a special tool.) The jugs in this style nearly always have rope handles. Rope handles are often denoted by the addition of the letter A to the shape code, e.g. 33A. The colours used do vary, but the semi-lustrous green was the most popular for the main bands of colour although sometimes it was replaced by a brown. Many colours are used in the decoration including a bright pink, bright blue and mustard yellow. This very attractive style which is nearly always found on major pieces continued in use until Collard sold the pottery in 1947. A particularly fine example of this type of work is shown in plate 29 which was made and decorated by Collard during the Second World War. He probably obtained the idea for this stippled finish from the barbotine style ware that he had decorated during his very early years at Aller Vale. It is interesting to note that similar pottery was produced occasionally by Harry Crute, the well known Torquay decorator, at the Dartmouth Pottery after the Second World War.

A range of styles being produced in 1940 can be seen in plate 64. The rather art deco style that had been used during the

1930s on pieces decorated underglaze had given way to the style illustrated by the large central vase which is decorated overglaze rather than underglaze. Perhaps the vase with its 'leafy' design in the top right of the plate still shows traces of art deco influence. As the photograph shows, Collard was still developing new designs whilst retaining the old favourites e.g. the Jacobean pattern in the bottom left-hand corner. Some of the designs would not have been out of place if produced during the 1950s, for example the polka-dot tea-set and the jug to the immediate right of the large vase. For comparison with the production of the mid 1930s see plate 62.

The pottery produced during these later years was on the whole the best produced at Honiton. At the Crown Dorset pottery Collard had an expert decorator in Jim Main to assist him from the start and therefore the standard of the decorating was good during the first few years. At Honiton however he did not have the benefit of a skilled decorator initially, all the girls he employed were new to the trade and had to be trained and this meant that any pieces which required skill had to be decorated by Collard himself, who was already busy with the day to day running of the business and the training of staff. As a result of this and the fact that he was experimenting and changing the techniques very few really good pieces of pottery were produced during the early years. Gradually the quality improved as he mastered the changed techniques and as his workforce became more skilful, so that by the time the Second World War interrupted the pottery's development some of the pieces produced were of a very high standard indeed. The early years of the Second World War gave those workers who had not at that time been called up a chance to really show their skills and produce pieces which gave them pleasure as so little pottery could be sold at that time. Therefore throughout Collard's period at Honiton the quality of the pottery was always improving and even in the last years new and imaginative styles were being introduced.

Other Wares

Not only did the pottery make jugs and vases it also met the then current vogue for all kinds of 'sets'; tea-sets, coffee sets, egg sets, fruit sets, sandwich sets, porridge sets, etc.! Other pieces included toast racks, pipe rests, denture boxes, cigarette boxes, candlesticks, wall brackets, tiles, electric lamps and children's mugs and model animals.

The model animals made for children seemed to be very popular at the time but are seldom found today; some of them are caricatures and others are natural representations; some were slipped in one colour and others were painted with several different colours. At least sixty different designs existed, they were made from moulds most of which were modelled by Collard or David Hickmott, although some were made by students who worked at the pottery in the summer. A range of these animals can be seen in plates 80 and 81, they nearly always have a hollow base and as a result of this are not marked with the pottery's backstamp. Other moulded pieces decorated only with a coloured slip, usually pink, turquoise, blue, black or white include all sorts of shaped vases including one in the shape of a fish with its head on the base and its back curving upwards so that the tail forms the opening of the vase. Models such as Anne Hathaway's cottage, a rather splendid lion and a comic fat fish with its mouth wide open were also made and moulded. In plate 62 some novelty face masks can be seen on the wall, these are the faces of real people. The moulds were made by putting plaster all over the model's face, with the exception of two air-holes for the nostrils, and then allowing the plaster to dry before removing it to use as a mould for the clay. Another rather unusual moulded line was that of garden animals. These were up to two feet high and were fired and painted but not glazed; the animals included ducks, rabbits, squirrels and penguins and were modelled by David Hickmott.

The pottery also made tiles, this was a new line for Collard as he does not appear to have made any previously at Dorset. Some were decorated in Jacobean style but animals seemed the most popular style of decoration and jumping lambs, leaping stags, fish, rabbits, etc. can be found painted in the clear simple brush strokes that were popular at the time and that are most effective.

In the early years the pottery made decorative plaques (plates) to hang on the wall. They were moulded and bore scenes such as a drinking house or the interior of a Tyrolean cottage and were partially painted underglaze in the typical blues, yellows and pinks of Honiton and are nearly always marked HONITON ENGLAND. Another piece decorated underglaze is a small dish or ashtray that is marked with the small COLLARD HONITON ENGLAND. It is painted inside with a pixie sitting between two toadstools and, rather surprisingly, has the sentiment 'Lest we forget' incised round the outside. This is one of the very rare motto pieces made at Honiton to bear this later mark.

Reading Lamps

Perhaps the most original line that proved to be very successful was the making of pottery lamp bases and matching shades. A range of these lamps, produced in the early thirties, can be seen in plate 82; although often found today they are unfortunately, but not surprisingly, very rarely found with their original shade. The lamps pictured in the plate were entirely hand-made at the pottery with the obvious exception of the electrical parts which were ordered from a company in London. The shades were cut out of parchment or linen and then handsewn to the frame and decorated to match the pottery base by Jessie Banbury. All of the Honiton lamp bases sold at the pottery had these special matching shades, but in addition thousands of lamp bases were sent to Elliott and Spears store in London where they were fitted with the store's own shades. The pottery also had contracts to supply Harrods and John Lewis with lamps. None of these lamp bases are known to be marked as they do not have a flat base on which the stamp could be impressed, however they are quite recognisable by the colour of the clay which shows through on the base rim.

Specialities

The pottery was always quite happy to make individual pieces even if they were as simple as egg cups for children with their own names on. Other special pieces made that can still be remembered today were ashtrays made for H.M.S. Exeter, two altar vases requested by the vicar of a church in Bristol and a dinner service bearing the coat of arms of the Egyptian ambassador, Dr Hassan Nachat Pasha. This was given as a gift on the occasion of his marriage to a local girl, Patricia Priest, who had taught at the junior school in Honiton. Honiton pottery seemed popular as a wedding gift, the Mothers Union presented a tall vase, thrown by Ernest Carnell, to Mr and Lady Evelyn Anstey on their marriage and Collard always gave his girl decorators a tea-set as a present when they got married.

Sir Frank Brangwyn, the artist, commissioned a series of sgraffito jugs in 1930 from Collard, presumably as part of an interior decoration he was working on. Collard put some original ideas into effect which appear to have pleased Sir Frank, and which were probably the prototypes of the normal sgraffito patterns produced at Honiton during the 1930s. Brangwyn in turn was commissioned by Doulton's in the 1930s to design some tableware, this also had a sgraffito design. Collard also produced pottery for other companies, which were filled with their products; for instance he made honeypots for a Somerset firm and little scent pots decorated with lavender and bearing the words Devon Lavender, in addition to the usual pots for violets.

Commemoratives

Just as he did at Crown Dorset Collard produced coronation mugs at Honiton. It is believed that two were produced for the coronation of George VI, one for Lyme Regis and one for Honiton. In addition he let his pottery workers make a coronation item for themselves, in one case a toilet bowl and in another a mug, these pieces can be recognised by the signature of the worker on the base. They are usually decorated with red and blue bands of colour and an applied shield with the royal coat of arms with a crown above and incised words such as 'George VI Coronation 1937'. Also a lamp base (the same shape as the base second from the left on the bottom row in plate 82) exists with a larger version of the royal coat of arms but without an inscription, the purpose of which is not known unless it was produced around that period for a patriotic buyer. Despite the fact that these coronation pieces were produced Collard was not keen on making commemorative wares, feeling perhaps that they were too similar to the motto ware from which he had striven to change his style. However one final commemorative item was made after the war to commemorate the victory. It was a mug marked 'Borough of Honiton/Victory Day June 8th 1946/J.M. Phillips, Mayor'.

Chapter 11

Success on the Tourist Route

Memories of Honiton during the thirties

In the late 1920s a new generation of workers began to join the pottery, one of them not surprisingly was Collard's daughter, Joan. By the time she left school at the age of fourteen she was already accomplished at drawing. Since she was eleven her father had encouraged her to draw a picture every day in a notebook and often gave her ideas for suitable subjects. Initially she worked part-time at the pottery going by train to Exeter Art School two or three days a week. Gradually she began to take more and more responsibility in the pottery taking some of the weight off her father's shoulders and becoming a partner in the business. It was just as well she took such an active part in the firm because, about ten years later, in 1938, her father got double pneumonia and she had to run the business entirely on her own for some months until he recovered. Not only was she an extremely capable decorator, as can be seen from plate 30 but she could also carry out all of the pottery processes which was obviously a great help in running the business. In particular she was in charge of the girls in the decorating room, as can be seen in plate 63, but in addition she kept the books, mixed the glazes, etc..

As at Dorset the glazes were made on the premises, as indeed was everything that was used and required in the pottery such as the saggars. Collard or his daughter prepared all of the glazes themselves, thus the composition of the glazes remained more or less a secret which is now forgotten. However it is remembered that the white leadless glaze contained a white powder which was used during the Second World War as face powder by the girls in the A.T.S.!

The men of Honiton

Another of the new generation of workers was Ernest Carnell who joined the pottery in 1929, again at the age of fourteen. His father, a local builder, was already well known to Collard as he had on many occasions carried out repairs to the pottery buildings and kilns. Carnell supposedly joined as an apprentice for five years but Collard was not one to formalise things and no paperwork to tie Carnell down was issued. He started by doing the labouring jobs such as mixing the clay and then progressed to helping the old thrower Freddie Jeanes by weighing the balls of clay and by filling his pipe which Freddie was unable to do with his hands dirty with clay! When Jeanes died of a heart attack Collard did the throwing himself for a while and then he asked Carnell to try it and Carnell found that he had, to use Collard's words, "a gift for throwing", and so he took over the job. In a normal day Carnell might throw eighteen dozen small six inch vases or twelve dozen of larger eight inch ones. He prepared the clay, a process known as wedging, himself most of the time; this process is explained on page 126. Although rather a menial task no one at Honiton considered themselves above such work and in this case if wedging was left to the boys they would usually not do it adequately, which meant that air bubbles remained in the clay and the thrower would not be able to get the clay to run true. At this time the pottery had three foot-wheels for throwing the pots and a big wheel that Collard or Carnell used to turn for each other on which large pieces such as those in plate 62, made by Carnell, were thrown.

Some pieces such as tea-sets were made on a jolly, or jigger, which was turned by hand often by Bert Nott in the early years. He found it very hard work and was glad when his elbow grease was replaced by a motor. The use of the jolly was rather looked down upon at Honiton being, as they thought, the first step towards mass production, therefore when ever possible pieces were hand thrown including all the candlesticks except one. The nozzles for the candles would be thrown one afternoon and left to dry and then the next day the bases would be made to which the nozzles were fixed. Only the candlestick with a flat base like a saucer was made on the jolly. The unusual bowl shaped vase, number 82 in plate 77, was made by throwing two open bowls, one with an open base, then when they were partly dry they were fixed together and a foot and a lip added.

Carnell also learnt all of the jobs in the pottery with the exception of decorating, Collard offered to teach him this in the evenings but Carnell declined, preferring to keep his evenings free. One of Carnell's other jobs was to operate the pug mill. The pugging was done once every three or four weeks and a horse was necessary to operate the mill as can be seen in plate 67. The horse was borrowed from Mr Madge who had a dairy round, and Joan Collard can remember as a child being sent along to Mr Madge to ask if her father could borrow the horse for a day in the following week. Mr Madge also used to do some work at the pottery, as required, mainly jollying. A few years before the Second World War the pug mill was mechanised and the horse was no longer required.

Walter Flood who was a school friend of Carnell joined the pottery soon after him and became the turner, and together with Bert Nott, the fireman, they were the three main male personnel employed at the pottery in the 1930s. They can be seen in high spirits at the gates of the pottery in plate 69. There was also a packer, and a handler, Les Skinner, who was replaced when he left by a young lad, David Hickmott, who graduated to throwing by the time Collard sold the pottery.

Anyone with some spare time helped in the packing of the pottery which was exported all over the world; to Australia, New Zealand, Canada, America, the Malay States, France, Africa, India, China, Denmark, Bermuda, British Columbia, etc.. Export orders had to be packed in wood chippings rather than straw and it was always a problem finding enough packing barrels. Collard would buy up casks from china shops or anywhere else he could lay his hands on them. He bought up a load of apple barrels on one occasion for 6d each which he invoiced to his customers for 9d, so if the barrels were not returned he at least made a profit!

British orders were obtained either from the pottery's agent in

London, F. W. Jukes of 15 Charterhouse Street, E.C.1 or by travellers employed by the pottery who went round from shop to shop to obtain orders. Many of the orders were for delivery at Easter and so throughout the winter pottery was made, packed up in casks and stacked in a storage shed to be despatched in the spring. The other main source of sales was visitors to the pottery. Collard had realised this potential when he bought the premises, saying to his family "Let's get on the main road so that we get visitors as well as orders". Sales to the general public, direct from the pottery, were of course more profitable than to shops and therefore were a very important part of the pottery's revenue. Hordes of visitors came to the pottery during the summer months, they could wander through the pottery and watch the employees at work and then could select their purchases from the showroom or from the pottery displayed in the courtyard.

Exhibitions

Occasionally, journalists and photographers would pay visits before writing articles for their magazines. On these occasions, a pottery worker recalled, Collard would make sure that everyone being photographed was wearing a clean white coat; this does not always appear to be borne out by the photographs existing today! These articles were of course good publicity for the pottery and were welcomed. Another way of attracting interest in the pottery was to give exhibitions at shows and department stores. Not that the pottery really needed to attract interest and custom by the 1930s because during the decade before the Second World War the firm always had a full order book even though many of its rivals were going out of business. The success of the Honiton Pottery was undoubtedly due to Collard's determination to change with the times and to continually update his wares, and to his innovative mind which was always full of new ideas and possibilities. As he had no need to attract more orders Collard did not bother with large exhibitions such as the Ideal Home Exhibition at which a number of his competitors exhibited. He felt that to stage a stand at such an exhibition would take two or three people away from production for quite some time and with only a total staff of thirty this was a very real consideration. However they did exhibit at County Shows and later they held several exhibitions in department stores such as Colsons of Exeter and Colmers of Bath. The first was in October

1936 at Colsons and was most successful judging by the amount of press coverage. Ernest Carnell was the centre of attention and for eight days he demonstrated the thrower's art, amongst a spectacular display of Honiton wares, to the shoppers who were fascinated by the proceedings and could not understand where the clay came from that was rising so skilfully under his hands.

When the Barton Pottery, which had been in business for about twelve years at Torquay, got into financial difficulties and had to close in the mid-thirties, Collard bought the contents of the pottery. Joan Collard drove her father, Bert Nott and Ernest Carnell down to Torquay where they set about sorting through the equipment and loading it on a lorry. Just when they were exhausted with all the hard work and the sleepy Torquay atmosphere Collard produced some beer to revive them. They took equipment such as jollies, saggars and throwing wheels from the Barton Pottery most of which they used at Honiton but the kick-wheels were resold to a pottery in Bristol.

The Decorators

Four years after Carnell started work at the pottery, Florrie Loving joined straight from school to train as a decorator. Initially she filled in, with blocks of colour, the outlines drawn by somebody else, for this she was paid 8/- a week. This was the normal method of work at Honiton for run of the mill pieces, one of the skilled decorators would outline a pattern such as the Jacobean and this would then be filled in by one or more of the younger, less skilled workers. This provided a good training for young girls who had had no formal training in drawing and helped them learn the most popular patterns. As the nearest art school was about seventeen miles away in Exeter Collard could not, as he had done at Poole, send the girls part-time or in the evening to art school. Readers will probably have noticed that some pieces of Honiton pottery are not very skilfully decorated which on occasion adds to their charm and sometimes does not. Collard was always keen that all his employees should have the chance to show their skills even though they might be limited, and he did not mind that the quality of some of the pottery produced was not always as high as it might have been. It was all handpainted, therefore spontaneous and true art pottery; this was far better in his eyes than an over studied piece of great precision that lacked life.

After a while Florrie Loving found that she and her widowed mother could not make ends meet on 8/- a week so she went to Collard and asked for a rise and received an extra 2/- a week. Later on she was still struggling financially and went back to Collard to explain her plight. Collard suggested to her that she could think about going on to piecework, when Florrie said "I don't think I would be able to do that Mr Collard", he replied "Well try, I'll put a proposition to you, if you can't make up your 10/- a week on piecework, I'll make it up for you". He did not have to make it up, Florrie Loving took home well over £1 in wages after her first week on piecework and was immensely pleased. He was, she said, such a fatherly boss, not at all like bosses today.

She was trained to decorate by Collard when she was sixteen or seventeen. There was no pattern book but a few vases made by Collard were kept as pattern guides; this meant that the decorators could not follow patterns slavishly but instead used and adapted Collard's ideas. Florrie Loving used to watch Collard draw Jacobean patterns, putting a flower each side. The art of it, he said, was spacing the work evenly around the vase and filling in the blank areas with leaves. She got on very well as a decorator and soon became one of the best, and in time took over the Persian pattern from Jessie Banbury. Both of these decorators can be seen at work in plate 63. Edith Readhead, who joined the pottery in 1932 is also to be seen in the same plate. She specialised in outlining the popular Jacobean and Woodland patterns and also remembers painting some of the border patterns such as 'pink scroll', 'posy', and 'zig-zag'. The hours worked by the employees were quite long. The men worked from 8am to 6pm on Monday to Friday with an hour's break for lunch between 12.30 and 1.30. On Saturdays they worked till 2pm. The girls had the advantage of starting half an hour later at 8.30 in the morning than the men, this was in order that the men could get the fire going first thing in the morning and warm up the premises for the girls. The girls stopped work at 1pm on Saturdays; at midday they would finish their decorating work and spend the last hour cleaning their benches thoroughly. In later years the men also stopped work at 1pm on Saturdays.

Collard had his own bench in the decorating room in front of which was an interior glass window through which he could keep an eye on the men in the throwing room! On this bench Collard decorated his own pots which were usually fired separately in a small kiln which took seven to ten pieces at a time. He also threw a number of his own pots and he can be seen at the potter's wheel in plate 66. Collard, we are told, never looked respectable while he was working at the pottery because he was always involved in production. He was also forgetful, or could forget the things he did not want to remember. On one occasion apparently he was called up for jury service at Exeter. When the day came he forgot to go and was working in the pottery in the old suit he used to wear with clay all over it, when a policeman arrived and took him off to Exeter without even giving him time to change his clothes. His whole life was wrapped up in the pottery by both financial necessity and enjoyment; even when he took time off from potting it was probably to go to pottery lectures, which were usually dinners, and when he returned he would discuss any possible new ideas with his daughter and his fireman. However he did find time to join the Honiton branch of the Rotary Club and regularly attended their meetings.

The Second World War

Ten very successful years were brought to an abrupt end by the war. Gradually the pottery workers were called up to join the forces or some other wartime occupation, including Joan Collard who went to work at Westlands, the aircraft manufacturers, at Yeovil. Even if the workers had not left, production would have been almost impossible, the big kiln could not of course be fired at night because it was the old fashioned open top type and since the firing process took nearly twenty-four hours this meant that the kiln could not be used. Restrictions were placed on potteries by the Government so that they were only allowed to make undecorated ware for sale in the home market, decorated ware was allowed for export but of course this market was very difficult to keep up under the circumstances. Therefore there was nothing to do but to close the pottery and only a very limited number of special pieces were made during the war, two of which are photographed in plates 26 and 29, one made by Collard and the other decorated by Joan Collard.

Collard was of course sixty-five in 1939 and with a war of uncertain length just beginning, he started to think about retirement and bought a house in Barton, Torquay for that event. However he could not leave the pottery to decay so he remained at Kingswood the house adjoining the pottery and let his new house in Torquay to the retired organist of Coventry cathedral. He might well have left the pottery to decay and been content to sell it after the war in a sad state, but the pottery workers had been so keen to return to the pottery at the first opportunity that Collard and his daughter felt obliged to keep the place in some kind of repair so that they could reopen again in peace years to provide the employees with the only work they knew. The employees felt that the pottery was like one big happy family, they all seemed to enjoy working there and remembered Collard as a very kind man who expected everyone to try their best. He would not even grumble too much if one of the girls dropped a whole board of soft pots, the crushed clay would just be put back into water ready for reuse. He was not however beyond pointing out the financial consequences of such negligence and even if one pot slipped off the end of a board he would comment pointedly "Well that's the profit on that lot gone!"

Unable to produce much pottery during the war Collard turned his artistic talents to painting and produced quite a few very competent watercolours, mainly still life, in particular of flowers usually arranged in a Honiton pot! He and his daughter also had time to do other things which they had not had time for previously. One of them was to set down a description of the pottery and its processes, which they did in November 1944, prior to giving a talk on it. Fortunately this still exists and is reproduced below in almost its entirety.

The Collards describe their Pottery

"Honiton Pottery is made from Honiton Clay, and everywhere in Honiton there seems to be plenty of good clay. There is the Brown and the Red, and Green and Grey, and the Dowell Street pure White, but they all burn the same colour, Red. The clay seam at the pottery is thirty-two foot deep and then becomes shale. After we dig our clay, we prepare it by washing it. We have a large tank, with a vertical shaft and beaters, called a Blunger. We half fill it with water, then the electrically driven machine is started, and as fast as a man can throw in clay, the machine beats it up into a liquid, then the machine is stopped, and a shutter plug lifted at the bottom of the tank, and the liquid clay flows through a fine lawn, which extracts the grit and all foreign matter. It is then lawned a second time into claybeds just over two foot deep. When the beds are full each morning the water is run off as the clay settles to the bottom, and then they are refilled and refilled until they will take no more, which means about 40 or 50 tons of clay. This is done in June and is allowed to stay there until the following April, when it is cut out and stacked in heaps. As required we take it about four tons at a time onto a cemented floor, and from there it is put through heavy iron rollers, and rolled out almost as fine as newspaper; it then passes on to a churn called the Pug Mill where a man stands and cuts it out in square lumps ready for the potter.

"The potter takes his clay and wedges it by cutting the blocks of clay in half and banging one half on top of the other like the baker and his dough, and he can tell in a moment by the cut of the wire if it is ready for working." (Normally this was done twenty times before the clay was ready to work.)

"Then comes the Making. There are four ways of making: *The Potters Wheel, Jigger, Pressing, and Casting.*
The Potters Wheel is the oldest method, and is reputed to be the first machine made, dating back over 6,000 years, the invention of the potter's wheel being the beginning of the machine age.

"First the Potter weighs his clay out; ie. if he is going to make an 8″ Jug he weighs out 2lb 10oz. balls of clay and for 4″ Jugs 10oz. He then fixes the gauge to tell him the height and width of the pot. He then dashes the ball of clay on the revolving wheel, sticks his thumbs in the centre, and in a couple of minutes he transforms the ball of clay into a vase or jug. Throwing is really a man's job. I have only had one girl thrower, a Honiton lass, who has come back after lunch, started at 2 o'clock, and by 6 o'clock she has made as many as 36 dozen vases in 4 hours, and good. A man working on teapots will make 5 gross teapots and 5 gross of lids in a day. That will give you some idea of the speed things are made on the potter's wheel.

"*The Jigger* is an electric machine which has a revolving steel cup in which moulds are placed, and is principally used for flat ware, such as plates and saucers, etc.; also for cups, teapots and bowls. This machine turns out about three cups a minute, which gives you the usual speed.

"*Pressing*. Dishes off the round, i.e. oval, square, etc., are made by this method. A piece of clay is balled out with a batter or a spreading machine, and laid on the top of the mould, and with a wet hand, the potter works it into shape, tools it around and with another small plaster mould works on a foot, which completes the dish. Animals and ornaments are done the same way." (The man who made the moulds for the Honiton Pottery for such pieces as shapes 63 and 65 came down from Staffordshire about once a year. He used to travel round from pottery to pottery in the area making moulds and used to stay about a fortnight at the Honiton Pottery making as many moulds as required. Rather predictably he was known as 'Mouldy'!)

"*Casting:* This is done by simply pouring liquid clay into a plaster mould. As the plaster absorbs the moisture the mould is refilled, this is repeated three times, then the liquid clay is tipped out of the mould and what is left adhered to the mould forms the pot.

"*Turning:* After the pots have been made by the potter, they are passed on to the turner in a semi-dry state; he slightly hollows up the bottom giving a slight foot, and a real finish to the article." (All Honiton pots were turned.)

"*Handling:* The jugs are then passed to the handler. He gets his handles from the handle press, a round steel box with a die at the bottom to give the shape and size required. By turning a handle similar to a letter press the clay is forced through the die and comes out in long strips, which he lays on his board a yard long. He cuts the strips up to the required length and sticks them on the article with liquid clay. The chief thing is to take the spring out of the handles, otherwise they will lift off in the drying." (The unusual 'rope' handles found particularly on the sgraffito jugs were made with a specially shaped die. The clay that was forced through the die was then twisted to give the required effect.)

"The pots are then dried and fired in an oven to a white heat, 2,200 degrees fahrenheit, and are then ready for glazing and decorating. The glazing of the pottery is very important, the chief glazes being transparent or opaque. *Glazes* are made from Borax, Felspar, Stone, Flint, Whiting, Malachite, Oxide of Tin, Zinc, and Titanium. The chief thing in glaze is to balance the ingredients to avoid crazing, pin holes and peeling etc.. If, for instance, we should hear a bang in the warehouse, we should expect to find a spiral crack, which would tell us at once there was too much Felspar in the mixture. If there were pin holes that would mean too much Whiting, and if the glaze runs too much, not enough flint. All these things have to be carefully watched.

"*Decorations:* In the case of transparent glazes the designs are put on before the article is glazed, and with the opaque the design is put on over the glaze. We use mineral colours, made from oxides of Copper, Tin, Manganese, Iron, Cobalt etc.. The designs are put on the pots, by each individual worker, and of which we have a great variety, and then we come to the final firing.

"*Firing the oven:* This being the final stage is naturally the most important one. We use 15" Saggars which we fill with our glazed ware, and the ware must be packed close together, to keep down the firing costs, but at the same time the articles must not touch or they would stick together. First we place on the floor of the oven a strong Saggar and make sure it is dead level, and, if anything, leaning away from the worker, as each saggar, as they are placed one on each other, would grow more and more out of line as the placer reached the 13 foot top, and would come over on the worker. In this way we keep rearing up these bungs of saggars until the oven is quite full, taking about 700 saggars all told. As the oven is being filled, little test bars are placed inside the oven, so that they may be seen from the outside by the fireman through little peep holes through the oven walls. These Thermoscope Bars are straight when placed in position and the fireman's skill is to get these bars to bend semi-circular at the same time. These bars are the first things the boss wants to see as they are drawn out of the oven. If the fireman gets these bent satisfactorily, he is not to blame if anything should go wrong. Firing an oven or Kiln is a very interesting job, although a rather black one. The skill is to work each fire according to the various heats. If, for instance, one side, the bottom, was hotter than the top, the fireman should at once select good coal and lift the fires off the bars, to send the heat to the top, if vice versa he should use poor coal such as slack."

After the Second World War

The pottery reopened in October 1945 and slowly went back into production. Instead of firing the kiln once a week as he had done previously Bert Nott recalled that after the war he went up only once every month or two to fire it. Thus production must have been much lower than it had been in pre-war years. Nevertheless there seems to have been considerable interest in the pottery and its products and several press articles were written about it during the period including the following rather 'flowery' paean.

"A gateway flanked by two busts is the entrance to a small oasis for the austerity-tired, for in the sun-brightened showrooms of the Honiton Potteries, Devon, are shelves of delightful, colourful and dainty articles ranging from ashtrays to large decorative vases and wall plates — there are vases of varying shape and size, mugs, jugs, lamp-stands, painted tiles, tea-sets, all beautifully designed and delicately coloured. It is like stepping into Dreamland, for all these articles are made for export and do not find their way into the shops of Britain. You hardly dare to enquire whether any of these, now almost forgotten luxuries are for sale, and on being told you can choose which you like, it is almost impossible to make a choice from the many objects displayed. These are all articles which have been made in excess of the quantity required for the export orders, and that is the only reason why they are available to the public. It is a real tonic to be able to browse around the showrooms picking and choosing pottery which is not just a plain white glazed utility shape.

"The Honiton Potteries have been closed for some years owing to the war and only reopened last October; their craftsmen are gradually returning from the Forces, their skill in throwing and moulding unimpaired, despite the fact that these skilled hands have had to do work which was likely to coarsen them and expose them to the risk of injury, and for a moment one should dwell on the hands which have fashioned these articles. Maybe the jug you are drinking from was formed by the thrower who went over to France on D Day and through all the hectic fighting from Normandy to the Rhine, and yet how graceful is the article, which his hands, one of them slightly injured, have created."

The impact of the decorated ware on the public seems almost unbelievable today, yet it was quite normal at the time. In the first years after the War occasional one day sales were allowed at potteries of pre-war stock, and queues formed in the early morning for a chance to purchase decorated ware.

The New Owners

In 1947, having put the pottery back on its feet, the Collards sold the business to two potters from Staffordshire; Norman Hull, a decorator who styled himself as "pottery designer" on the company documents, and Harry Barratt, a mould-maker. The pottery was registered as a limited company under the name Honiton Art Potteries Ltd with a nominal share capital of £6,000, but Hull and Barratt held only one share each in the business. A Nissen hut was erected over some of the buildings to give more space and the pottery produced was also 'improved'. An article written in 1961 for the Pottery Gazette compares the pottery made by the new proprietors with that during Collard's period in the following terms "the coarseness of shape and finish have long since disappeared". In addition the pottery ceased to use the local red clay and replaced it with white clay that has no local characteristics. The reason for this was explained in the same article. "That its use has been discontinued is no reflection on its quality but is rather a practical decision dictated by the need to have a thoroughly dependable body of known chemical analysis and constant physical properties. Unless these conditions can be guaranteed absolutely, which with the local clay it cannot, then all manner of body and glaze troubles such as pinholing, dunting, spit-out, fire-cracking and so on are always a possibility. These troubles can be eliminated by using a blended body."

The first eighteen months after Collard sold the business were a period of change for the pottery. Almost immediately much of the production was pressed rather than thrown by hand and gradually the use of the local red clay ceased in favour of bought in white clay, so that by 1949 red clay ware was no longer produced. Initially Mr Hull used Collard's paints and glazes but these too were gradually phased out during the first year or so and replaced by paints and glazes purchased from a potters' merchant. Florrie Loving regretted this change as the range of colours she was allowed to use was cut considerably and she could no longer use different colours to produce shading in the leaves and flowers. Another change that occurred after Collard left was that many more pieces started to be initialled on the base by the decorators. Some say the reason for this was that if anything went wrong with the colours in the firing they would know who to blame!

Not surprisingly with all the changes taking place when the new owners took over many of the workers felt unsettled and left the pottery. David Hickmott went to the Axe Vale Pottery and Ernest Carnell left to work in a sawmill for two years before Collard helped him find a new job as a thrower for the new Dartmouth Pottery. This was very much a typical Torquay type pottery started by Messrs Koppenhagen and Miller and managed by Harry Crute who had owned his own pottery in Barton before the war with a Mr Lemon. Florrie Loving was married and did not rejoin the pottery at Honiton for some years after the war. When she did she, of course, returned as a decorator particularly skilled in the Jacobean and Persian patterns which have remained popular over the years. When she retired in 1979 she took her knowledge of the Persian pattern with her, and so ended almost a century of production of that pattern by one man and the employees he had taught.

Visitors to the pottery today will find the premises and methods much changed from Collard's day. If it had remained unaltered it would have been a living museum of the traditional potting methods used since biblical times.

Chapter 12

Home Again

Retirement at Torquay

After selling the pottery Collard and his daughter moved to their house in Torquay, which he had bought during the war, and he settled down to an active retirement. The first thing he did was to buy a small automatic electric kiln which he fixed up in his garden shed, and with clay dug from the garden he continued to produce pottery. An example of a pot made at home and fired in this little kiln can be seen in plate 31.

Some pieces he produced were experimental, testing different glazes such as lustre ones, etc., which he could not have afforded to experiment with whilst running the business. He was particularly fond of producing pieces with a pink lustre glaze and with handles which give the impression of being plaited during these later years. He also produced quite a large quantity of small pieces such as dishes, ashtrays etc. which he painted with stylised flowers, triangular patterns and suchlike, reminiscent of Honiton pottery. These were decorated in bright sunny colours and have quite a shiny glaze. Collard gave these away to friends and visitors and even sold some by the box load to an acquaintance who ran a gift shop in Newton Abbot! Sometimes these pieces were impressed or stamped in black paint CC TORQUAY, see Appendix I, mark 26, but some were unmarked. Collard would have perhaps changed the kiln at the Honiton Pottery to an electric one had not development at the pottery been interrupted by the war because, although he was so keen that all pieces should be handmade, he was not against modern equipment where it was necessary. He was certainly very impressed with this little kiln. "It's wonderful" he said one day to Ernest Carnell who was visiting him, "all I have to do is put the pots in, then I go and have a game of bowls and when I return it's done the firing and switched itself off". Bowls was Collard's other main interest in his retirement, he had taken it up during the war finding time on his hands and in his retirement he became an avid player. In addition of course he had the pleasure of looking up all the old friends he had made at the Torquay potteries many years before. Harry Birkbeck who came from a distinguished family of pottery decorators was one, and another was Ernest Brimson who had worked with him at Aller Vale and had been one of his closest friends in those early years.

Unfortunately at about the age of eighty Collard gradually went blind, which to a large extent curtailed his active life. Although this was obviously a terrible blow, especially to someone who had loved the visual arts, Collard made the best of life he could. No longer able to pot or to bowl, he would rise late in the morning about eleven o'clock to give his daughter a chance to work undisturbed, he would then walk up and down the drive to get some exercise. After lunch, most days, he and his daughter would drive out into the country for a walk and in the evening he would sit by the radio keeping himself up to date with the world's news whilst his daughter went out. Nothing in the house was moved so that he could walk around easily and he was even able to help his daughter by drying the dishes. Thus he kept himself as active as possible, both physically and mentally, until the day before he died at the age of ninety-five on March 20th 1969.

His had been a long life and a contented one and on many occasions he said to his daughter "if ever I had my life again I'd be a potter". He obviously obtained great enjoyment from his work just as we may do today.

APPENDIX 1 POTTERY MARKS All marks are shown to size.

1. 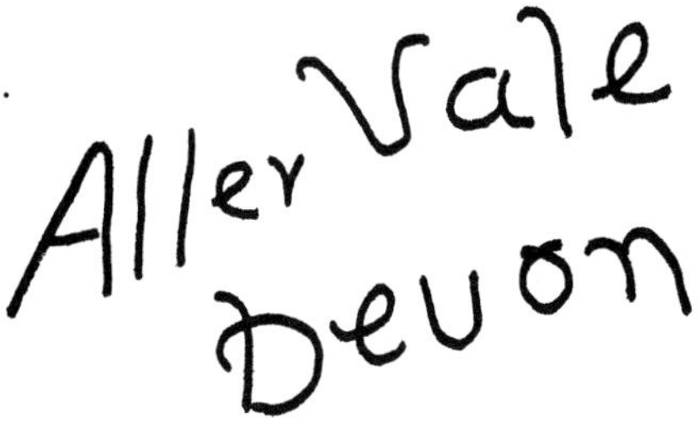

Rare incised mark sometimes omitting 'Devon'. Used on red clay wares, usually major pieces with an unglazed base. c. 1885-95.

2. 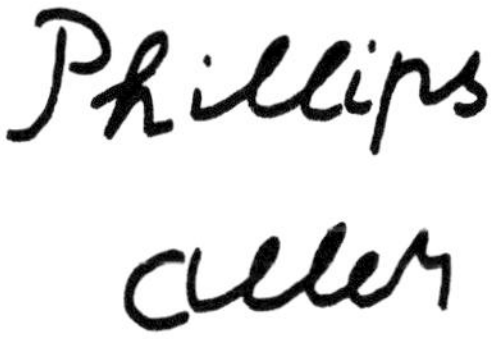

Rare incised mark sometimes with 'Newton Abbot' rather than 'Aller'. Used on terracotta ware. c. 1881-87.

3. 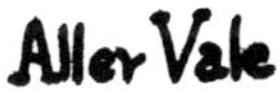

Rare impressed mark. c. 1881-87.

4.

Impressed mark on 'folksy items' made of red clay with unglazed bases. c. 1881-87.

5.		ALLER VALE	Impressed mark used on white and red clay pieces with glazed and unglazed bases. c. 1885-93 and sometimes thereafter on pieces with a heavy, coloured glaze. In addition the word 'England' is sometimes added after 1891 as shown in mark 6.
6.	(a)	ALLER VALE	Impressed. c. 1891 onwards.
	(b)	DEVON	Sometimes incorporated in the above mark under 'Vale'.
	(c)	ENGLAND	Impressed. Often added to the above mark with a separate stamp.
	(d)	ALLER VALE H. H & Co	Impressed mark used between c. 1897-1902. Again the word 'England' is sometimes added.

Later Aller Vale marks were often painted in black.

7. Watcombe

Incised mark c. 1901-1920. Sometimes with the words 'Torquay' and 'England' added. An impressed mark with 'Watcombe Torquay' in capitals was also used during the same period.

Many other marks were used during the life of the pottery, between 1871 and 1962.

8. H M EXETER

Impressed. 1896-1935. The only pottery mark with the exception of a circular black rubber mark 'Royal Devon Art Pottery' found occasionally on later pieces.

9. LONGPARK TORQUAY

Rare impressed mark. c. 1903-04.

10. LONGPARK TORQUAY

Impressed. c. 1903-09. Later marks were stamped in black. 'Tormohun' was a name used by the pottery for a few years from 1908, other pieces were marked 'Longpark Torquay' during this period.

11. COLLARD POOLE DORSET — Rare impressed mark found on small items. 1905 – c. 1908.

12. COLLARD POOLE DORSET — Normal impressed mark. 1905 – c.1909.

13. Poole — Rare incised mark. 1905 – c. 1909.

or, POOLE — Rare incised mark. 1905 – c. 1909.

14. Collard Poole — Rare incised mark found on large items. 1905 – c. 1909.

15.
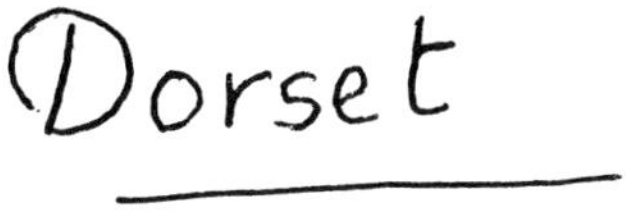

Incised mark found on cottage and similar ware. c. 1908-15.

Very occasionally this mark is painted in black rather than incised.

16.
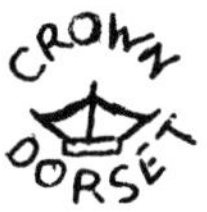

Impressed.
Believed to be 1910-12.

17.

Normal impressed mark.
c. 1909-15.

18.

Impressed.
Often found with impressed rather than incised shape numbers.
c. 1915. Possibly post Collard.

19.
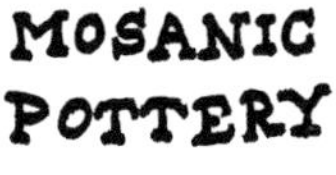

Impressed.
Alternative to mark 20.
c. 1910.

20.
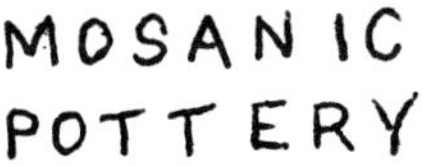

Impressed.
c. 1908-15.

21.	**HONITON ENGLAND**	Impressed. c. 1920-29. Revived briefly post Collard: 1947-48 on red clay ware 1947-49 on white clay ware.
22.	**COLLARD HONITON ENGLAND**	Impressed. c. 1927-37.
23.	**COLLARD HONITON ENGLAND**	Impressed. c. 1935-47.
24.	**HONITON**	Either incised or in black paint, used on special pieces during the whole period. c. 1920-47. Not to be confused with a similar black painted mark used post Collard on white clay ware.
25.	**MADE IN ENGLAND**	A very rare mark found on early Honiton pieces.
26.	**CC TORQUAY**	Pottery made by Collard at his home in Barton. Impressed or stamped in black. c. 1948-56.

APPENDIX II *ALLER VALE PATTERN CODES*

A 1 Persian pattern on a cream ground (see plates 3 and 4)
2 Persian pattern on a blue ground
3 Persian pattern on a green ground
4 Crocus pattern (stylised)

B 1 Coloured scrolls on a cream ground (see plate 37)
2 Coloured scrolls on a green ground
3 Coloured scrolls on a blue ground
4 Yellow and cream scrolls on a green ground
5 White scrolls on a blue ground

C 1 Sandringham pattern, blue scrolls on a white ground
2 Forget-me-not pattern (stylised) on a cream ground
3 Dark green scrolls on a mid green ground
4 Parrot's head
5 Donkey's head

D 1 Narcissus pattern (stylised) (see plate 5) on a blue ground, sometimes the design consists only of coloured scrolls on a blue ground.
2 ?
3 White scrolls on a green ground

E ?

F 1 Daisy pattern (stylised) white on a green ground
2 ?
3 Daisy pattern (stylised) white on a blue ground
4 Scandy pattern cream on a green ground
5 Sprays of white flowers on a blue ground

G 1 Normandy pattern plain green translucent glaze on white slip

H 1 Butterflies and forget-me-not pattern on a cream ground

I 1 Scandy pattern on a blue ground
2 Scandy pattern on a green ground
3 ?
4 Abbotskerswell or daisy pattern under amber glaze

J	1	?
	2	Cream coloured flowers on a blue ground
K	1	Natural flowers on a cream ground
	2	Natural flowers on a green ground
	3	Natural flowers on a ginger ground
	4	Natural flowers on a blue ground
	5	Natural flowers on a chocolate ground
	6	Plain green ground with place name in yellow slip
L		?
M	1	Plain green translucent glaze on red clay body
	2	Edward VII coronation pattern ALSO Plain green glaze pitted with 'pinholes' deliberately induced during firing
	3	Wading bird on green ground
N	1	Scandy pattern on a cream ground (see plate 38)
	2	Coloured cockerel on a cream ground
	3	Black cockerel on a cream ground
	4	Plain green ground
	5	?
	6	Honeysuckle pattern yellow flowers and scrolls on a green ground
	6	Later. Princess or ladybird pattern (stylised) on a blue ground
	7	Princess or ladybird pattern (stylised) on a green ground
O		?
P		?
Q	1	Coloured sgraffito patterns of flowers, leaves, etc. on a cream ground
	2	?
	3	Geometric pattern reminiscent of an Aztec design on a cream ground
R		?

S 1 ?
2 Scandy on a green ground
3 Late scandy pattern with intertwining tendrils on a cream ground
4 Scandy on a pink ground

T ?

U 1 Yellow scrolls on a chocolate ground
2 ?
3 Sgraffito scrolls with dolphin head terminals on a cream ground

V ?

W ?

X ?

Y 1 Partially covered in white slip with sgraffito motto

Z 1 Blue coloured sgraffito scrolls on brown ground

APPENDIX III

DORSET MOTTOES

One of the most popular, and used on early pieces usually jugs:

1. Vor Do'set dear
   Then gi'e woone cheir,
   D'ye hear? woone cheir!

The traditional motto for the puzzle jug:

2. In this jug there is good liquor
   Fit for Parson or for Vicar
   But how to drink an' not to spill
   Will try the utmost of your skill.

Early seaside humour:

3. Now goo away you
   Crabbed, jealous chap
   You shan't kiss me you shan't
   I'll gi'ye a slap.

   An' as for kissen
   O' – me if he did, I
   didden ax' en' to, nor
   zay he mid.

On useful objects, in these cases candlesticks:

4. Blessed are the drowsy
   for they shall soon drop off.

   Many are called but vew get up.

General:

5. I slept an' dreamt that life was beauty,
   I woke an' found that life was duty.

   Wi'out money man is a shadder.

   Ah gie me if I wer a squire
   Th' settle an' a girt wood vier.

   The little busy bee
   Is a mighty little thing
   First it steals your honey
   Then it pays you with a sting.

6. Good Luck to the Hoof an Harn,
   Good Luck to the Flock an th' Fleece,
   Good Luck to the Growers o' Carn,
   Wi' blessens of Plenty an' Peace.

APPENDIX IV

DORSET HANDLES

cross section of handle | terminal

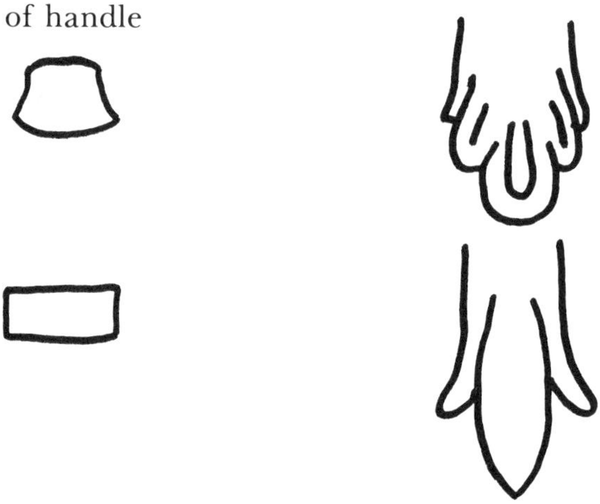

TYPICAL DORSET LETTER FORMATIONS

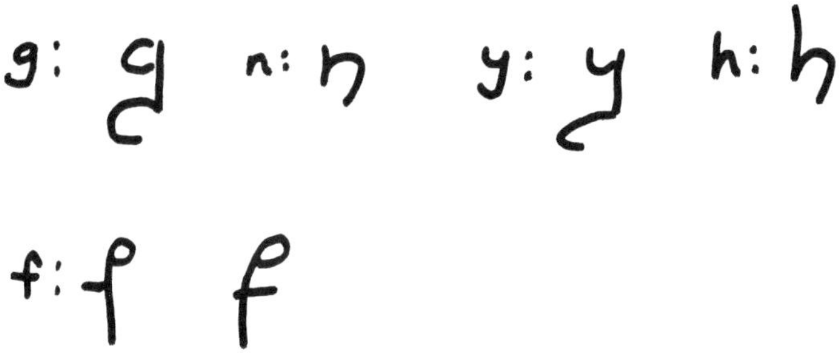

Capital letters:

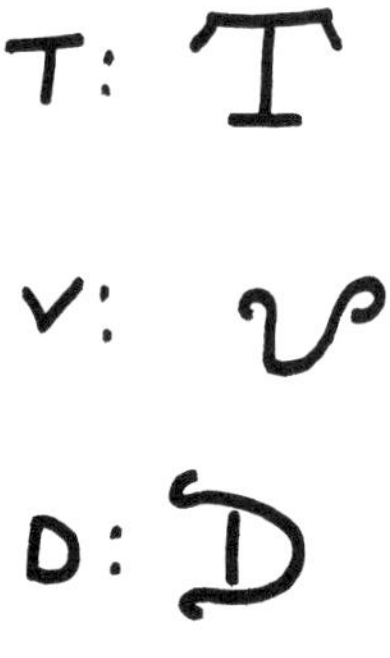

Note: One or two very early pieces are in a hand of a different style particularly notable for its rather fancy lower case k:

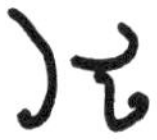

INDEX

Plate 1
A 10″ Aller Vale barbotine flask made of pink-buff clay and decorated with a rather unusual stylised flower. The only mark is an impressed crescent. Circa 1890.

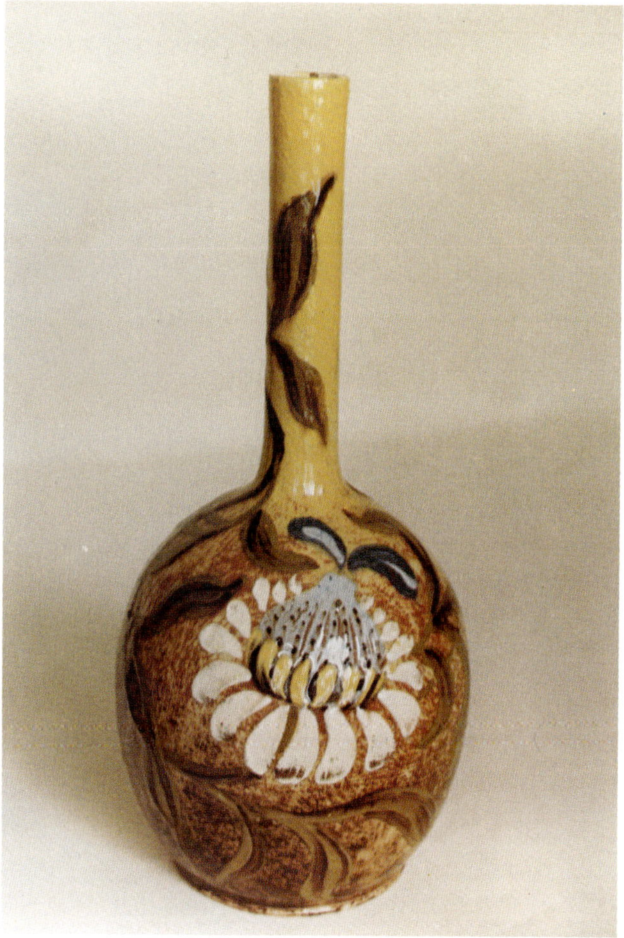

Plate 2 (below)
An Aller Vale barbotine vase 5½″ high made of pink-buff clay. Decorated by Collard and marked on the base with his incised initials and an impressed crescent. Decorated with a dragonfly on the reverse. Circa 1890.

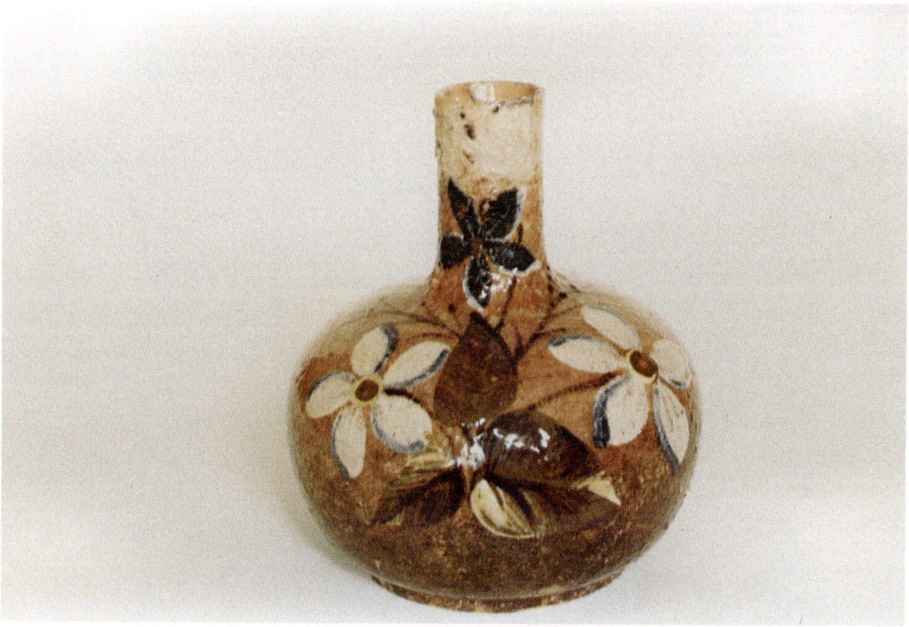

Plate 3
Two views of an apprentice piece made by Collard at Aller Vale. Made of white clay the Persian pattern mug is 5″ high and bears his incised signature and the small impressed turner's mark T on the base. Circa 1889.

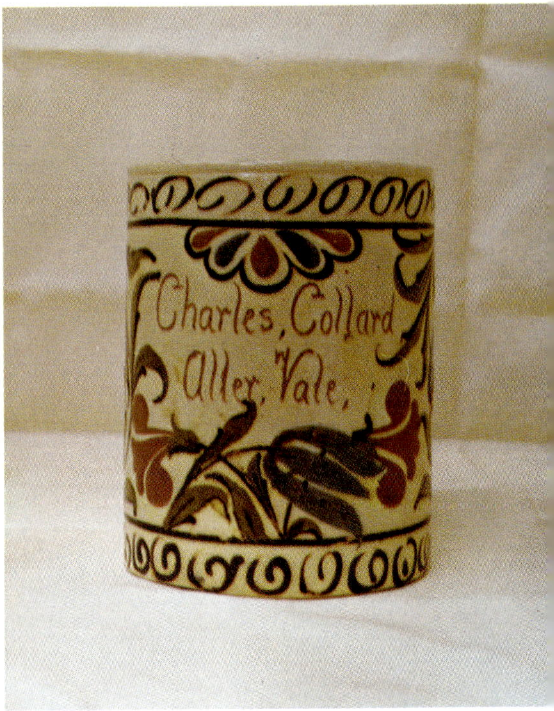

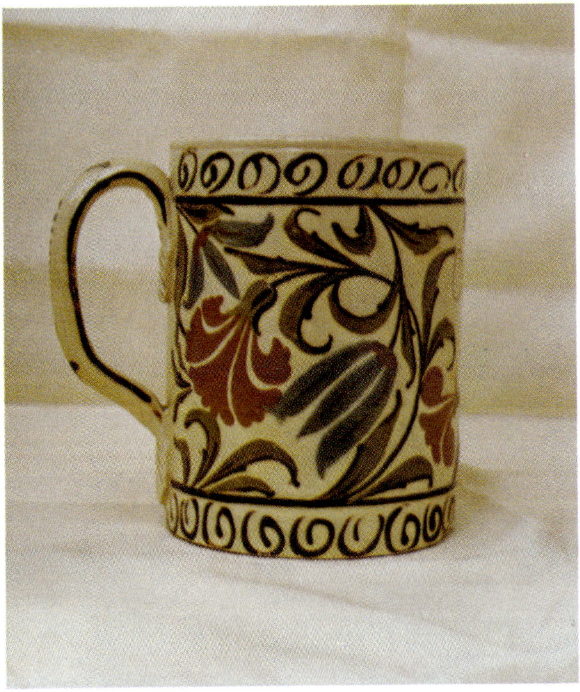

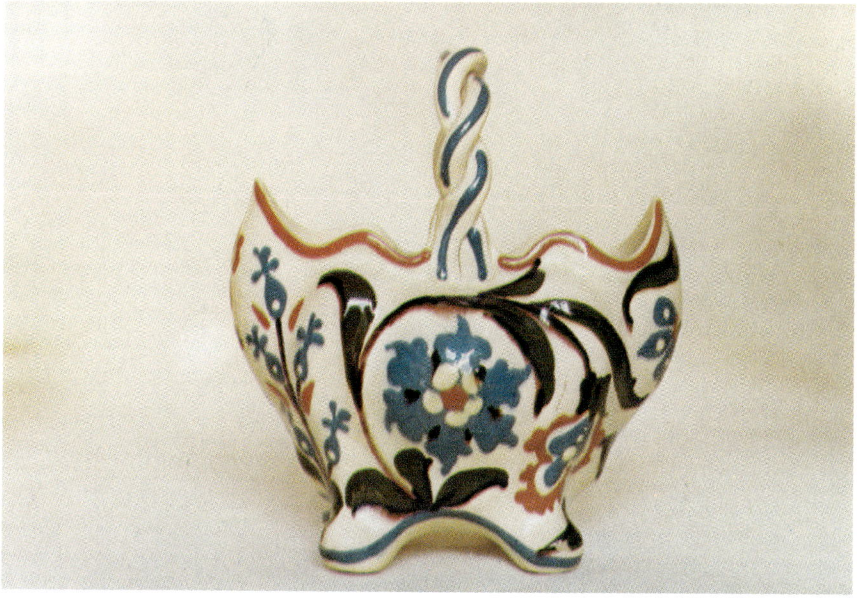

Plate 4 A basket 6½″ high in the later Persian pattern with the decorative blobs on the tulips in pale yellow rather than brown. Mark no 5 with pattern and shape numbers A1 and 1019 scratched on the base. White clay. Circa 1897.

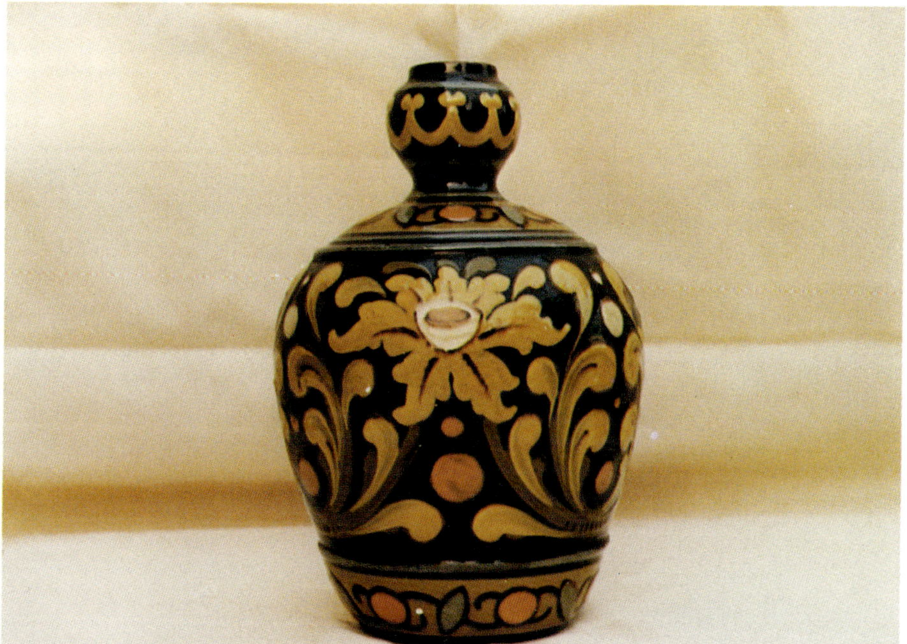

Plate 5 A D1 pattern 8″ vase made of red clay with mark no 5 and incised D1 1111 on a glazed base. Circa 1893.

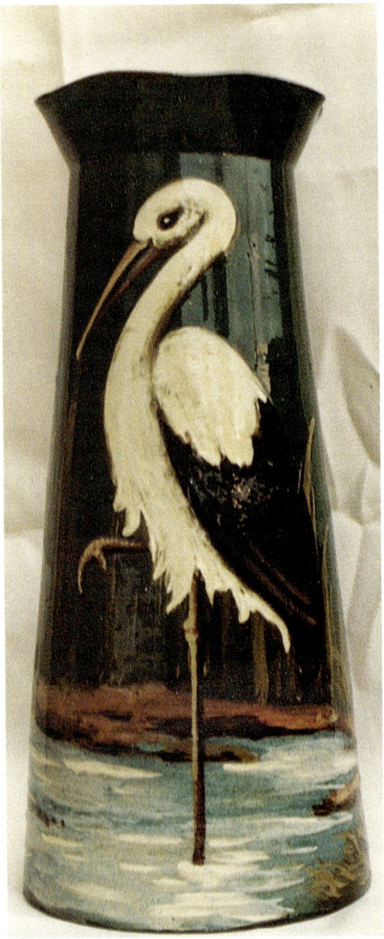

Plate 6
A 12″ Watcombe vase in red clay believed to have been decorated by Collard. Mark no 7. Circa 1902.

Plate 7 (below)
An 8″ Watcombe jardiniere in red clay decorated by Collard. Incised with mark no 7 and 824 B2. Circa 1902.

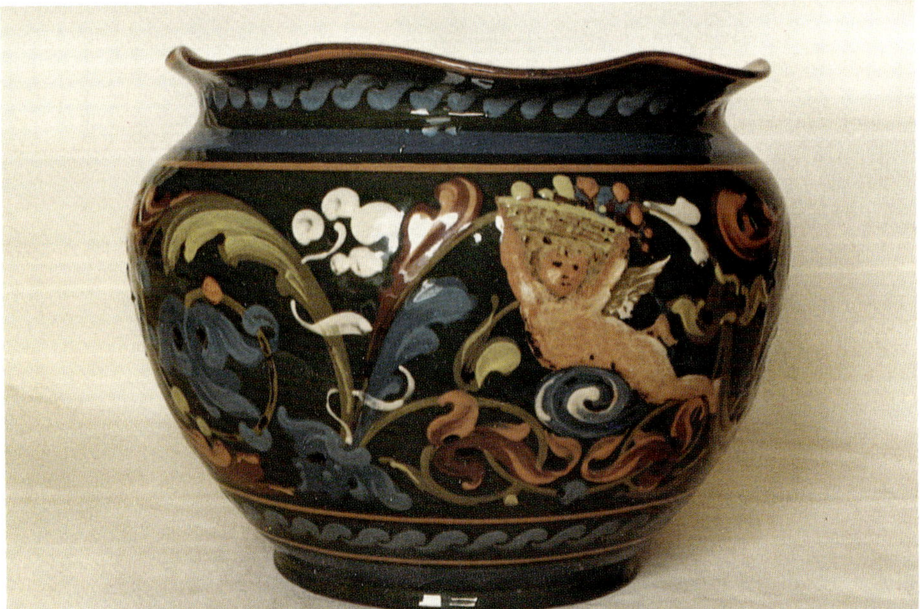

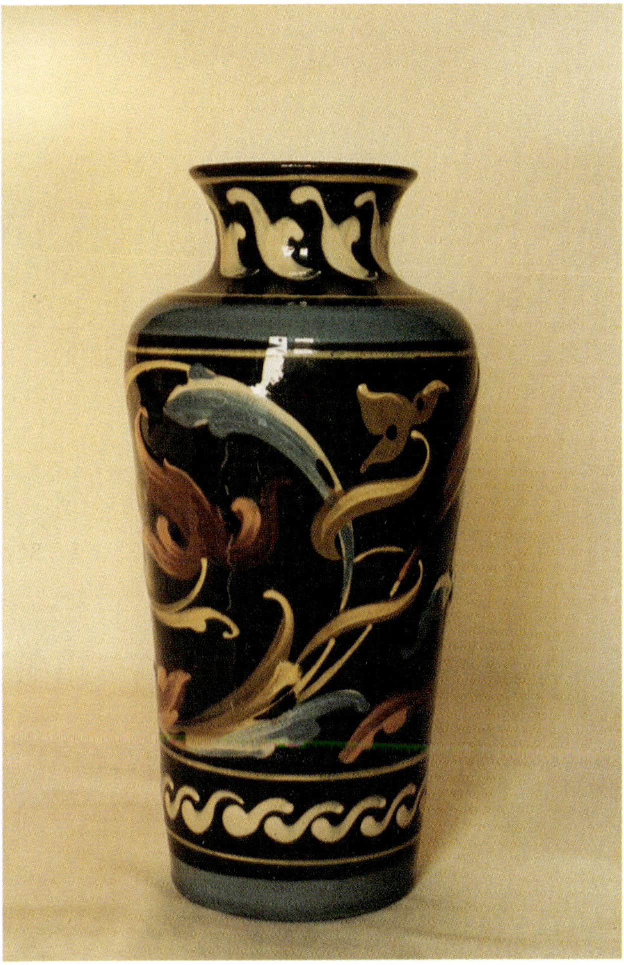

Plate 8
An 8″ Hart and Moist vase decorated by Collard. Mark no 8. 1903.

Plate 9 (below)
A jardiniere, 11″ high, made at Longpark by Collard. It has 3 moulded dolphin shaped handles and each of the three panels has a slightly different mythical sea creature surrounded by scroll decoration. Compare the scrolls with those in plate 10 and the sea creature with that in plate 16. Circa 1904.

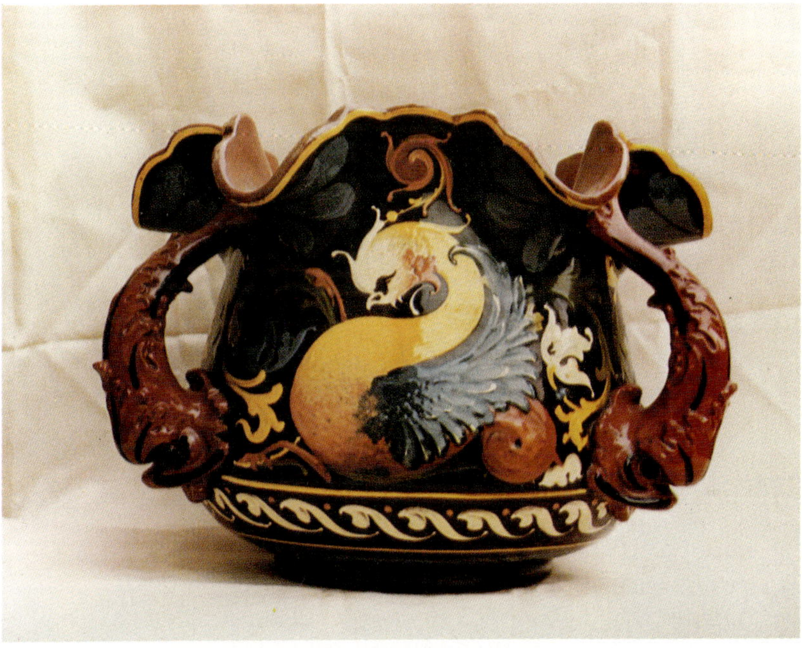

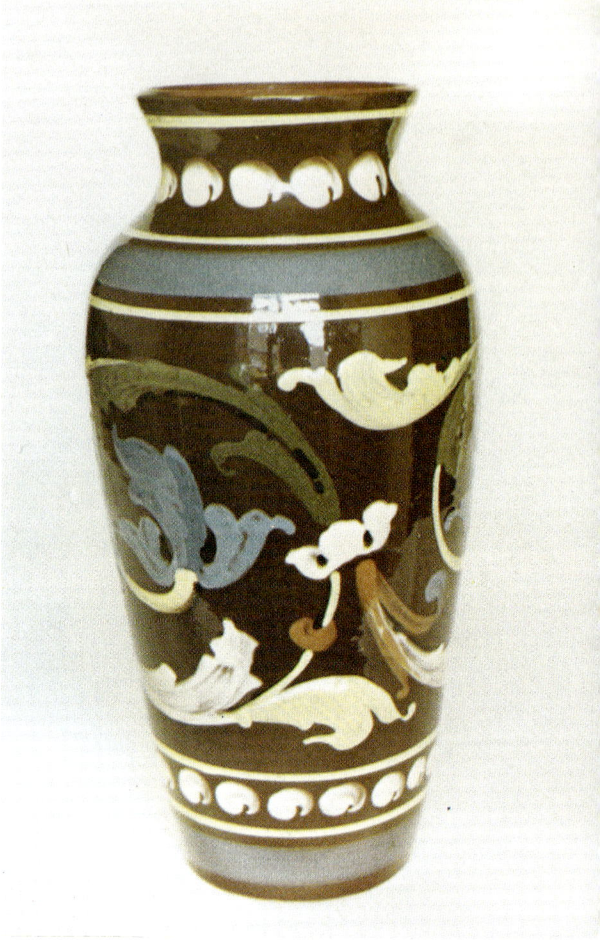

Plate 10 (right)
One of a pair of 10″ vases made by Collard at Green Road. Made of red clay, mark no 12. Circa 1906.

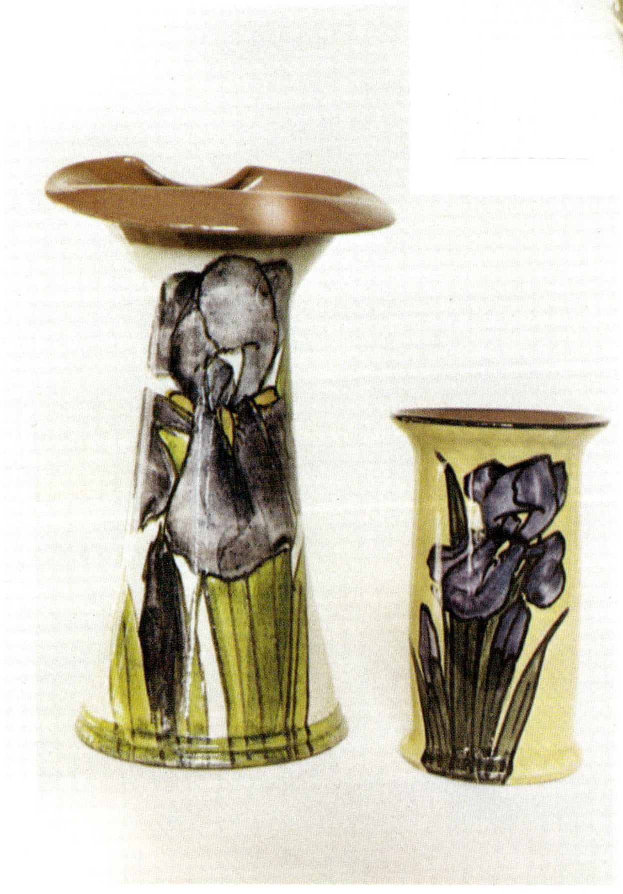

Plate 11 (left)
Left — A 7″ Dorset 'flip over lip' vase. Mark no 12 and incised number 438. Circa 1907.

Right — A similarly decorated 4″ vase of red clay made at the Watcombe pottery about the same period.

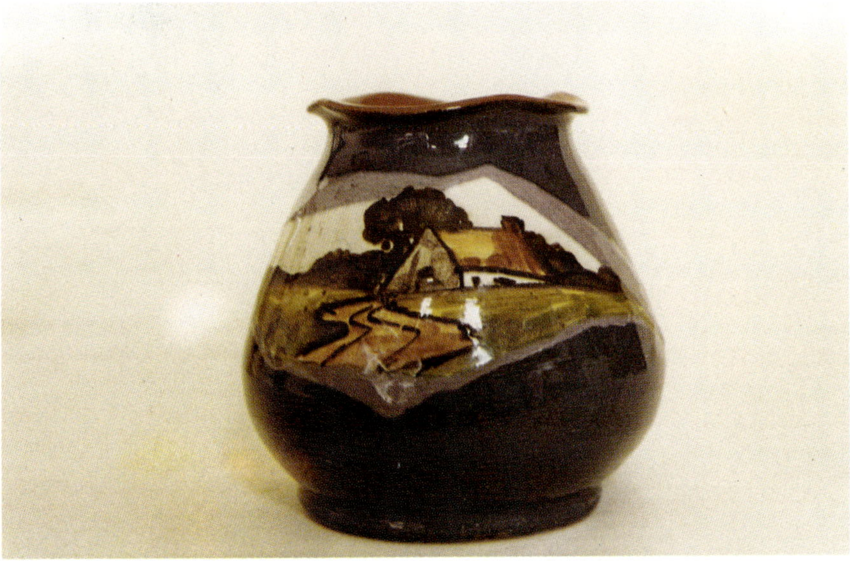

Plate 12 A 3″ posy bowl, a popular Dorset shape. Mark no 12 with incised number 421. Circa 1907.

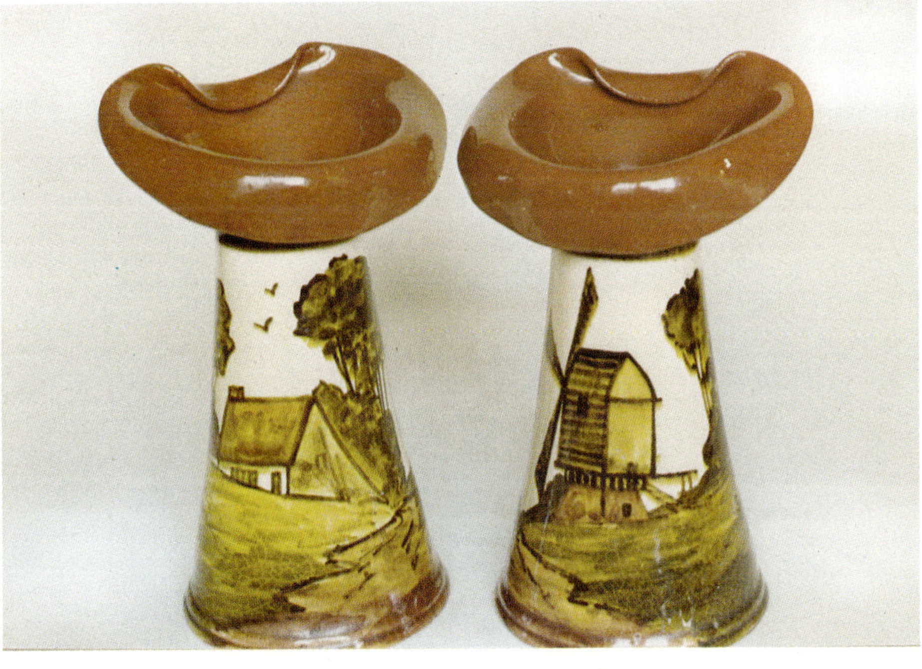

Plate 13 A pair of 8″ 'flip over lip' vases in Crown Dorset's most popular pattern. Mark no 14 with 438 incised on the base. Circa 1908.

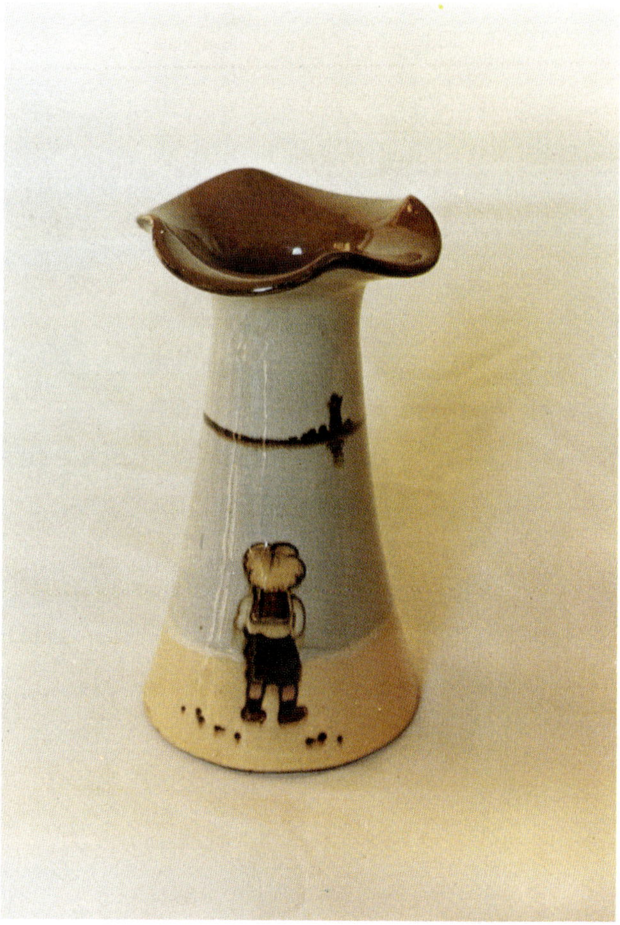

Plate 14
A 6″ vase of typical Dorset shape. Incised 36/6″ R on the base. Circa 1910.

Plate 15 (below)
A Crown Dorset George V 3″ Coronation Mug with applied busts of the King and Queen. Handle no 1 appendix III. No marks. 1911.

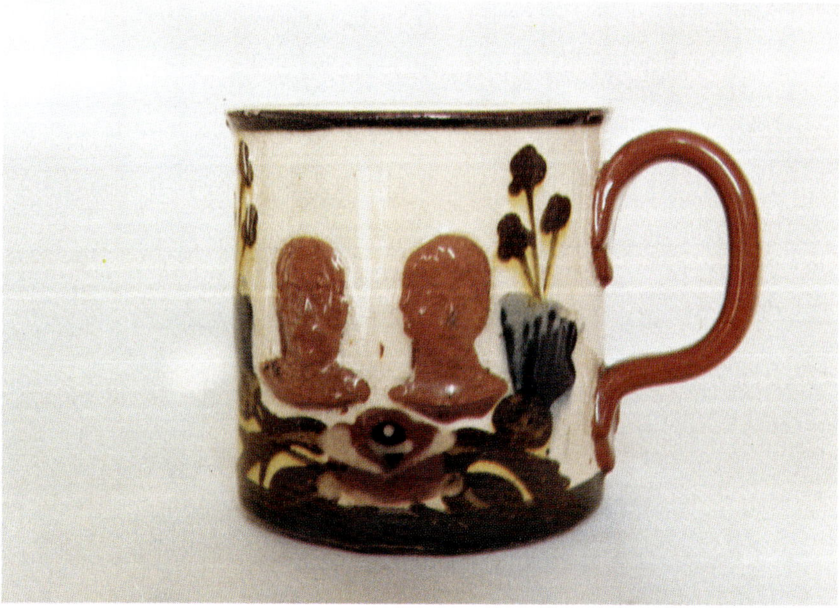

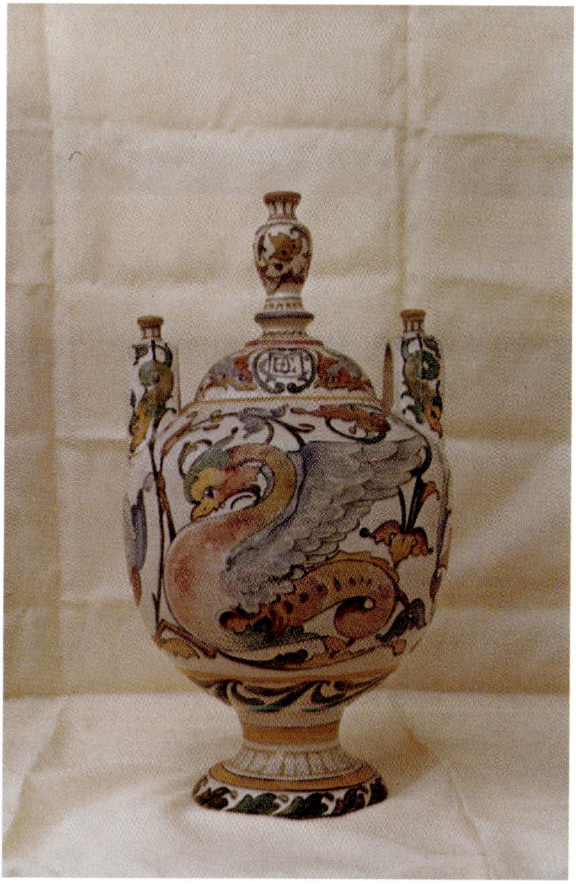

Plate 16
A 13″ covered vase thrown and decorated by Collard at Ilminster. Made of a beige clay and incised on the base 'C Collard 1916'. Decorated in one of his favourite themes and bearing his wife's monogram on the lid.

Plate 17 (below)
A 6″ Honiton jug made of grey-fawn clay which shows the result of over firing as discussed on page 98. Mark no 22. Circa 1933.

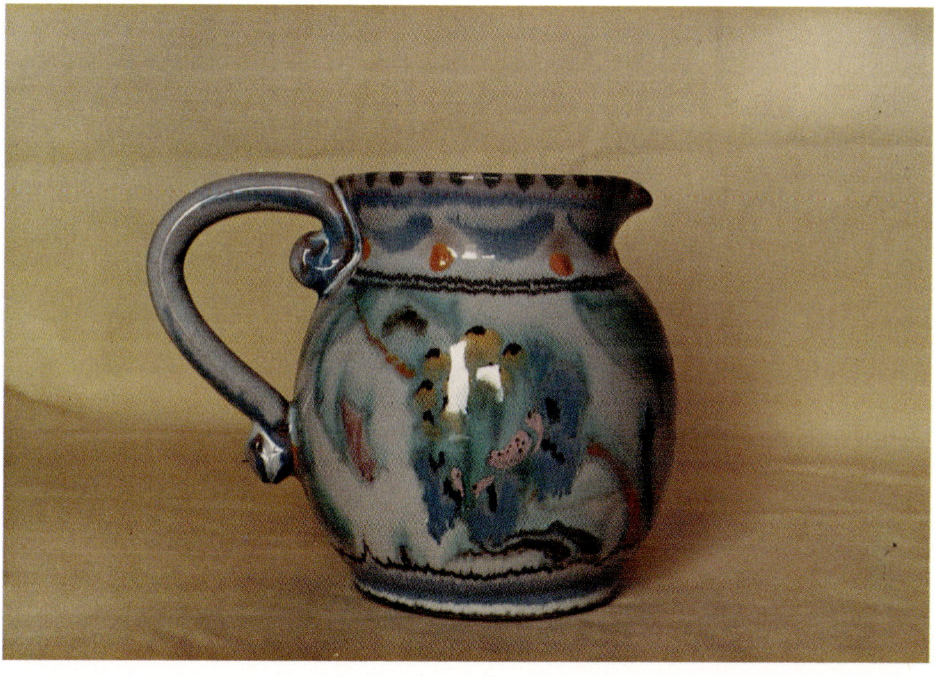

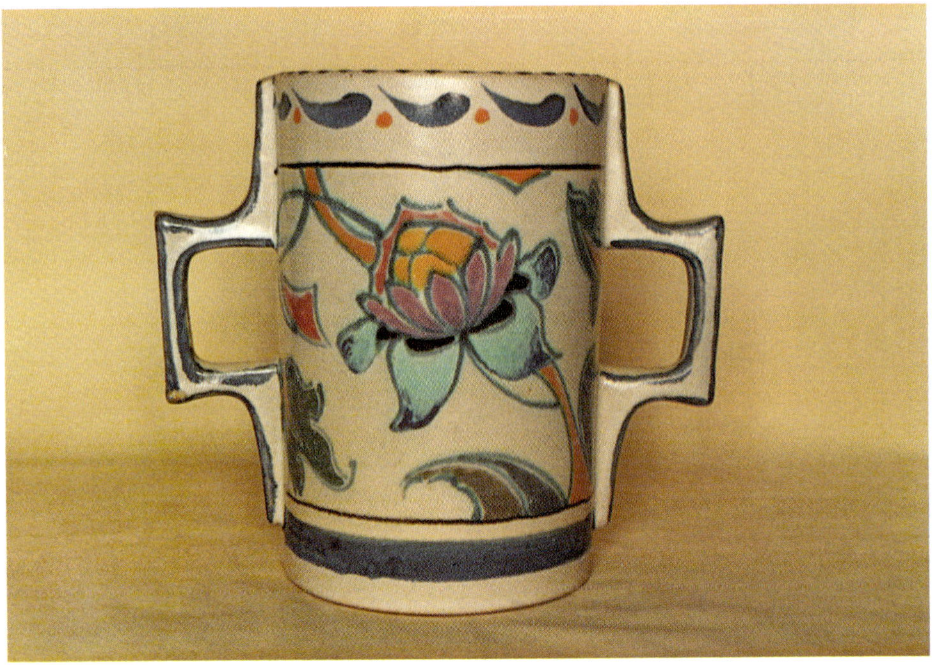

Plate 18 (above)
An 8″ two handled mug decorated with a typical Honiton Jacobean pattern. Mark no 22. Circa 1933.

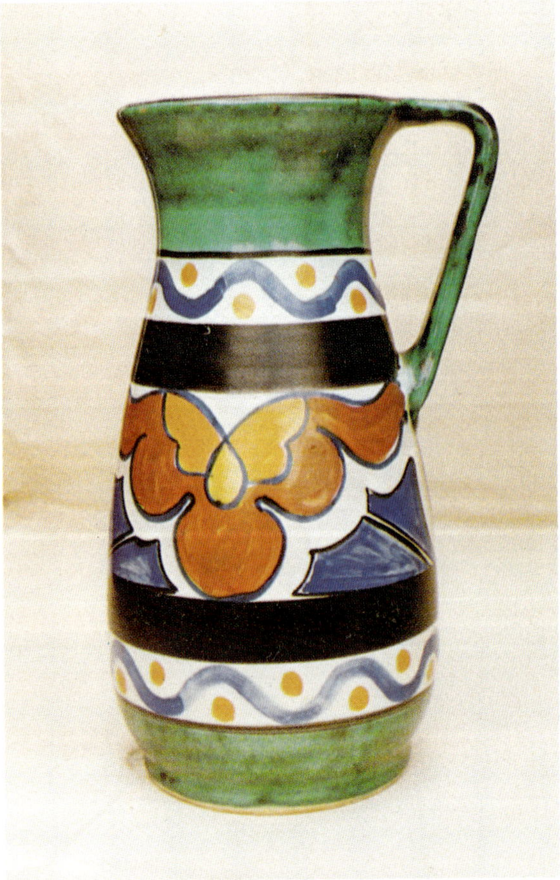

Plate 19
A 10″ Honiton pitcher decorated in the Stuart pattern showing the distinctive lustrous Honiton green. Mark no 22 and painted shape no 32. Circa 1935.

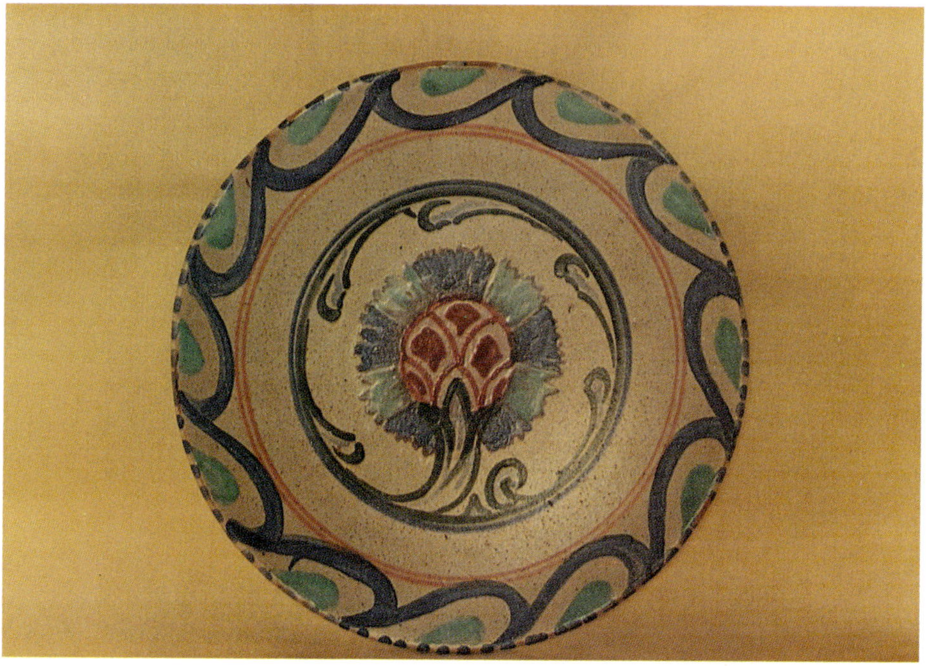

Plate 20 (above)
A 9″ diameter Honiton plate in the de Morgan pattern. Mark no 21. Circa 1926.

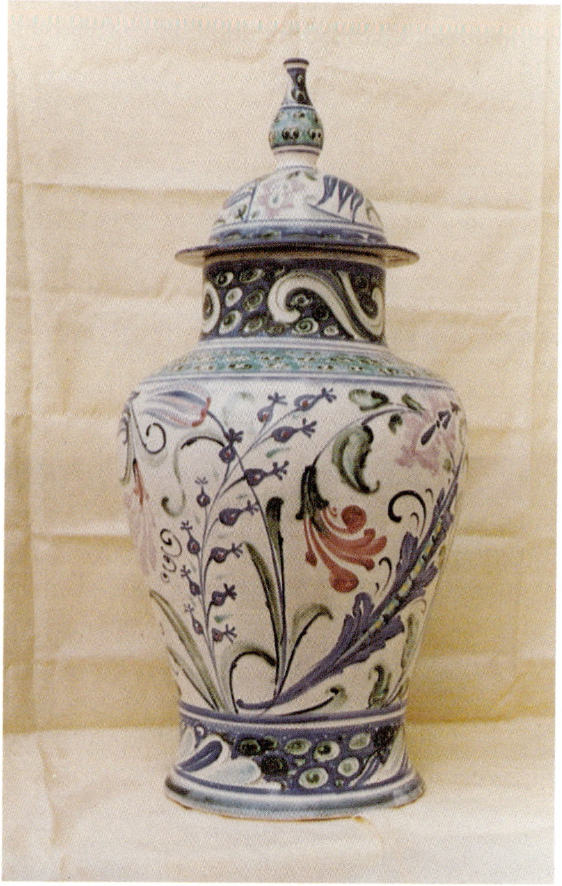

Plate 21
A 22″ covered vase decorated in the Persian pattern. Thrown and decorated by Collard at Honiton and signed on the base 'C. Collard 1927'. The reverse is decorated with a large 'saz'. The blue scroll-leaf rising from centre bottom is also similar to a 'saz'. The swirl decorations on the borders are typical of Isnik pottery.

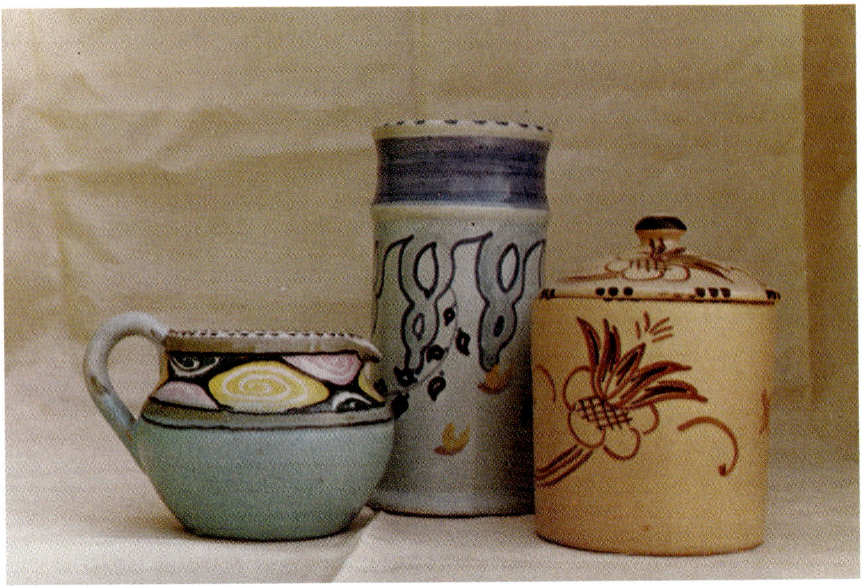

Plate 22 (above)
Three pieces showing different coloured slips used at Honiton. On the left is a 3″ turquoise jug, mark no 22, circa 1930. The 6″ spill vase with blue slip bears mark no 21 and shape no 3 in black paint, circa 1927. (Compare design with plate 32.) On the right is a salmon coloured jam pot, mark no 23 and painted shape no 13, circa 1940.

Plate 23
A 4″ beaker, part of a water set, decorated in a standard pattern. It has a butterfly on the reverse and the inside is deep green. Mark no 21. Circa 1928.

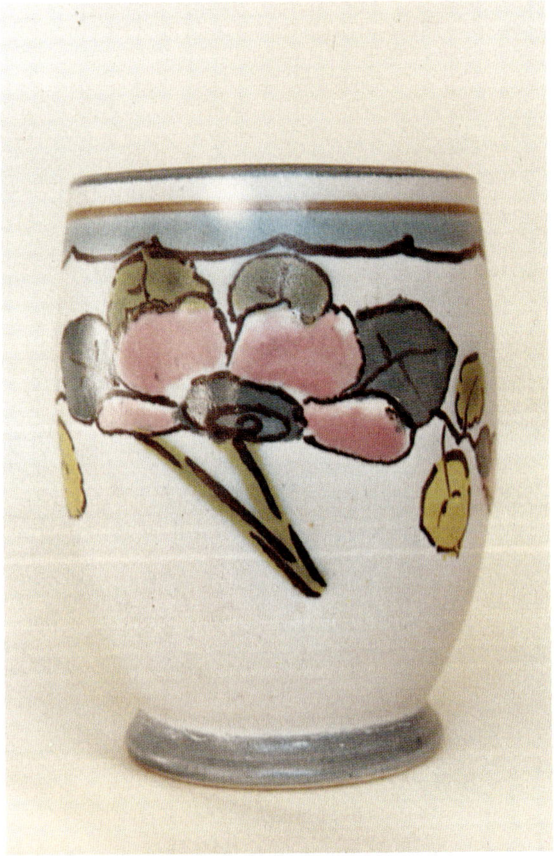

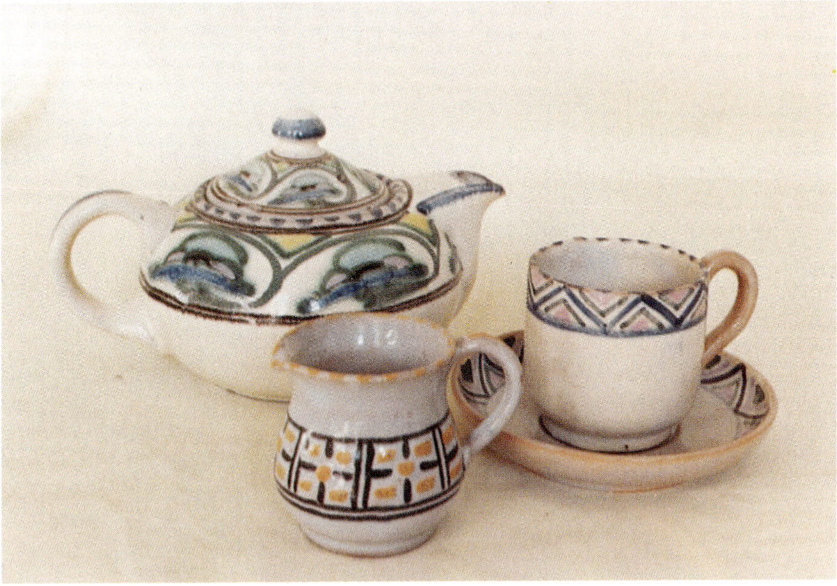

Plate 24 (above)
Three examples of Honiton's banded decoration. A 3″ teapot in the adapted Jacobean pattern, page. Mark no 23. Circa 1933. The 2½″ jug bears mark no 22, circa 1933. The coffee cup, part of a set, has mark no 21, circa 1927.

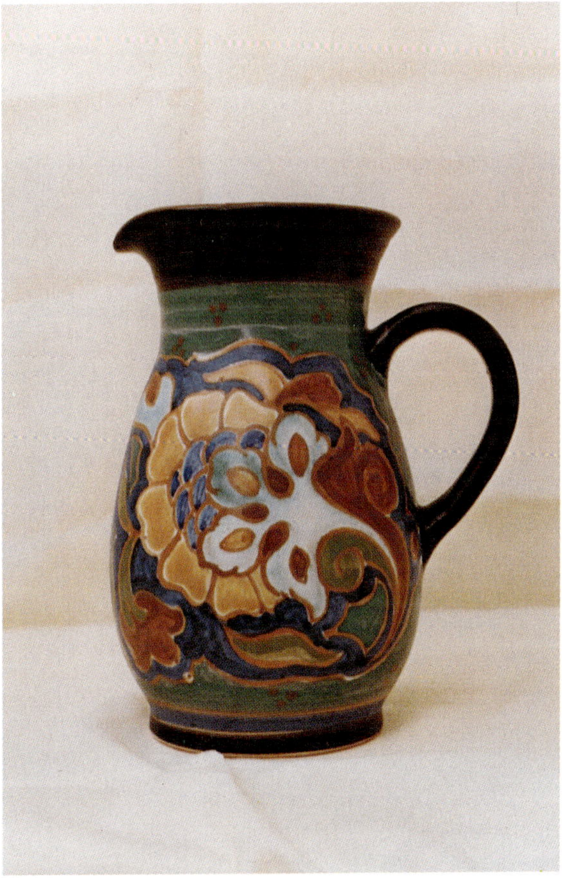

Plate 25
An 8″ Honiton jug in Dutch style. Mark no 23 and shape no 33. Circa 1939.

Plate 26 (right)
A Honiton 11″ lampbase made totally of pottery and decorated by Collard. No marks. Circa 1941.

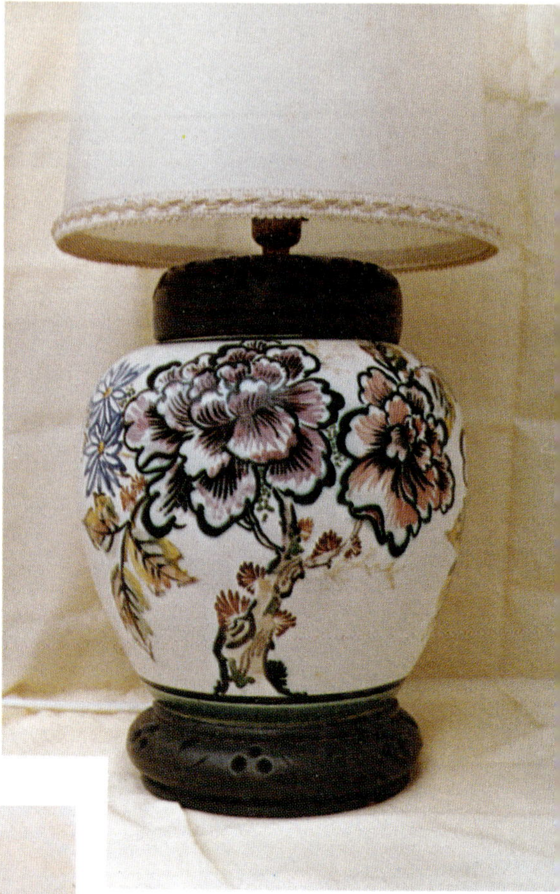

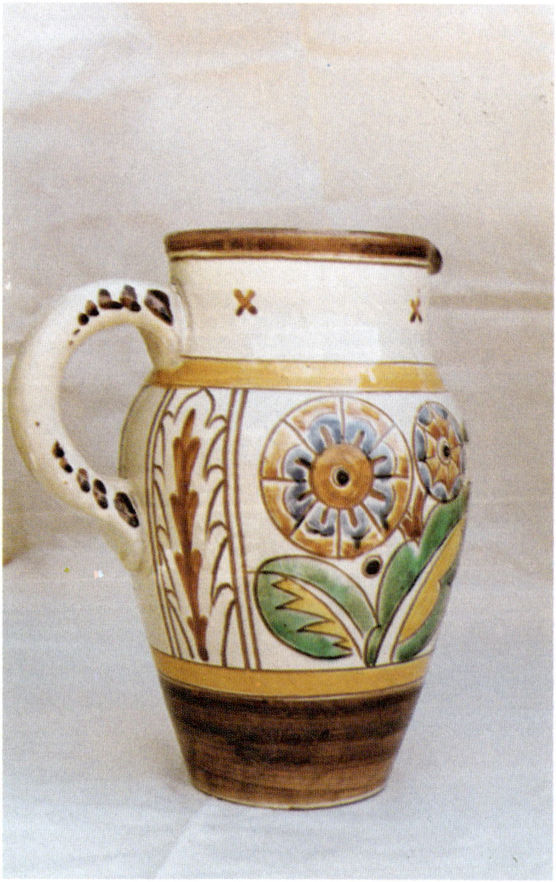

Plate 27 (left)
An 8″ sgraffito Honiton jug with geometric floral design and underglaze decoration. Mark no 23 and black shape number 34. Circa 1935.

Plate 28 (right)
A rough textured 8″ Honiton sgraffito jug with underglaze decoration. Black Shape no 34 and mark no 23. Circa 1937.

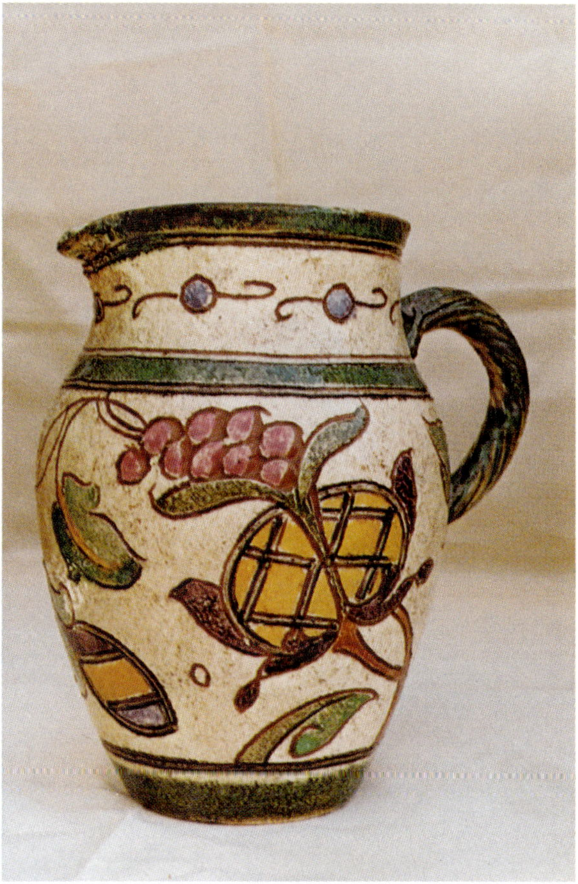

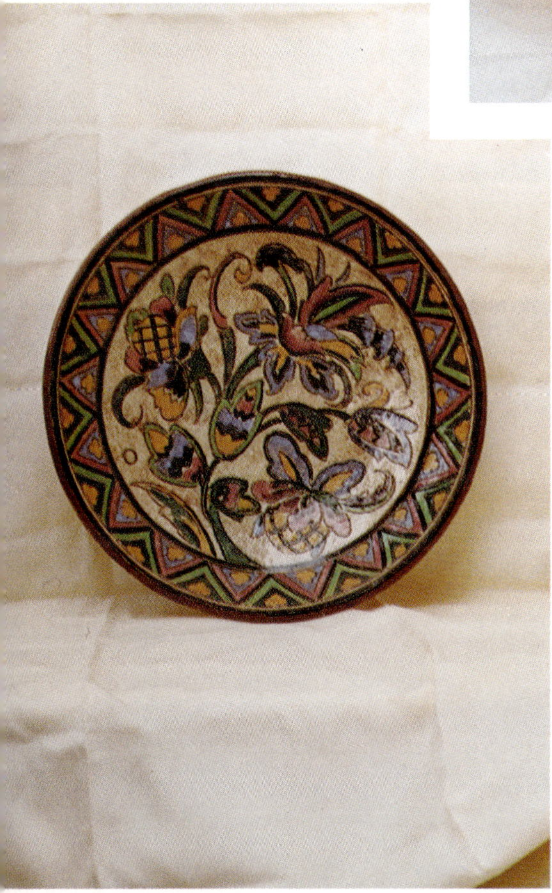

Plate 29 (left)
A rough textured Honiton sgraffito charger 13″ in diameter with underglaze decoration, made and decorated by Collard. Mark no 23. Circa 1940.

Plate 30 (right)
A fine example of a late Jacobean pattern vase decorated by Joan Collard. 17" high, signed on the base 'B. J. Collard, 1942' with a painted mark in capital letters 'Honiton Pottery' and also bearing mark no 23.

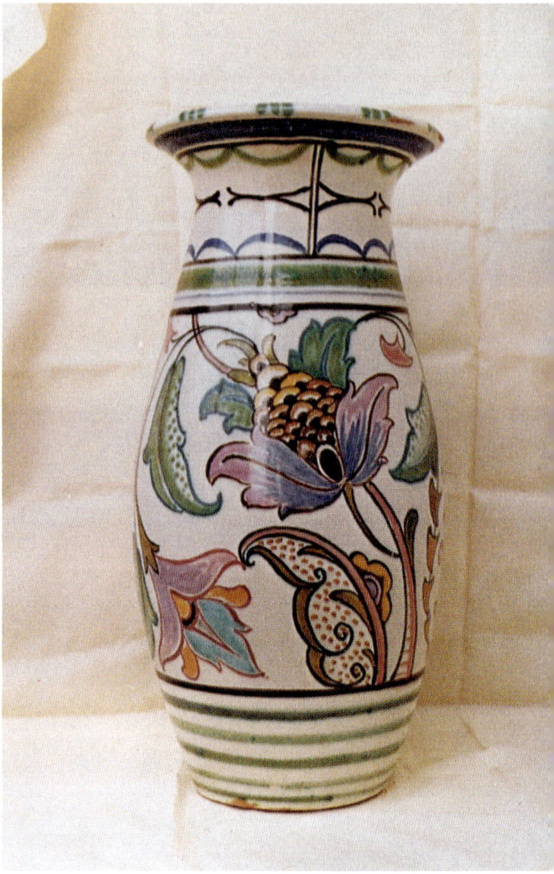

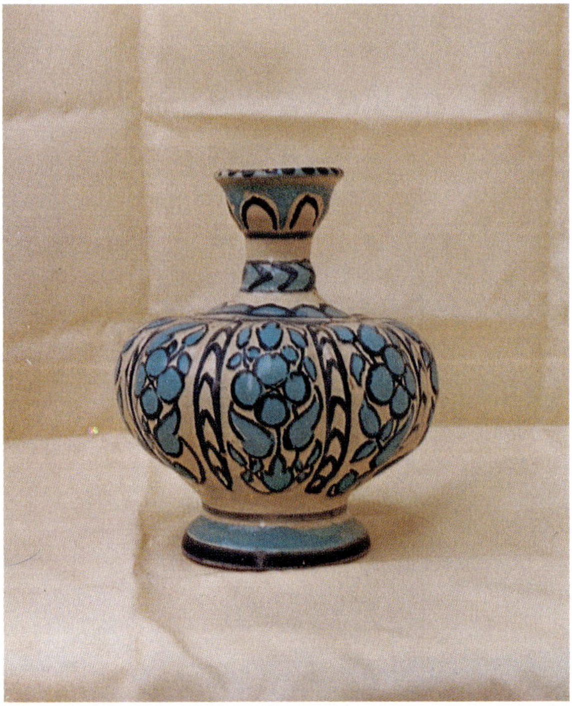

Plate 31 (left)
A 5½" vase showing Eastern influence made by Collard during his retirement at Barton, Torquay. Made of local red Torquay clay. Circa 1950.

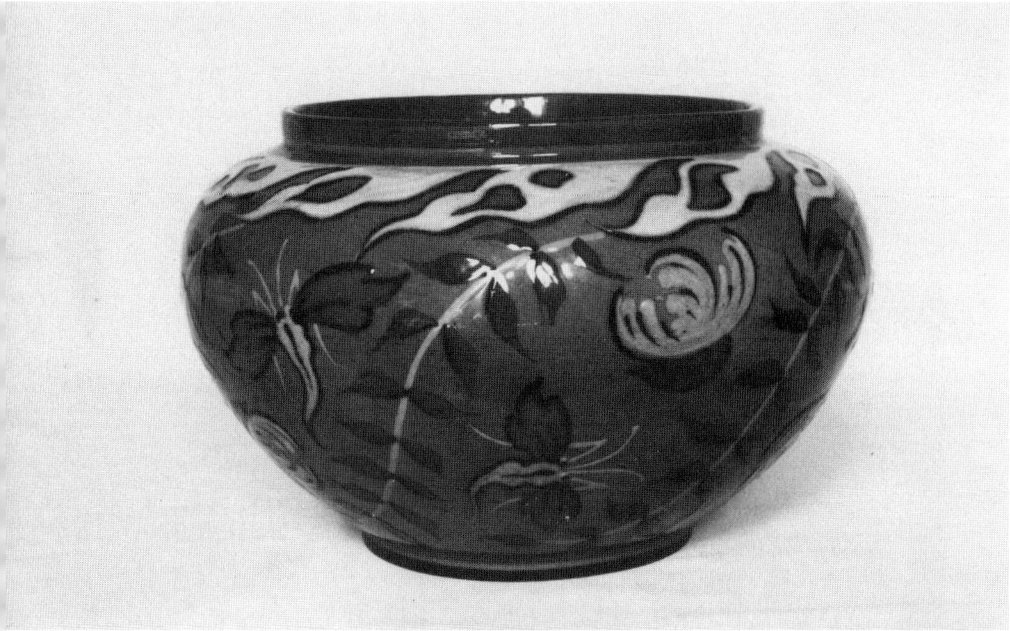

Plate 32 (above)
A 6″ high unmarked Aller Vale jardiniere, stamped only with a small Maltese cross. Made of red clay covered in blue slip. The design is outlined in black and blocked in with cream, green, red-brown, white and pale blue. Circa 1897.

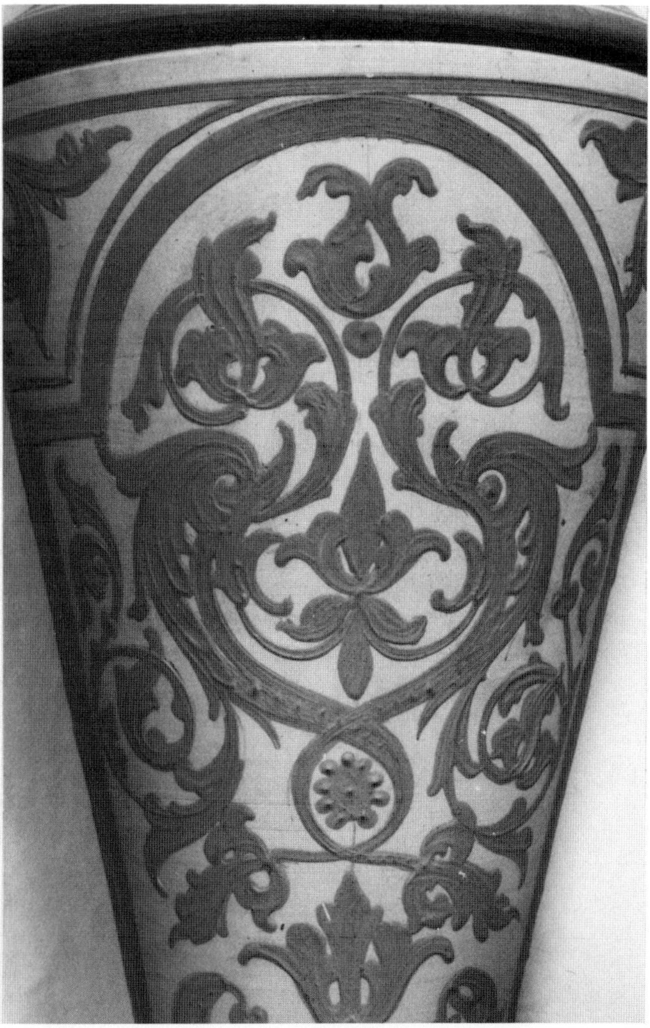

Plate 33 (right)
Detail from an unglazed Aller Vale jardiniere stand 2′6″ high, decorated with Wedgwood blue scrolls on a white ground. Made of white clay and incised 'Marcucci' both inside the base and top. No pottery mark. Circa 1890.

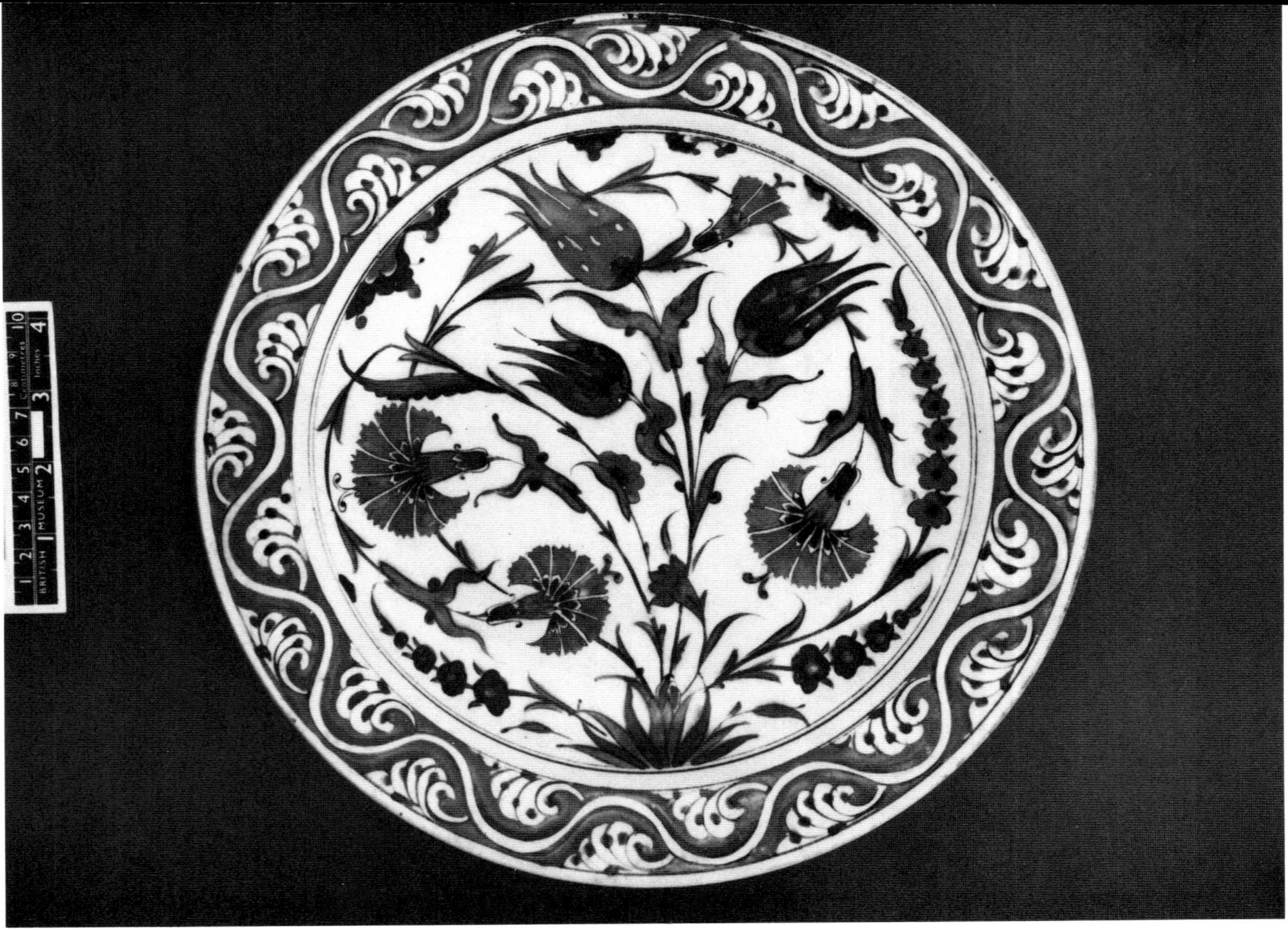

Plate 34
A mid 16th Century Isnik plate, 13″ in diameter. Decorated in the 'quatre fleurs' pattern in red-brown, blue and turquoise. Reproduced courtesy of the British Museum.

Plate 35
An 8″ Aller Vale harvest jug in the sgraffito Q1 pattern with motto on reverse. Painted in mustard yellow, olive green and dark blue on a cream ground. Made of red clay and unmarked. Circa 1895. (Compare with plate 27.)

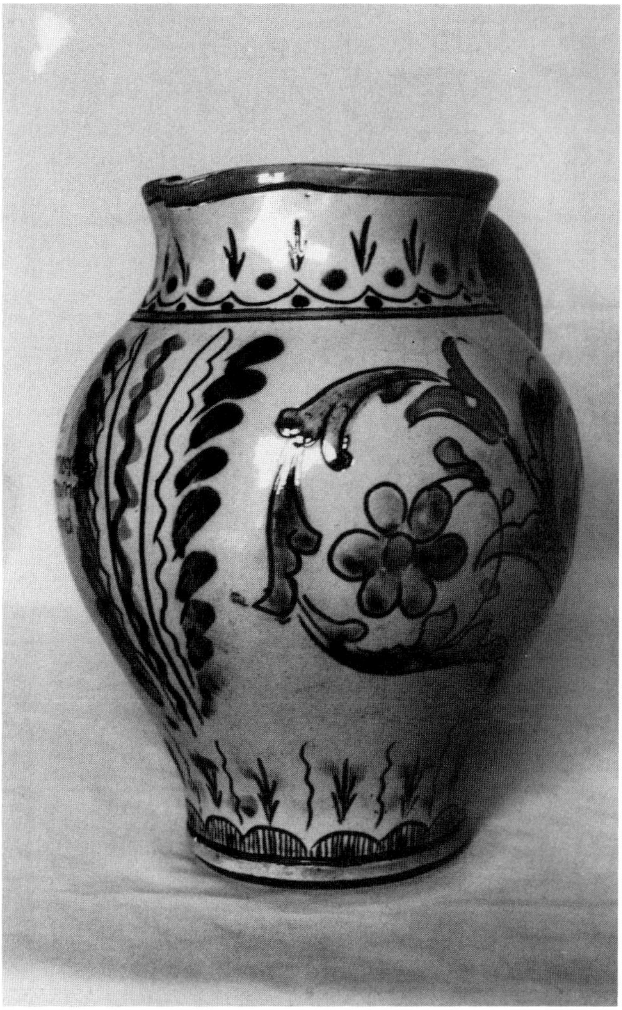

Plate 36 (below)
A 7″ high Aller Vale Egyptian style bowl made of white clay. Decorated, possibly by Collard, in an abstract pattern which includes the heads of dolphins on a sage green ground. Other colours include beige, red-brown, white, pale blue and mid-green. Unmarked. Circa 1893.

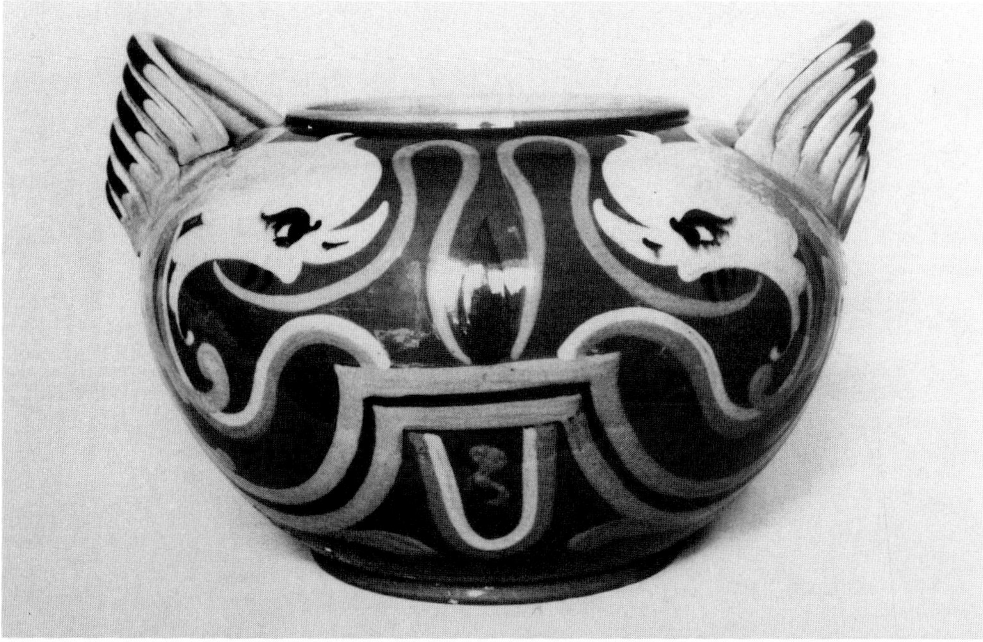

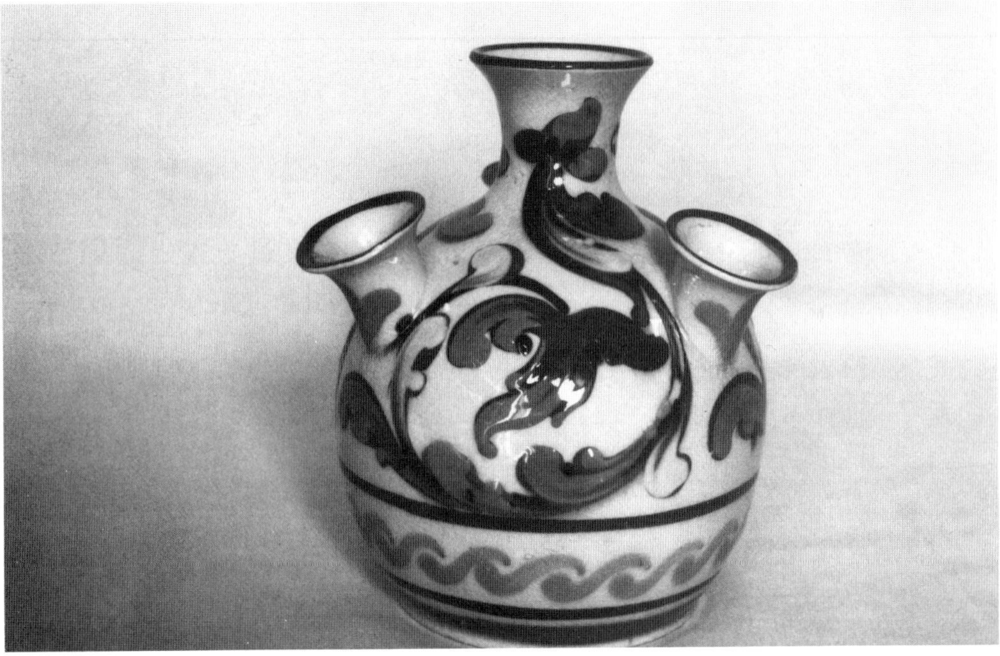

Plate 37 (above)
A 6″ four funnelled tulip vase in white clay. Mark no's 6a, b, c, and incised 901 B1. Made at Aller Vale circa 1902.

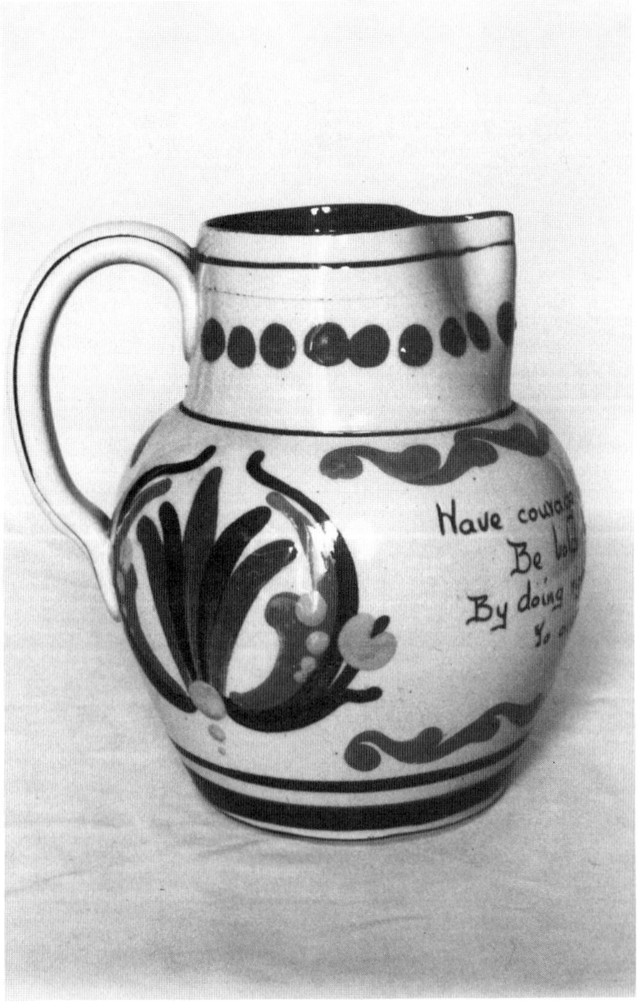

Plate 38
A 7″ Scandy pattern jug with patriotic Boer War motto, made of red clay. Decorated in dark and light green and lemon yellow with blue and red-brown 'feathers'. Mark no 6a with 154 N1 incised on base. Made at Aller Vale circa 1900.

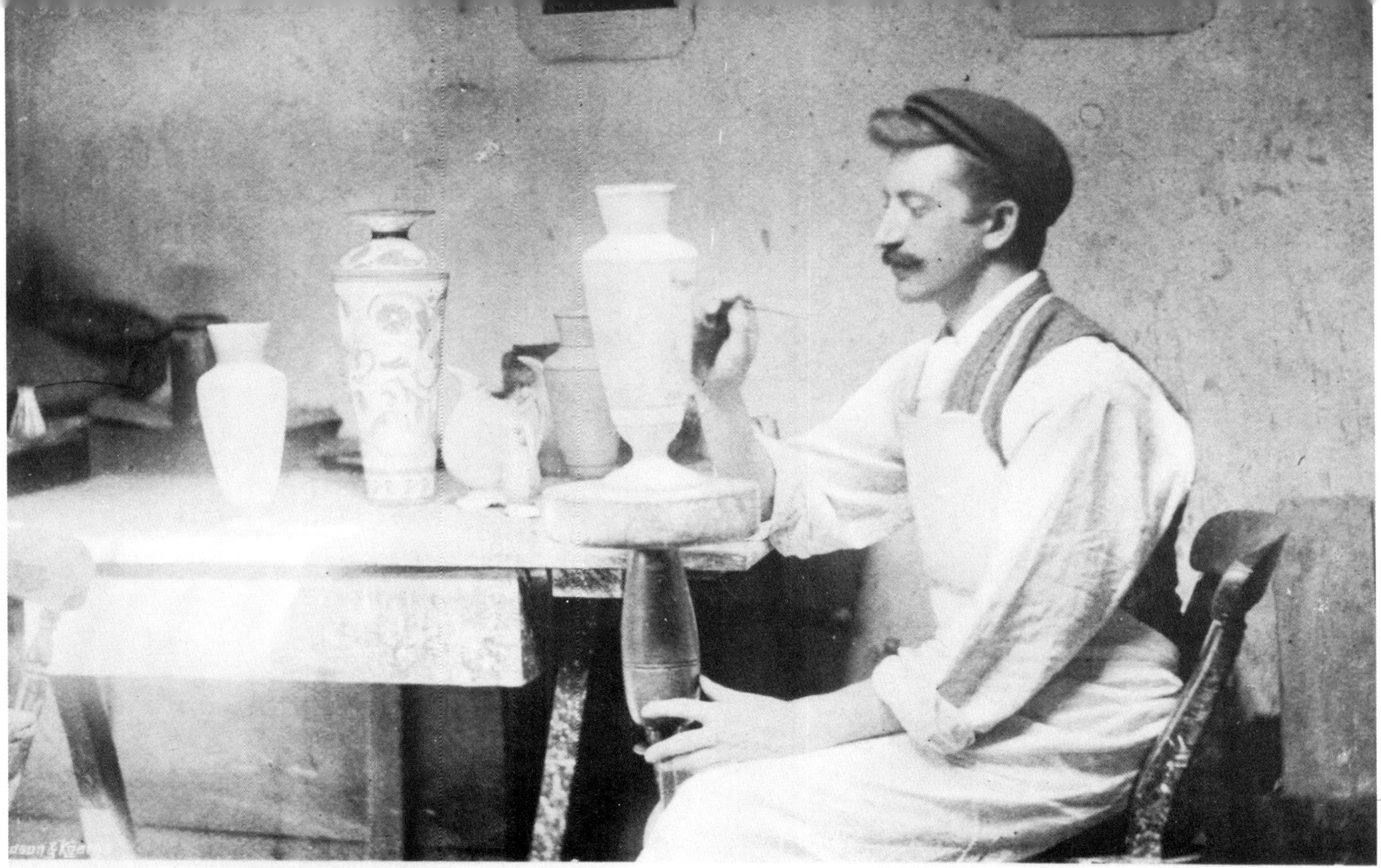

Plate 39
Charles Collard decorating at Aller Vale in 1901. Originally in the Country Life Magazine. Reproduced courtesy of the City of London Guildhall Library.

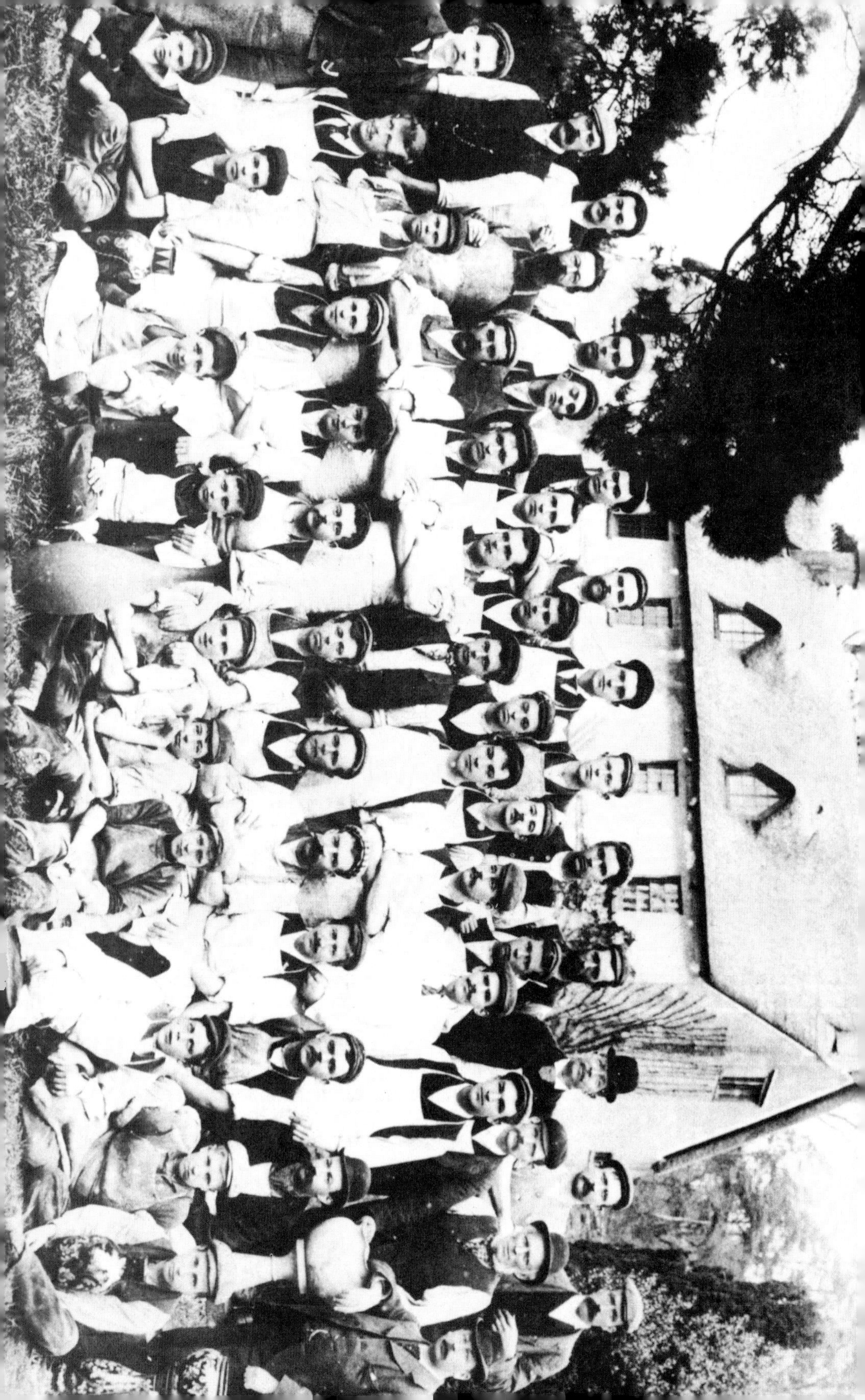

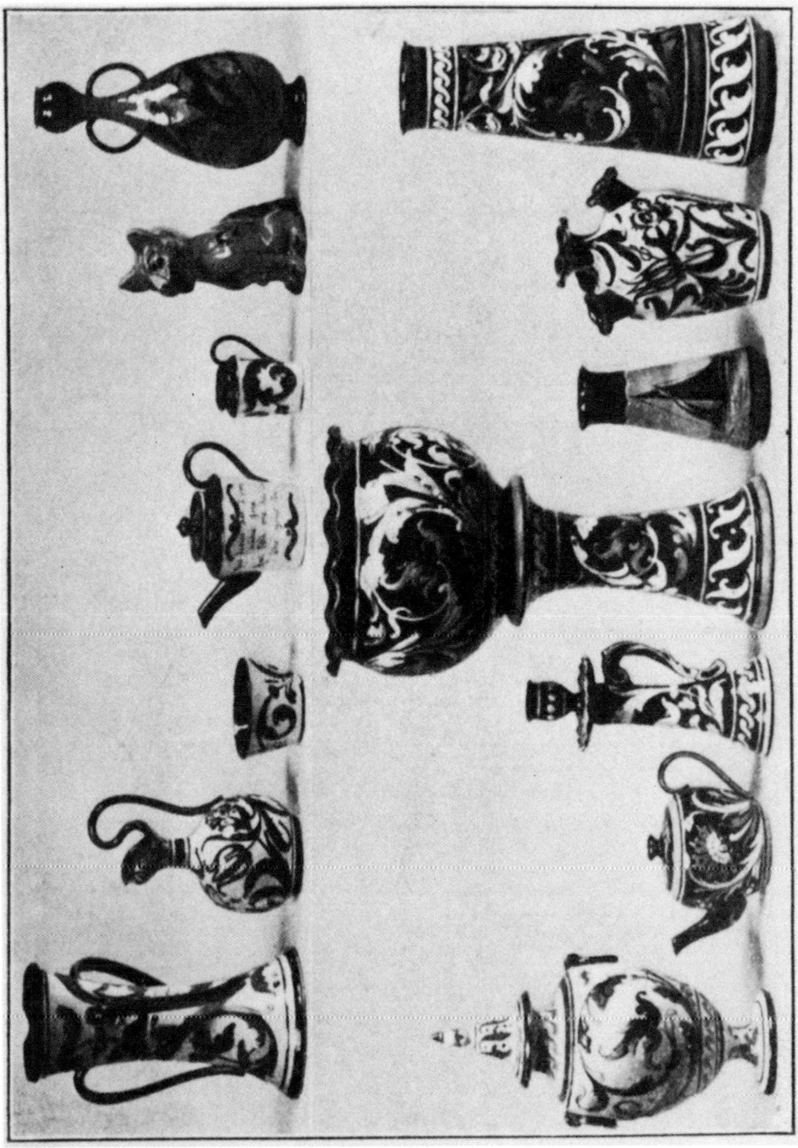

Plate 41
From an advertisement placed by Hart and Moist in the Pottery Gazette in January 1904. Many of the pieces are attributed to Collard. Reproduced courtesy of the British Newspaper Library.

Plate 40 (opposite)
The staff of Aller Vale photographed in the grounds of Moor Park just after Phillips' death in 1897. Those referred to in this book are, from left to right: Second Row Up: standing Herbert Bulley, next to him Samuel Bradford, sitting third from the right Charles Collard and next to him Sam Main. Fourth Row Up: second from the left Thomas Lewis. Top Row: second from the left James Main.

Plate 42
An 8″ Longpark Persian pattern mug. Made of red clay and decorated in red-brown, dark blue, green, black and yellow on a cream ground. Attributed to Collard. Mark no 10 and incised 25 A1. Circa 1904.

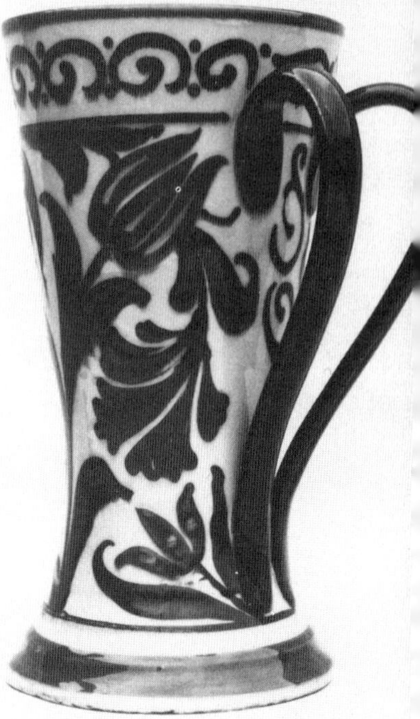

Plare 43
Sam Main at the potter's wheel at the Crown Dorset Art Pottery circa 1911.

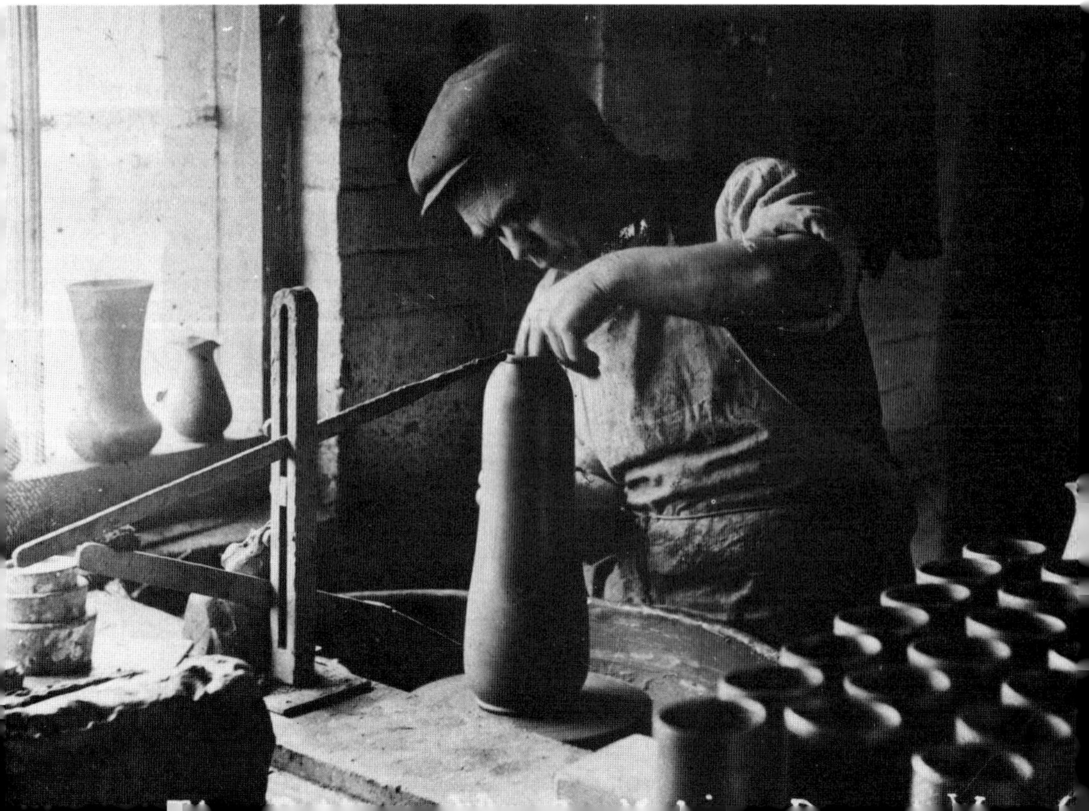

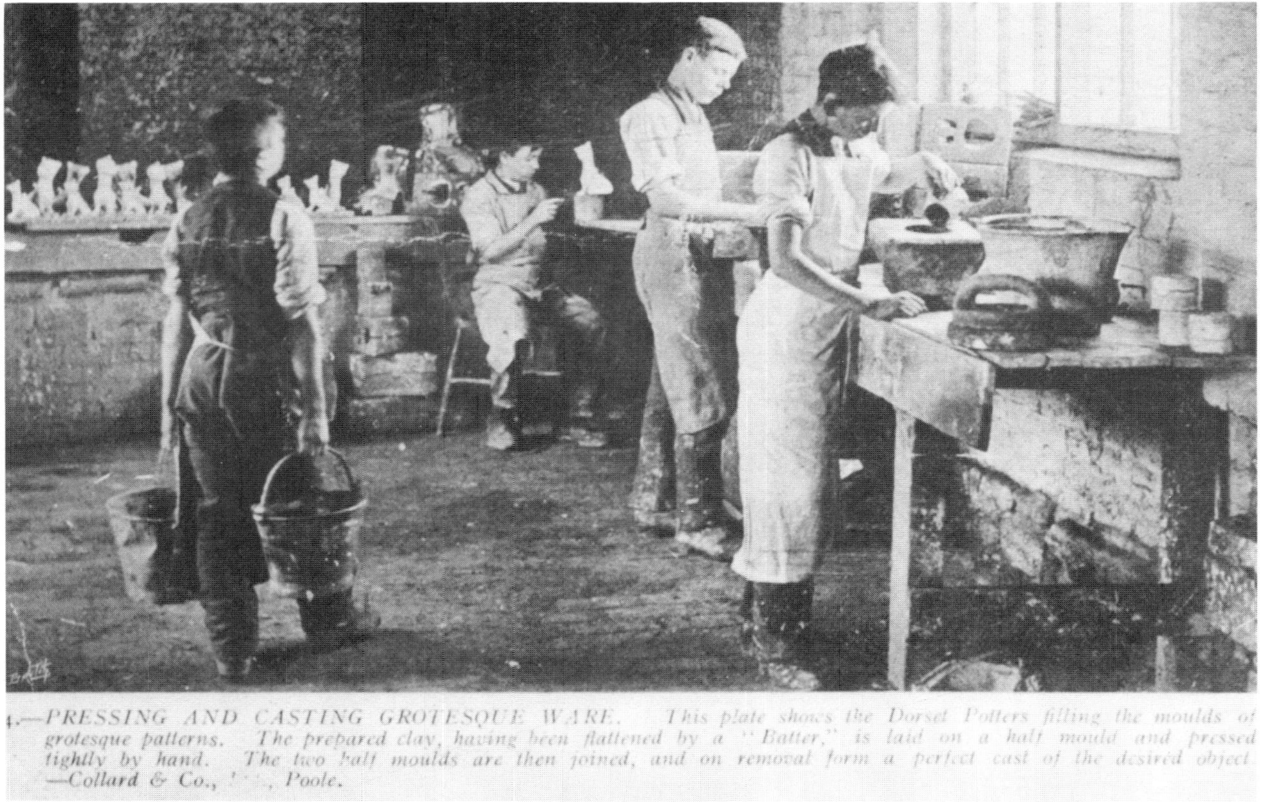

Plate 44
One of a series of postcards produced around 1909 showing the different stages of production at the Dorset Art Pottery. This photograph shows the lads filling the grotesque cat moulds.

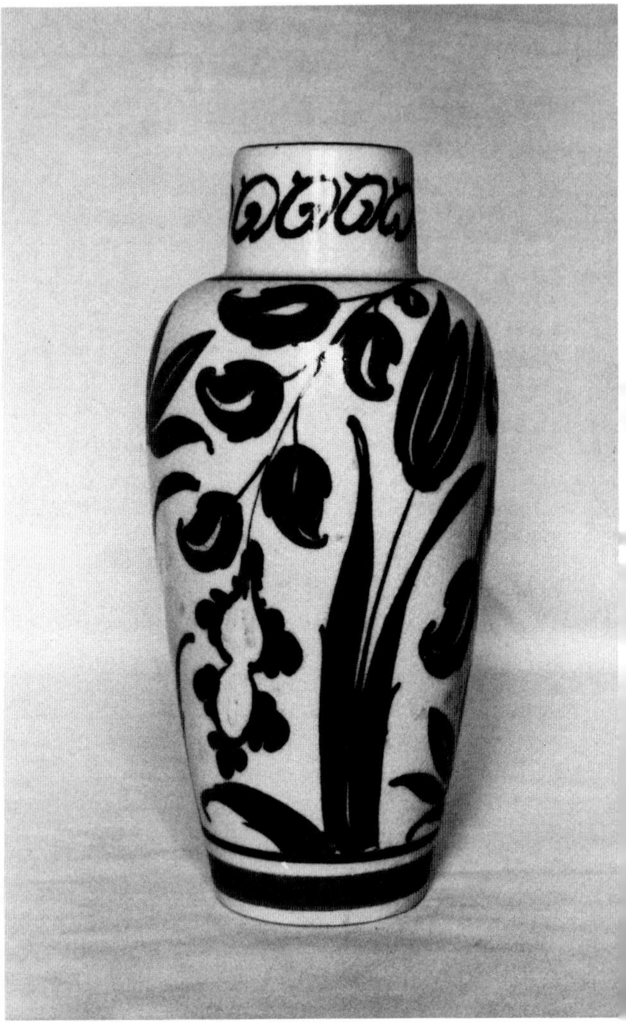

Plate 45
One of a pair of 8″ Crown Dorset vases in the Persian pattern, circa 1914. Made of white clay and decorated in mid-brown, sage green, French blue, cream and black on a white ground. Mark no 17 and 8-159-P incised on the base.

Plate 46 (below)
Left — A 4″ Dorset jug with ribbed handle decorated in pink, green and dark brown on a cream ground. Made of red clay with mark no 13 and 94 B incised on the base. Circa 1906.

Right — A Crown Dorset pot-pourri vase 4″ high. Made of red clay and unmarked. The sgraffito decoration is filled in with a transparent dark blue and the stone coloured rough background is unglazed. Circa 1911.

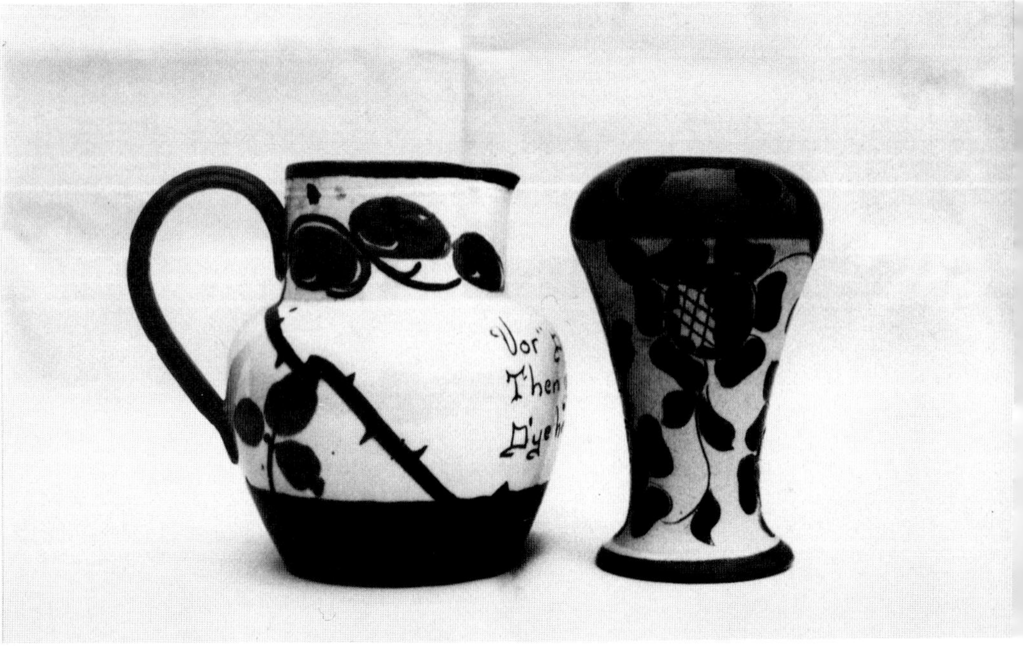

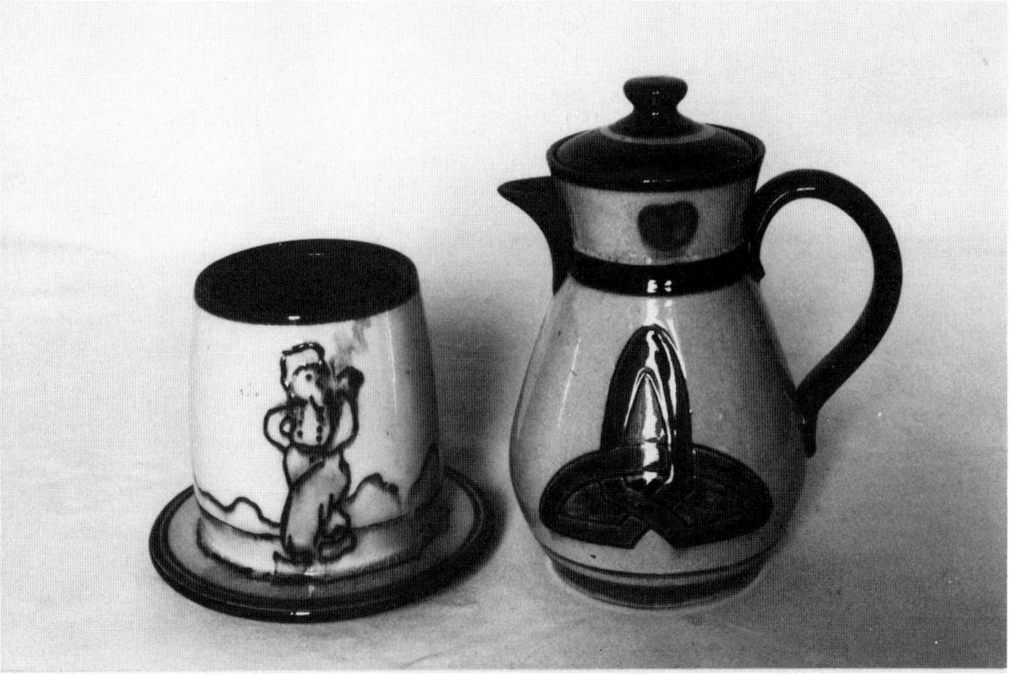

Plate 47
Left — A Mosanic Pottery tobacco jar with a Dutch boy depicted in brown slip and pale 'wash' colours, mainly green on a cream ground. 4″ high without its lid. Made of red clay. Mark no 20. Circa 1911.

Right — A 6″ Dorset hot water jug in a sgraffito pattern. Painted in orange, blue, yellow and green on a cream ground with motto no 6, appendix III. Mark no 15 with 'No 13' on the red clay base. Handle shape no 1, appendix IV. Circa 1911.

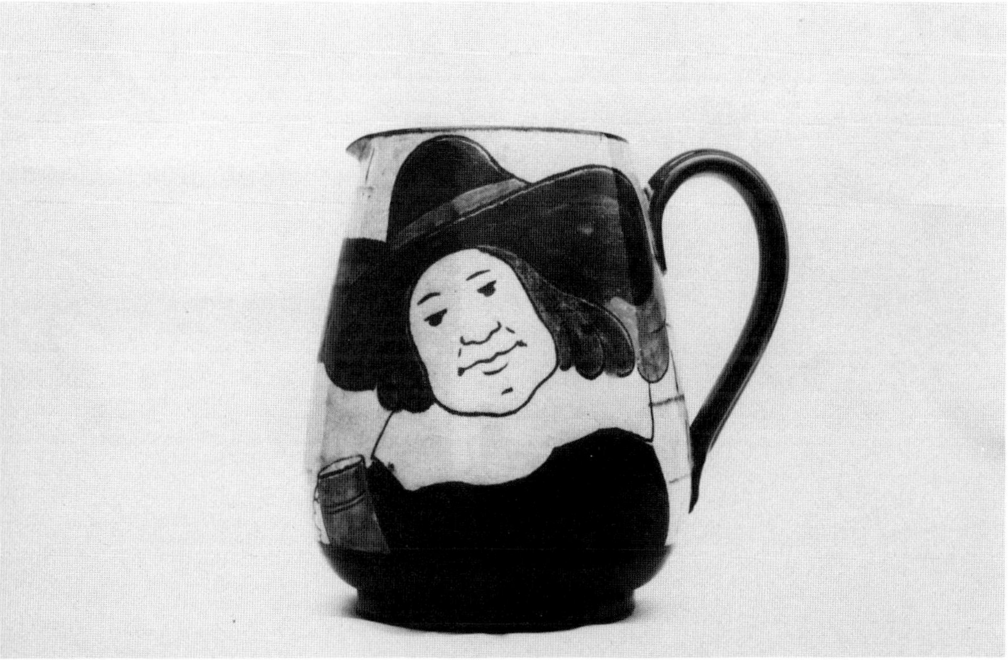

Plate 48
A 5″ jug of red clay with sgraffito design of a man holding a tankard. In typical Dorset colours of dark olive green, mustard yellow, red-brown and black. Motto no I, appendix III on reverse. Mark no 12 and incised 474 on base. Circa 1908.

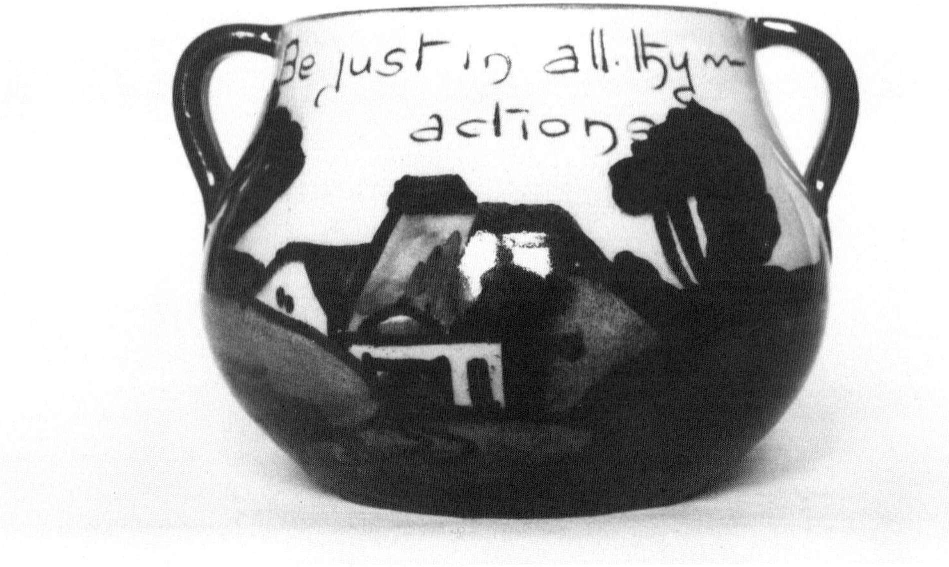

Plate 49
A 3″ bowl with 'fleur de lys' handles. In typical Dorset colours of greens, browns and yellow with the addition of a pink (!) field on the left. Incised 463/24 on the red clay base. Circa 1911.

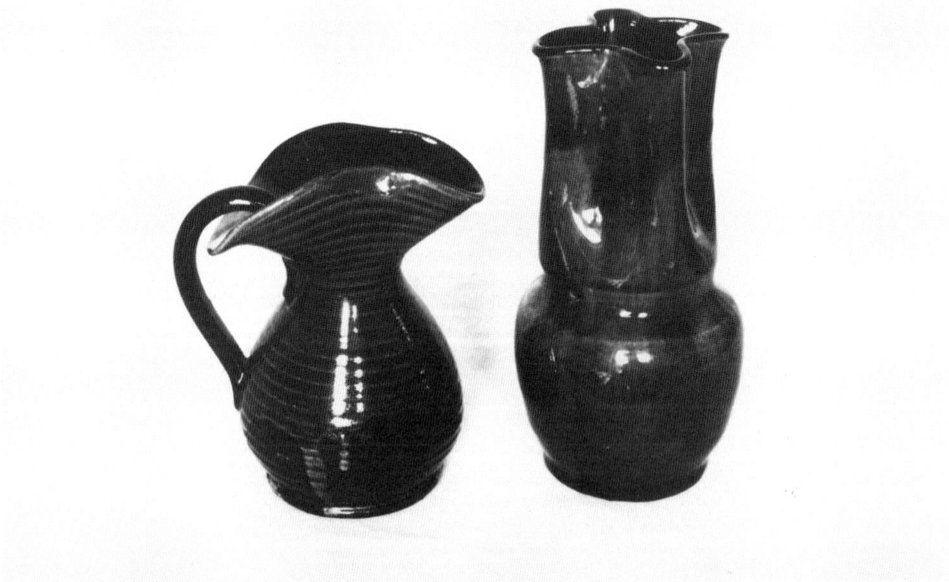

Plate 50
A 5″ Dorset jug whose handle fits through a hole in the jug's large rim. Bottle green with the exposed red clay appearing almost black under a dark green glaze. Mark no 12 impressed. Circa 1906.

Right — A 6″ Crown Dorset vase whose fluted neck is also reminiscent of Aller Vale and Exeter shapes. Red clay with impressed mark no 17. Sea green with blue flecks under a very glossy glaze. Circa 1910.

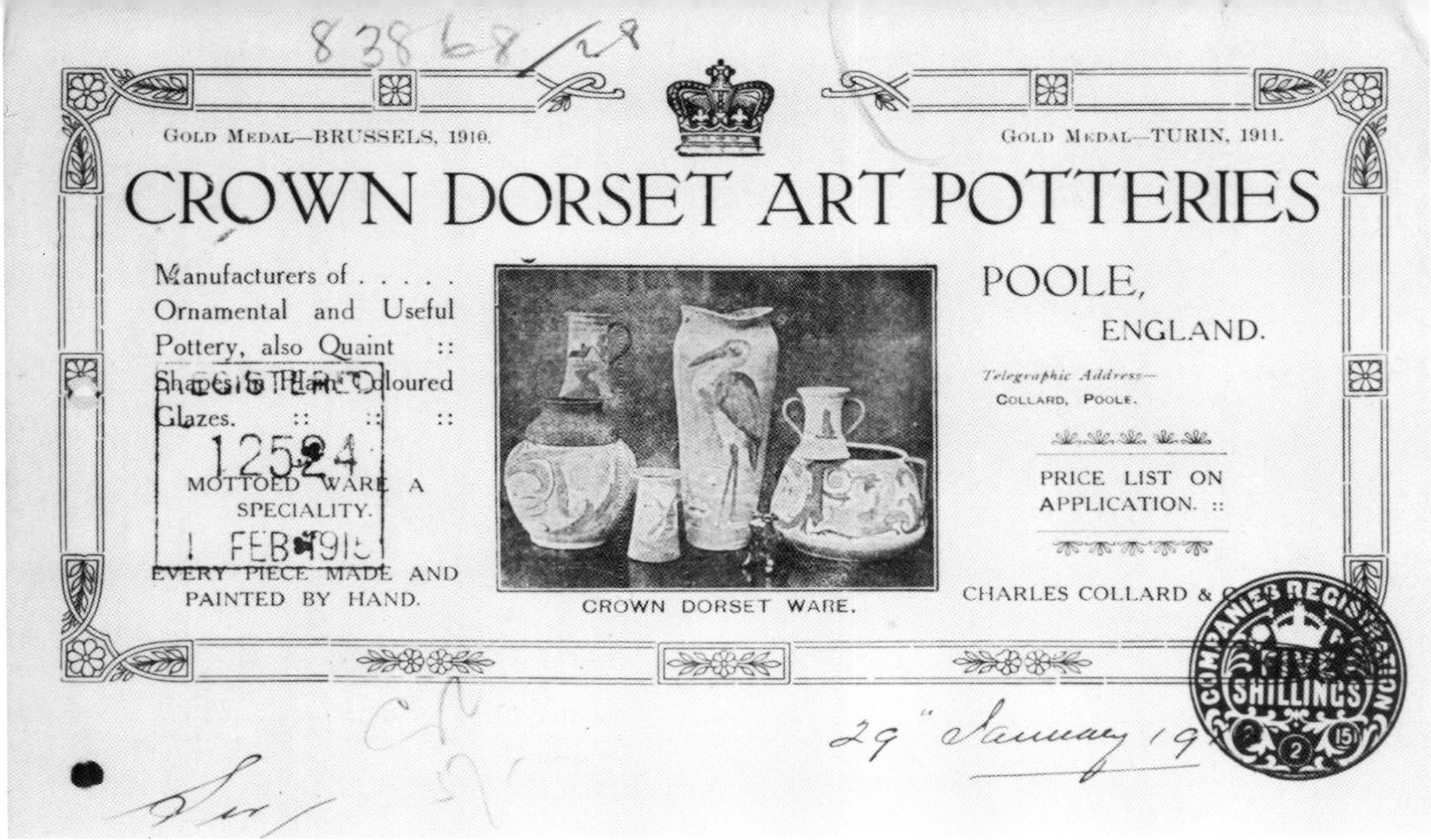
GOLD MEDAL—BRUSSELS, 1910.

GOLD MEDAL—TURIN, 1911.

CROWN DORSET ART POTTERIES

Manufacturers of . . . . .
Ornamental and Useful
Pottery, also Quaint ::
Shapes in Plain Coloured
Glazes. :: :: ::

REGISTERED
12524
1 FEB 1915

MOTTOED WARE A
SPECIALITY.

EVERY PIECE MADE AND
PAINTED BY HAND.

CROWN DORSET WARE.

POOLE,
ENGLAND.

Telegraphic Address—
COLLARD, POOLE.

PRICE LIST ON
APPLICATION. ::

CHARLES COLLARD & C

COMPANIES REGISTRATION
FIVE SHILLINGS

83868/28

29" January 19

Sir/

Plate 51
A letter heading used in 1915 and printed soon after 1911. Note the Aller Vale influence still on the major pieces of: left a Persian pattern, centre a wading bird and right a mythical beast and scrolls. The shape of the central vase was also popular at Watcombe and Longpark at the time. Reproduced courtesy of the Public Records Office.

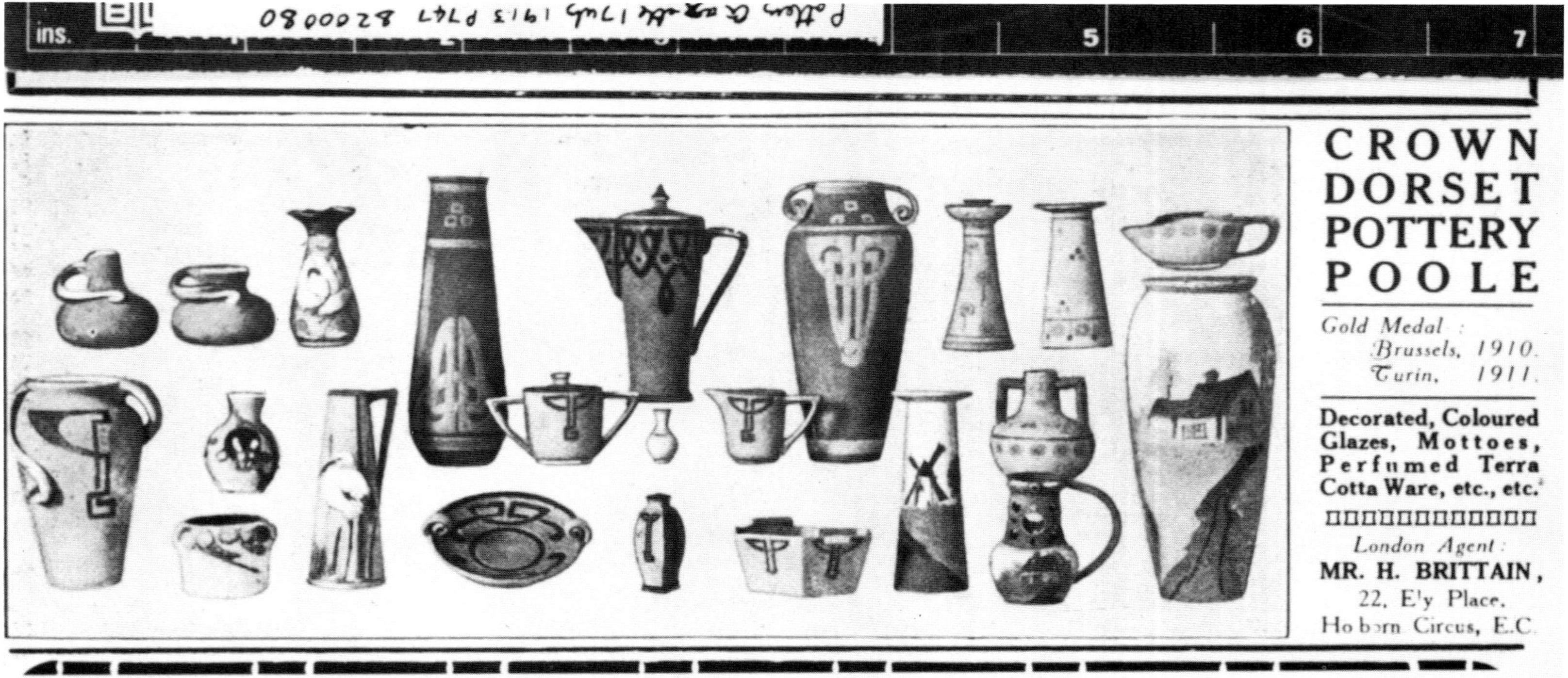

Plate 52
An advertisement from the Pottery Gazette, July 1913, showing a range of new Crown Dorset patterns and shapes. Reproduced courtesy of the British Newspaper Library.

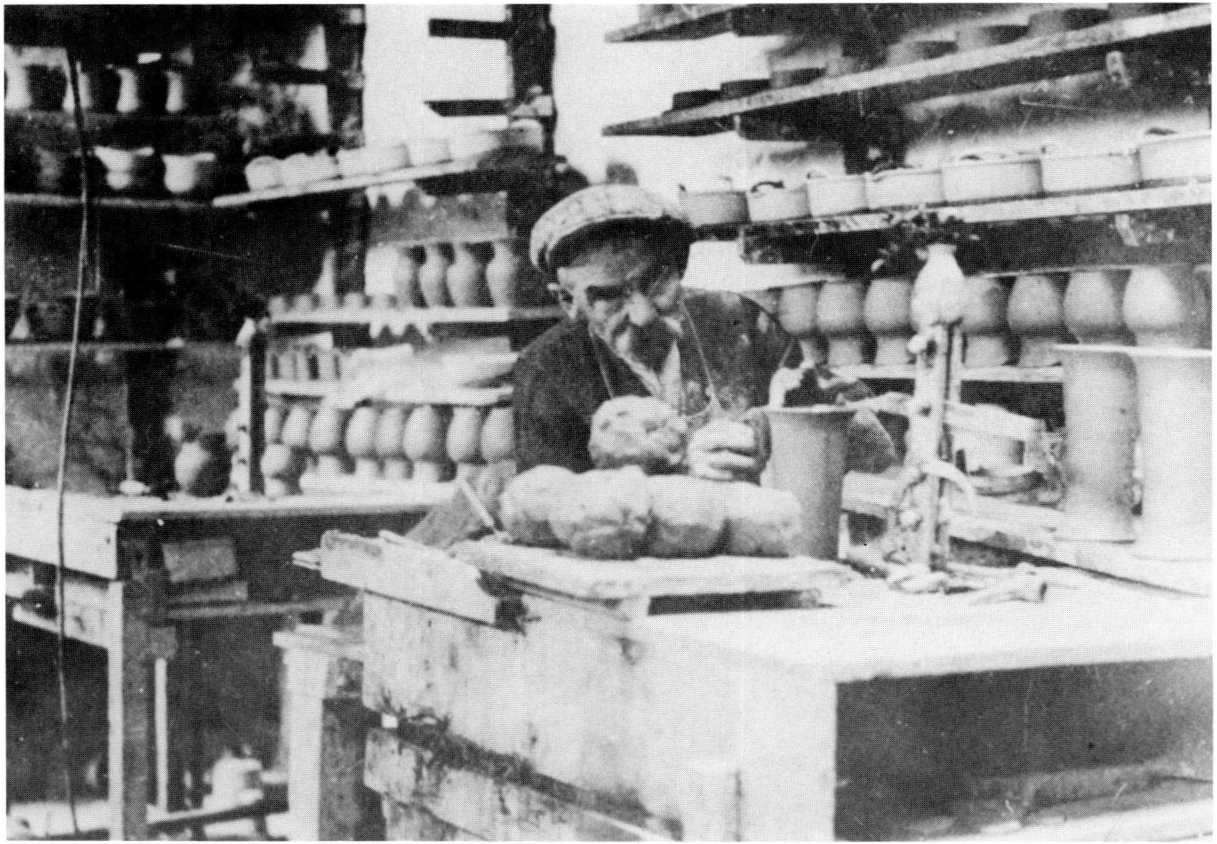

Plate 53
Freddie Jeanes, nicknamed 'The Walrus', at the potter's wheel at Honiton in the 1920s.

Plate 54
A 10″ Mosanic vase with sgraffito decoration of a man with a pig on a rope set against a typical Dorset background of trees, a cottage and a winding path. The man wears blue-green breeches and hat and a pink jacket. Mark no 19 and impressed no 463 3 on red clay. Circa 1910.

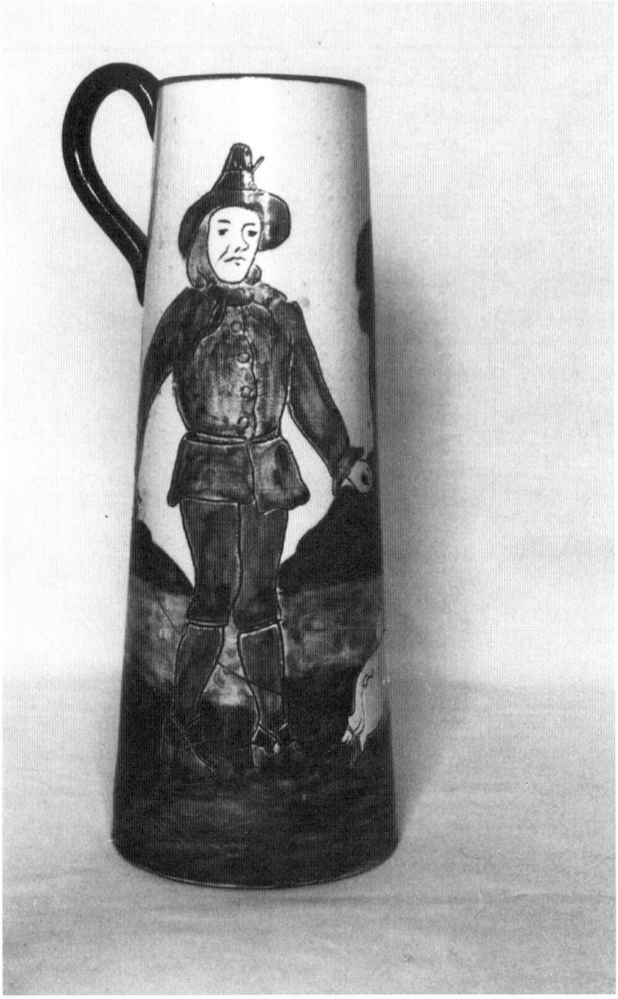

Plate 55 (below)
A small Honiton jug made entirely of the local red clay without the addition of any white clay. Showing the 'duck egg' effect discussed on page 97.

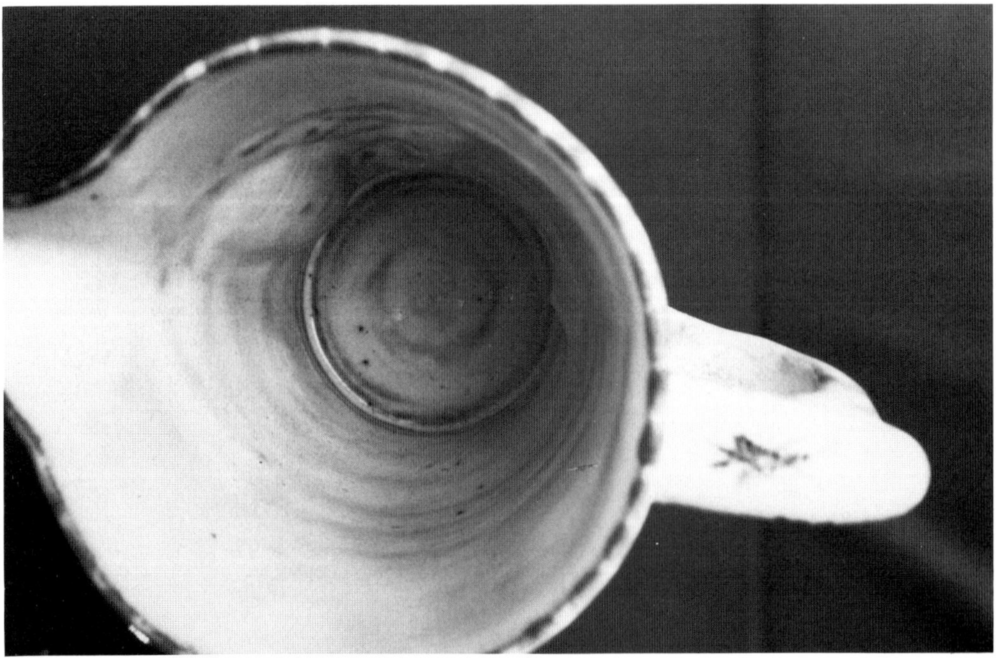

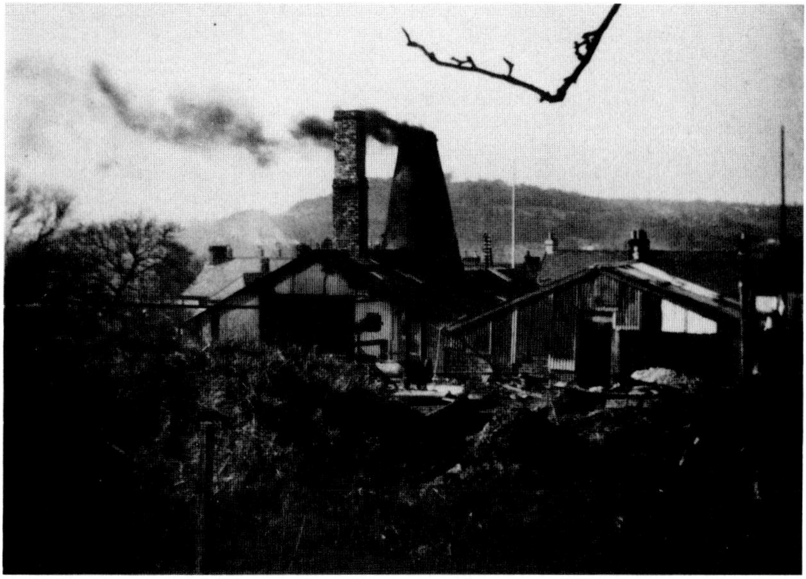

Plate 56
The Honiton pottery kiln during firing in the 1930s.

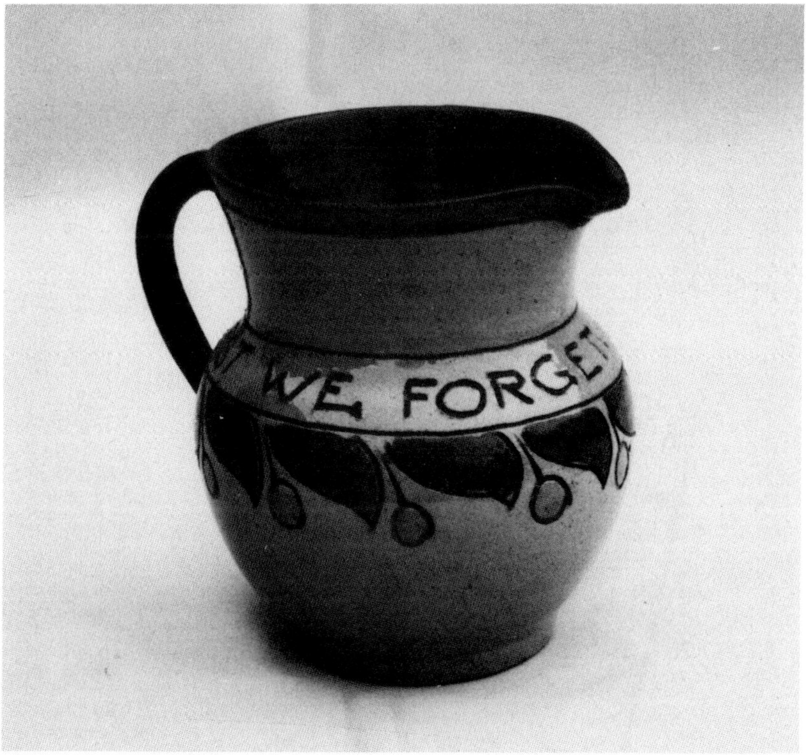

Plate 57
A 3½" Honiton jug decorated in a sand coloured slip with a sgraffito design in green, yellow and blue. Marked with an unusually small version of mark no 21 on orange-brown clay. Circa 1922.

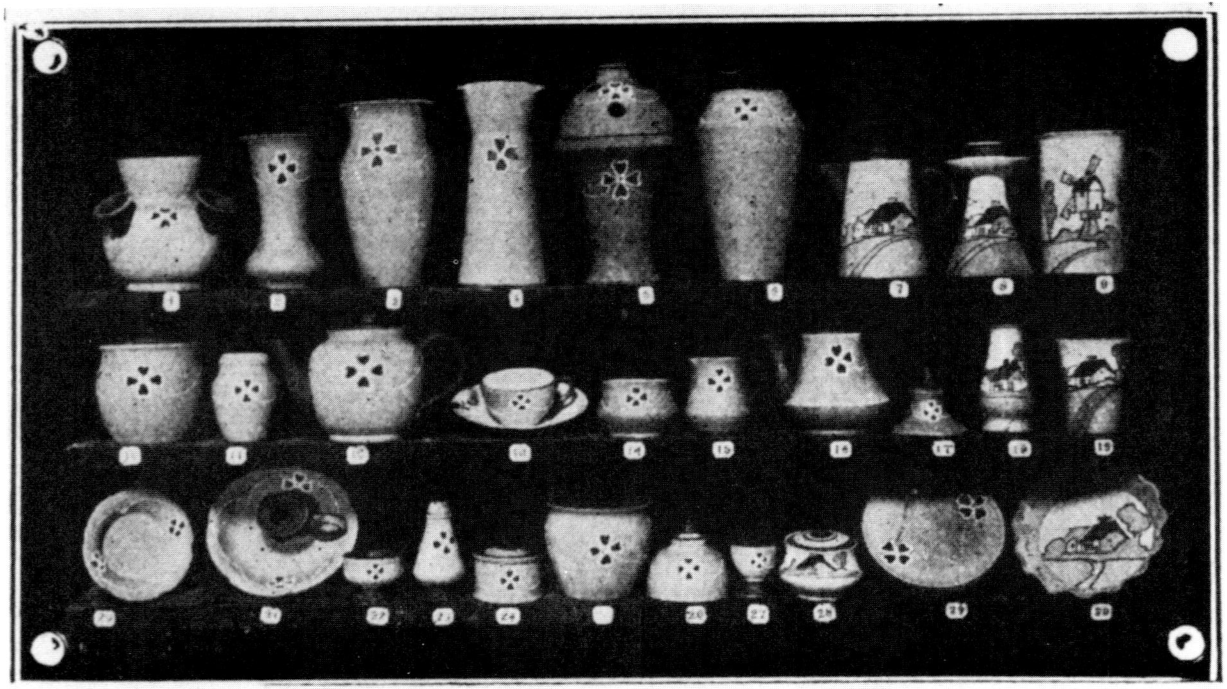

Plate 58
A photograph used for advertising by the Honiton Art Potteries in 1921. This type of pottery was only produced for a few years. Courtesy of the British Library.

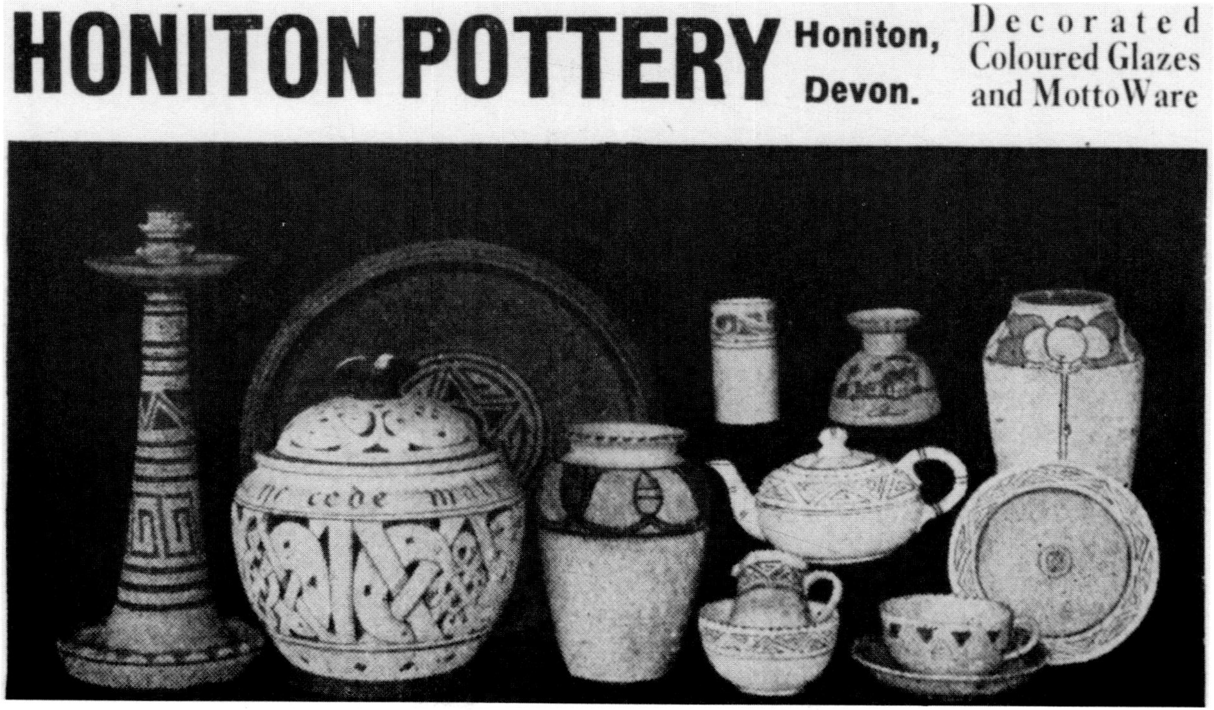

Plate 59
An advertisement from the Pottery Gazette, February 1924, showing early examples of Honiton's "new style" with the exception of the solitary piece of cottage ware. Courtesy of the British Newspaper Library.

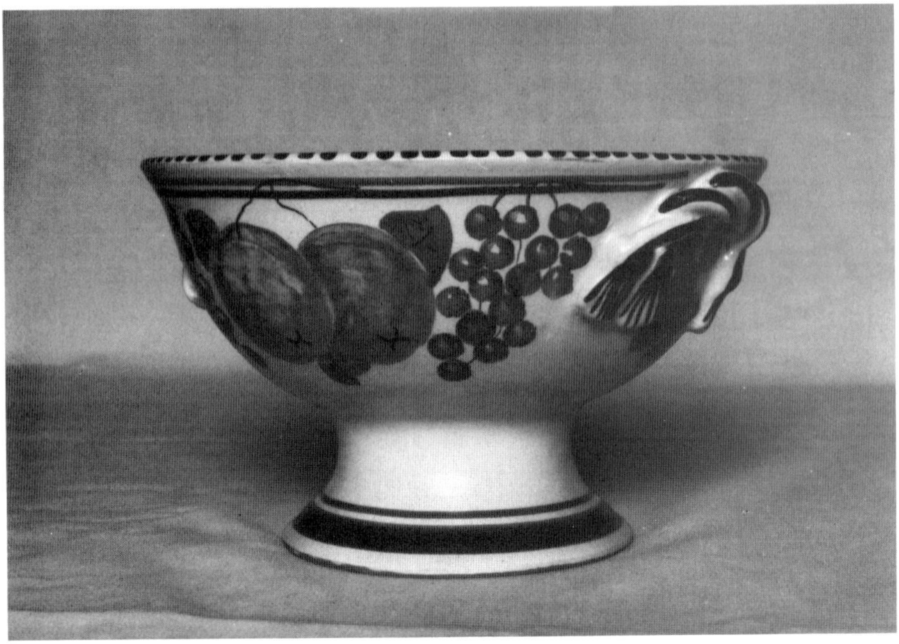

Plate 60 (above)
A 5″ high fruit bowl decorated by Florrie Loving and dated on the base 4/3/41. The fruit were put on with different size sponges and the leaves and stems were painted free-hand. The handles are sepia, the bands sepia and green. The fruit are in natural colours: purple, red, yellow and salmon.

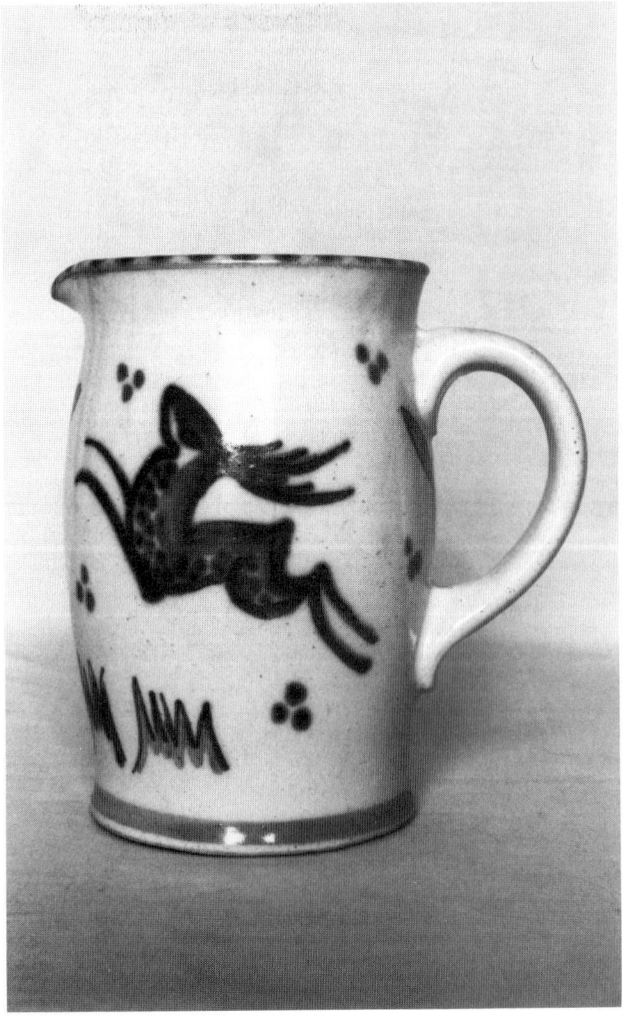

Plate 61
A 6″ jug decorated in the well-known Honiton Woodland pattern. Painted in greens on a white ground. Black painted shape no 27. Mark no 23. Circa 1935.

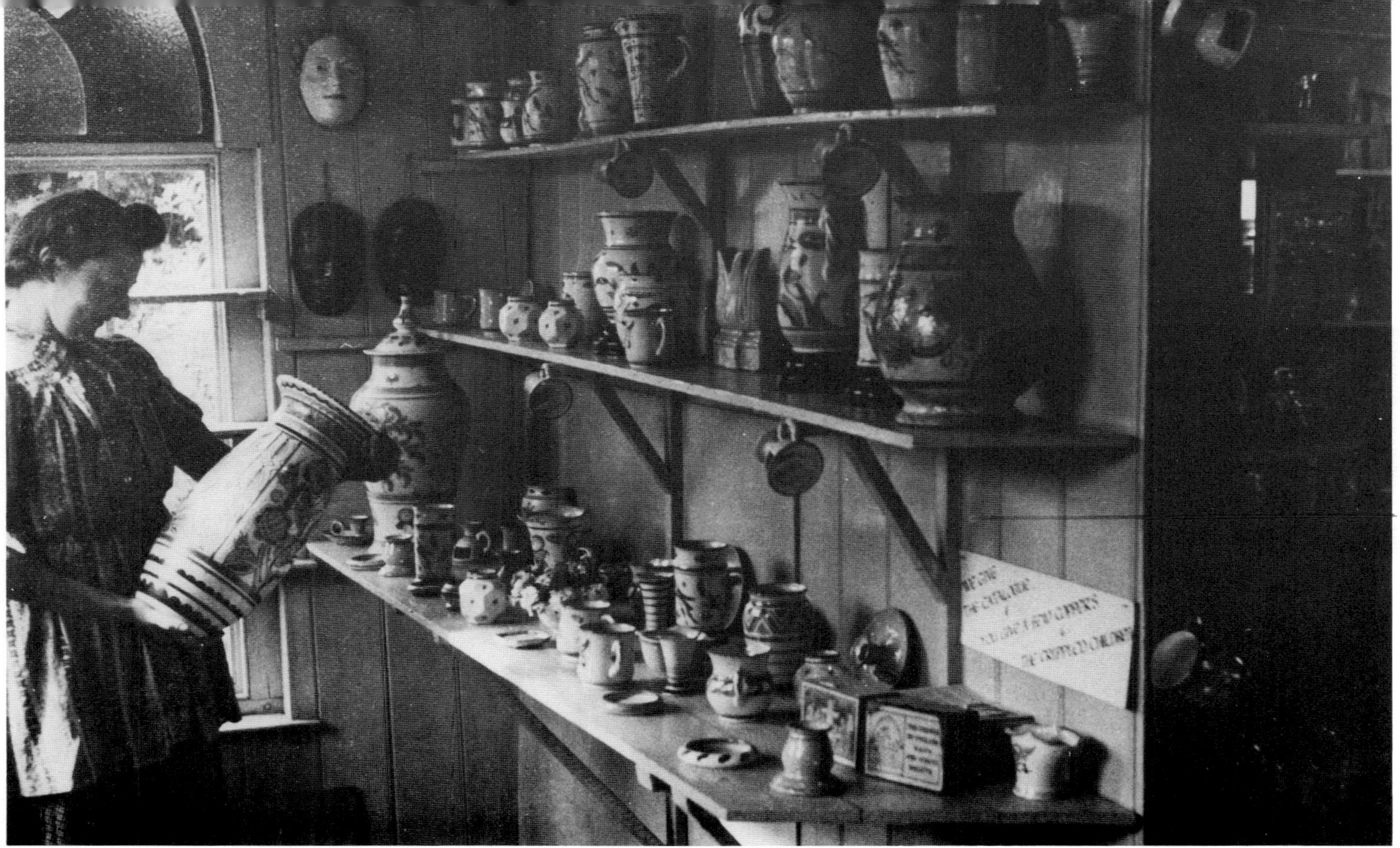

Plate 62
Joan Collard inspecting a particularly fine Jacobean vase from a selection of mid 1930s ware in the Honiton showroom. Note the pottery face masks on the wall.

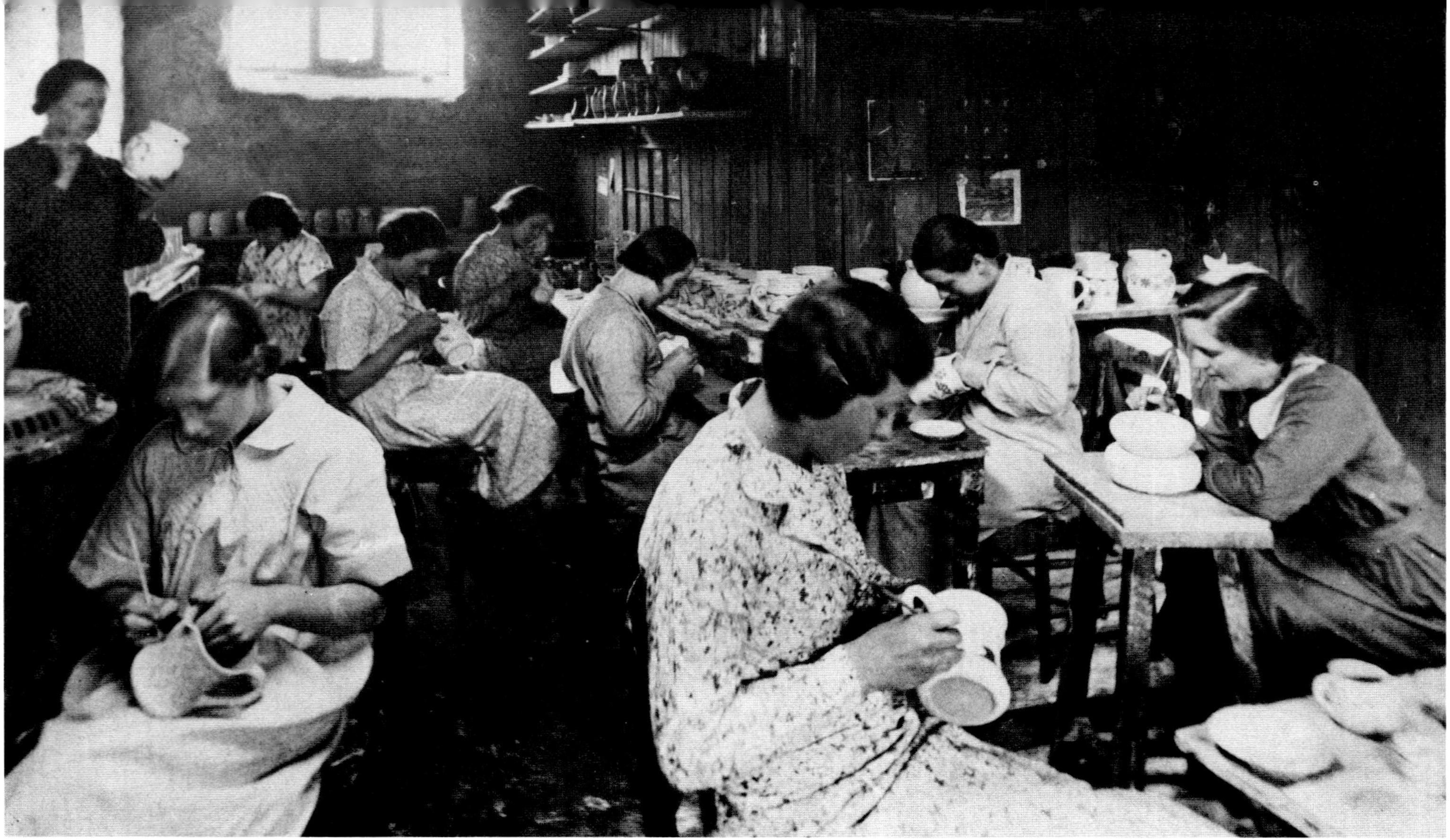

Plate 63
The decorators of Honiton in the mid 1930s. They are from left to right:
Front Row: Peggy Cooper, Florrie Loving, Jessie Banbury.
Middle Row: standing Joan Collard, seated Edith Readhead, Dorothy Channon, Vera Stuart.
Back Row: Beryl Radford, Linda Marks.

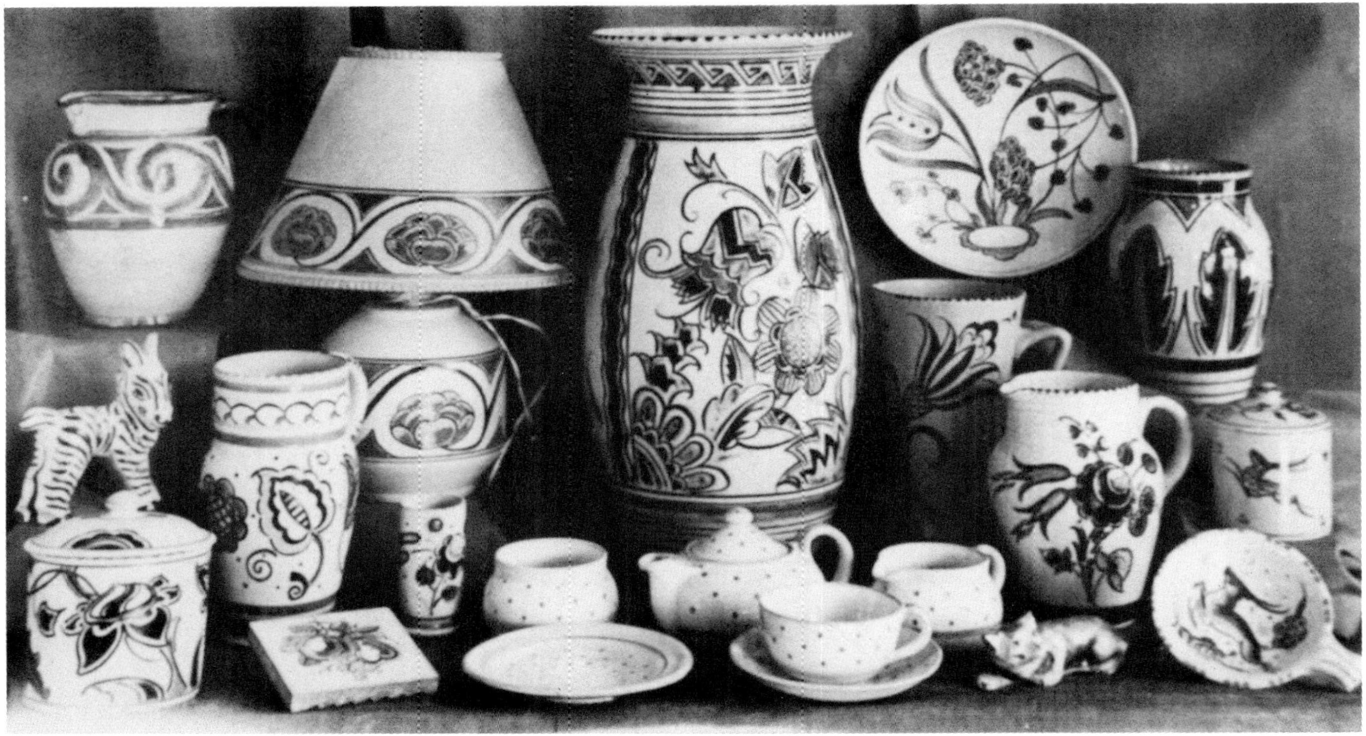

Plate 64
A range of Honiton ware from a publicity photograph taken in 1940.

Plate 65
A 10″ Honiton pitcher decorated in royal blue, black, yellow, red-brown and lustrous green. Mark no 22. Circa 1929.

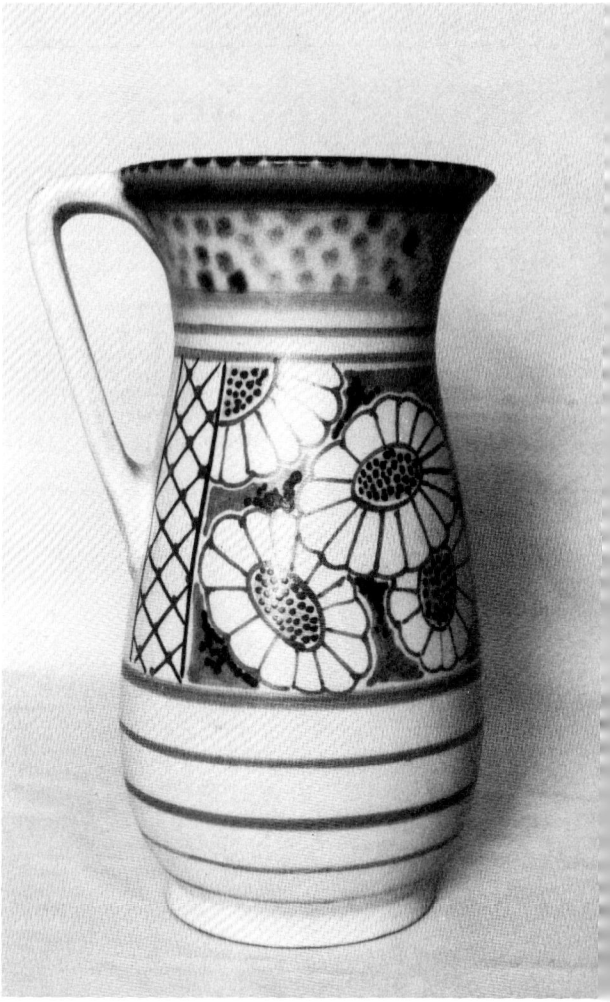

Plate 66
Charles Collard at the potter's wheel at the Honiton Pottery around 1940.

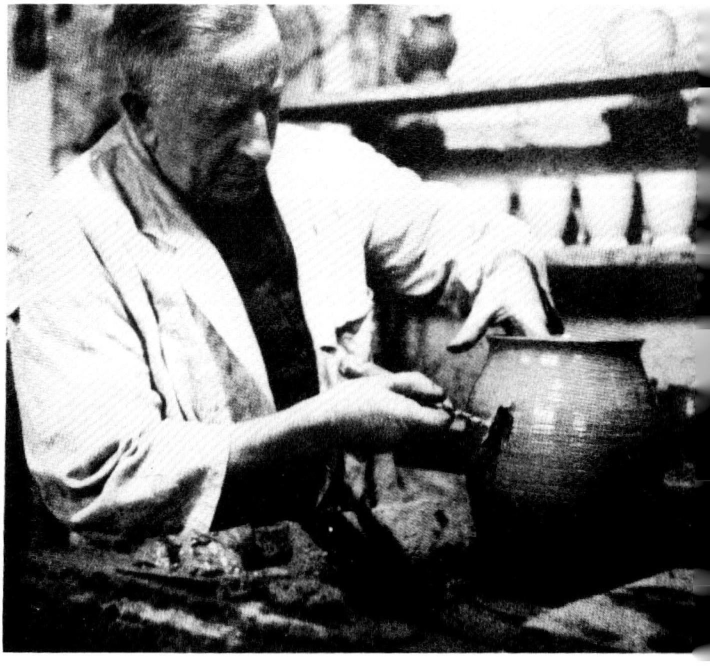

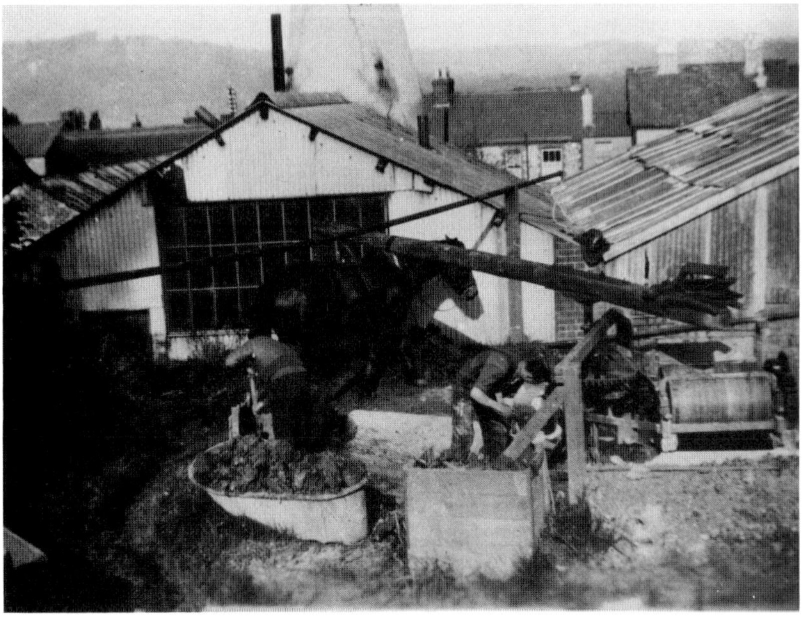

Plate 67
Walter Flood and Ernest Carnell operating the pug mill at the Honiton Pottery in the mid 1930s, with the help of Mr Madge's horse.

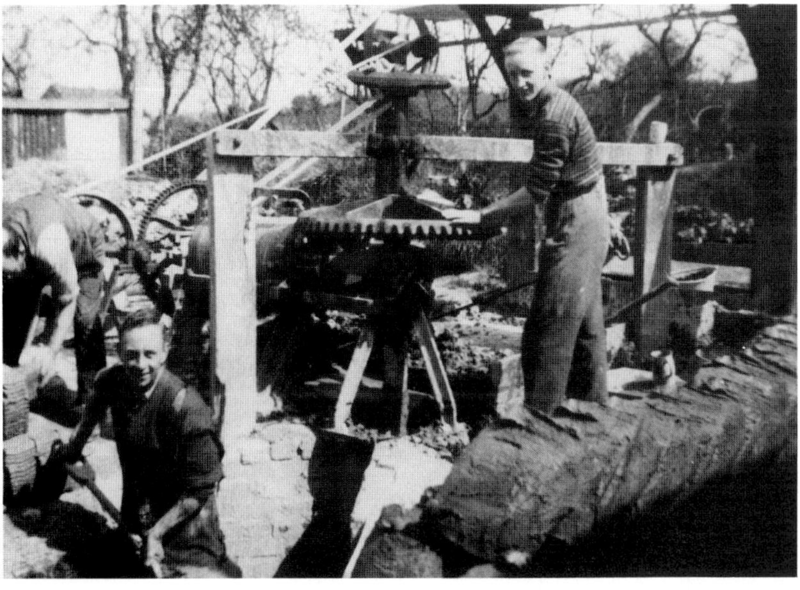

Plate 68
A closer view of the pug mill with Bert Nott, left, Ernest Carnell, centre and Walter Flood, right.

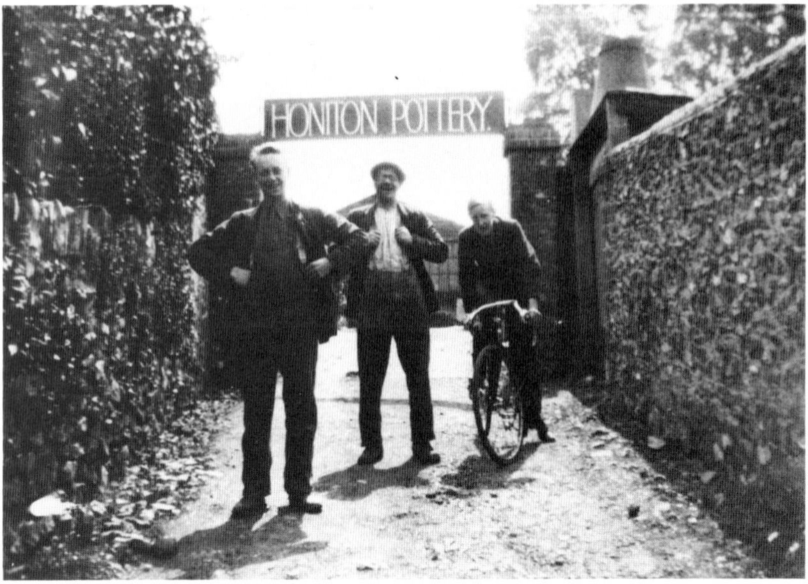

Plate 69
Ernest Carnell, Bert Nott and Walter Flood in jovial mood at the gates of the pottery in the mid 1930s.

The following plates (numbers 70 to 82) are from a catalogue produced by the Honiton Pottery circa 1934. The numbers refer to the shape of the piece, these are painted in black on the base of the majority of pots. The catalogue shows as many of the different patterns as possible from the selection in the showroom at the time.

Plate 70

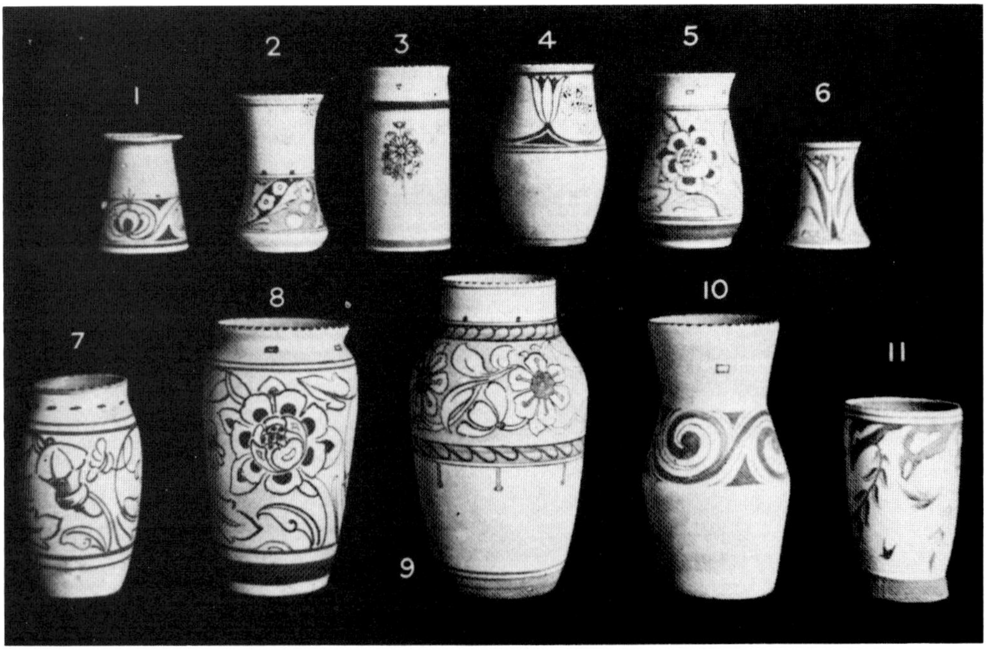

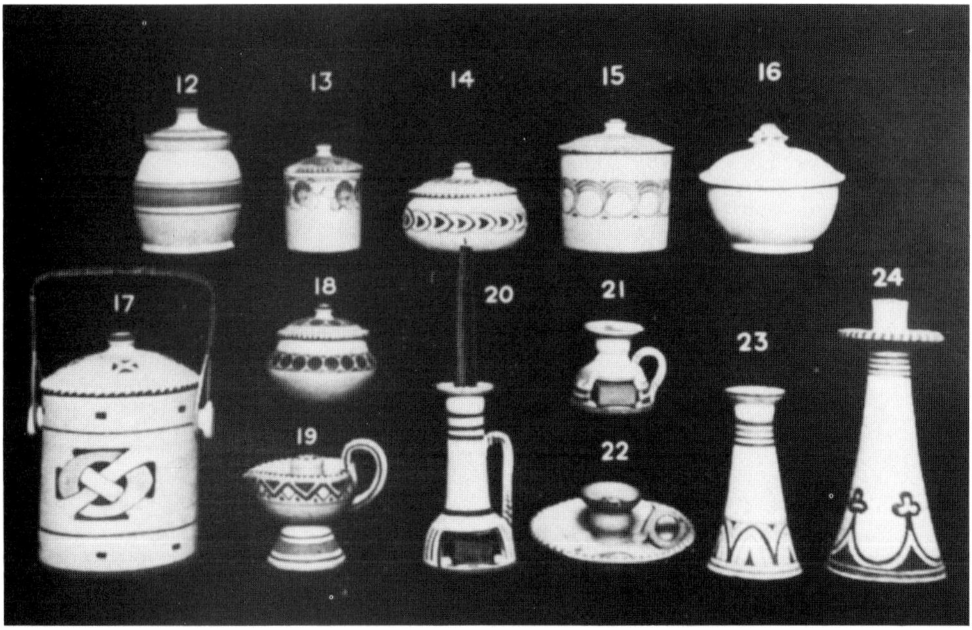

Plate 71

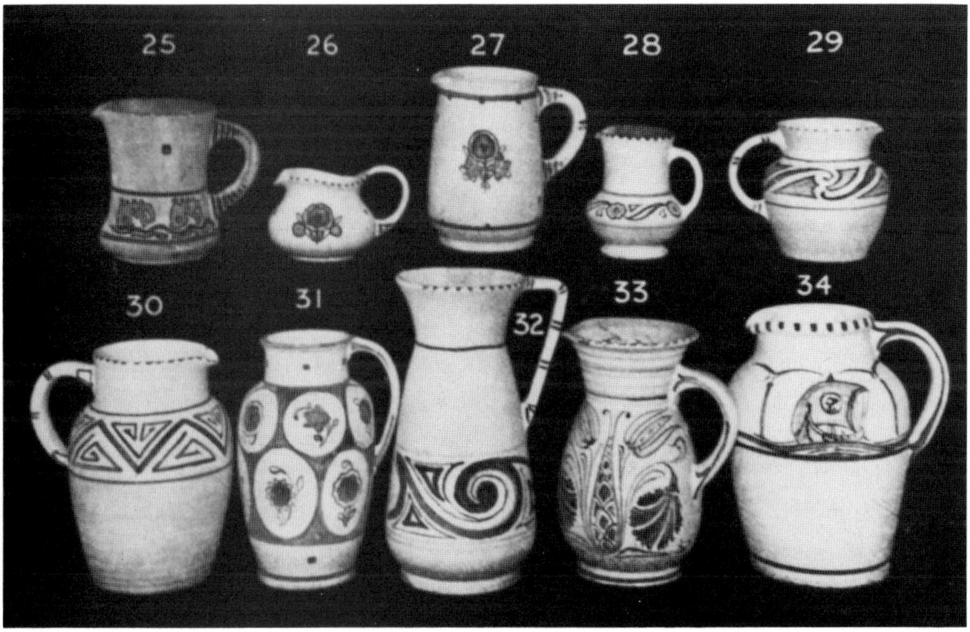

Plate 72

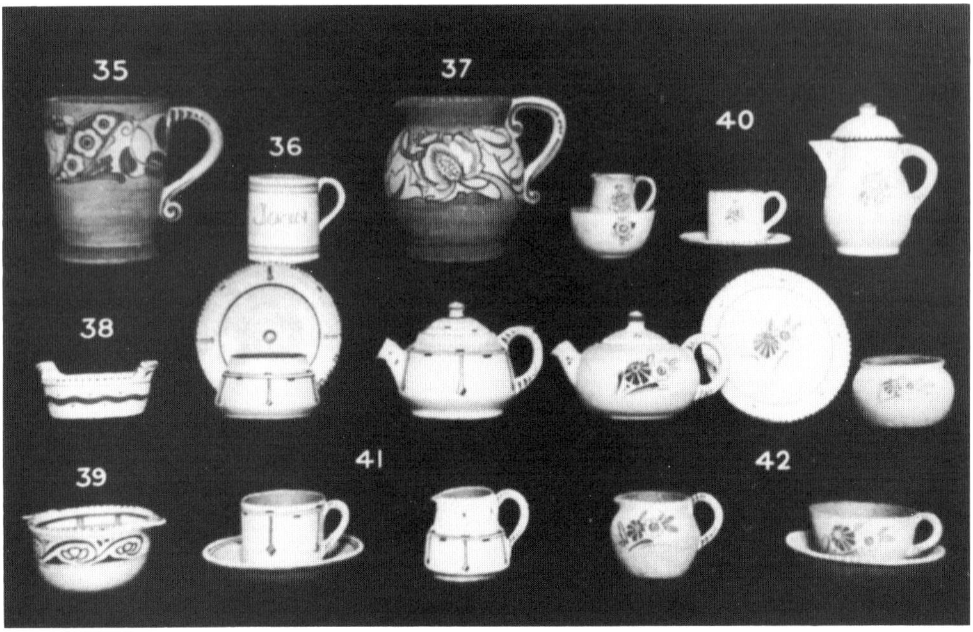

Plate 73

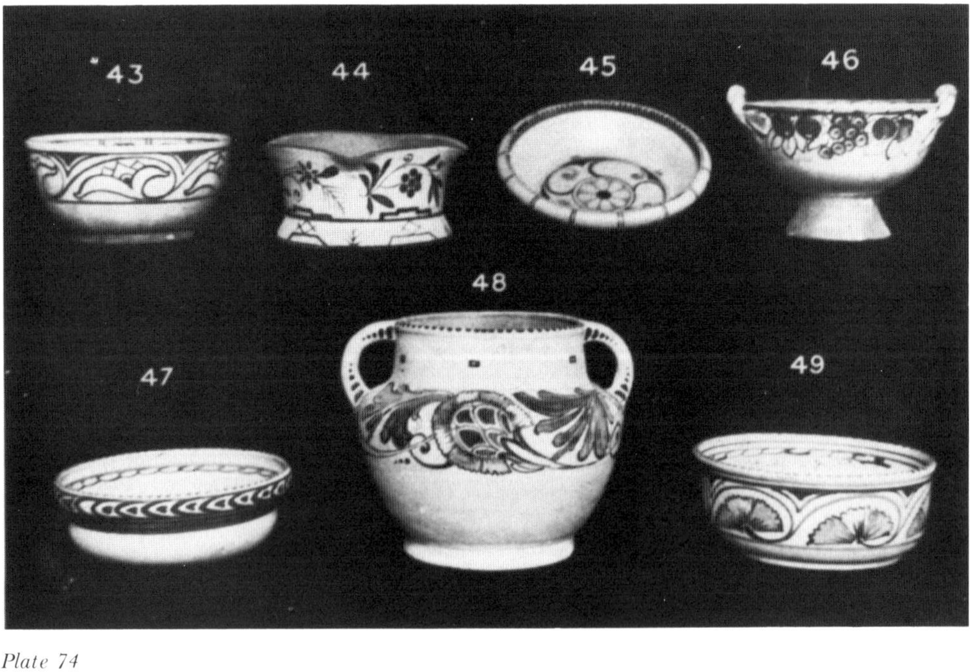

Plate 74

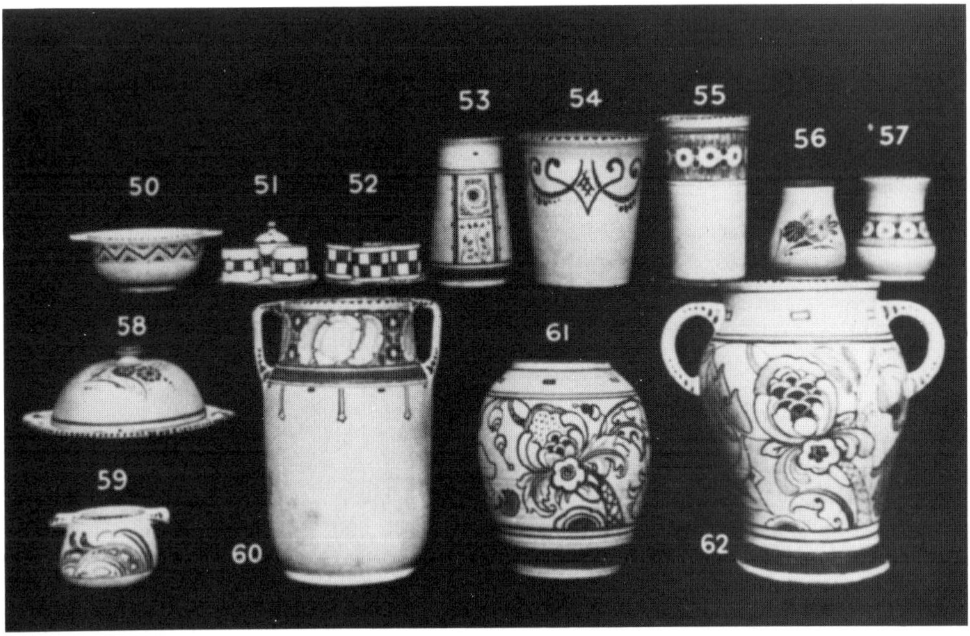

Plate 75

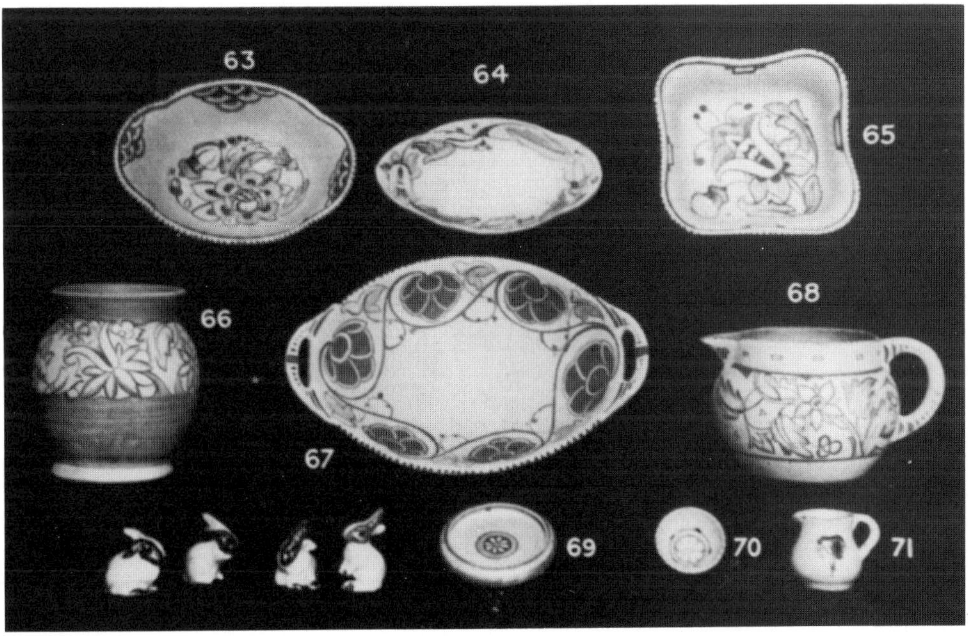

Plate 76

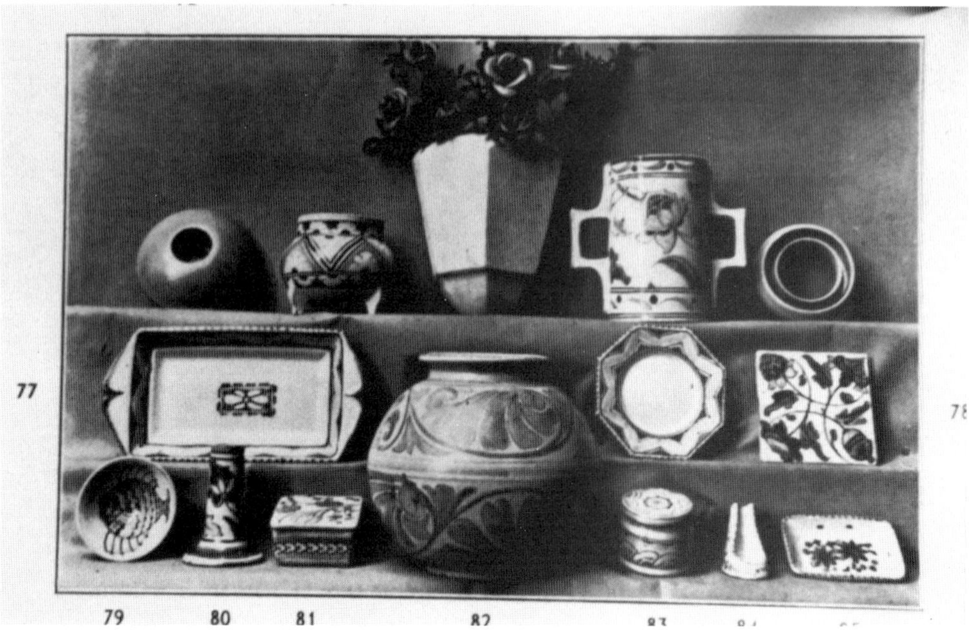

Plate 77

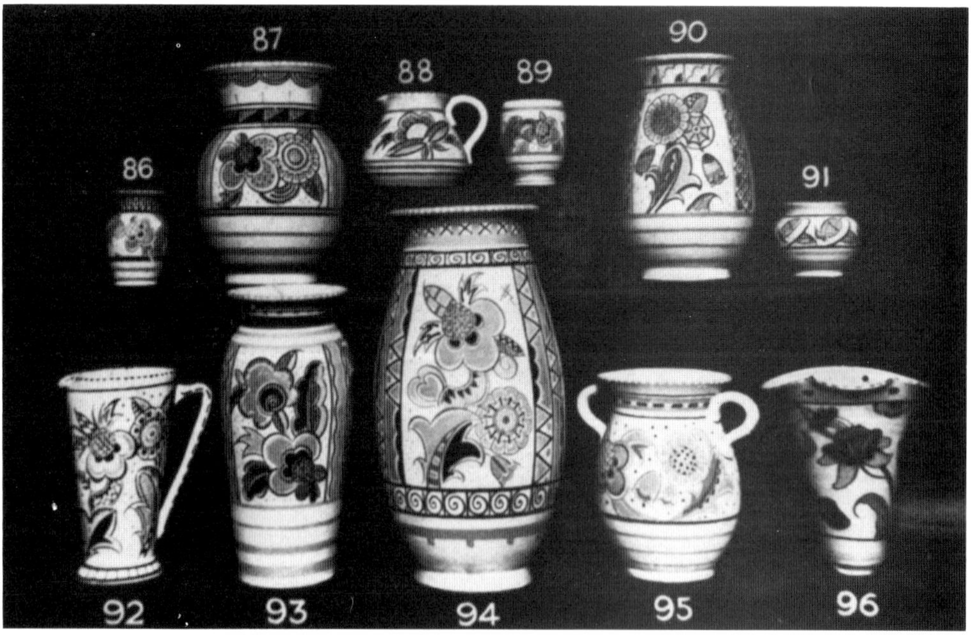

Plate 78

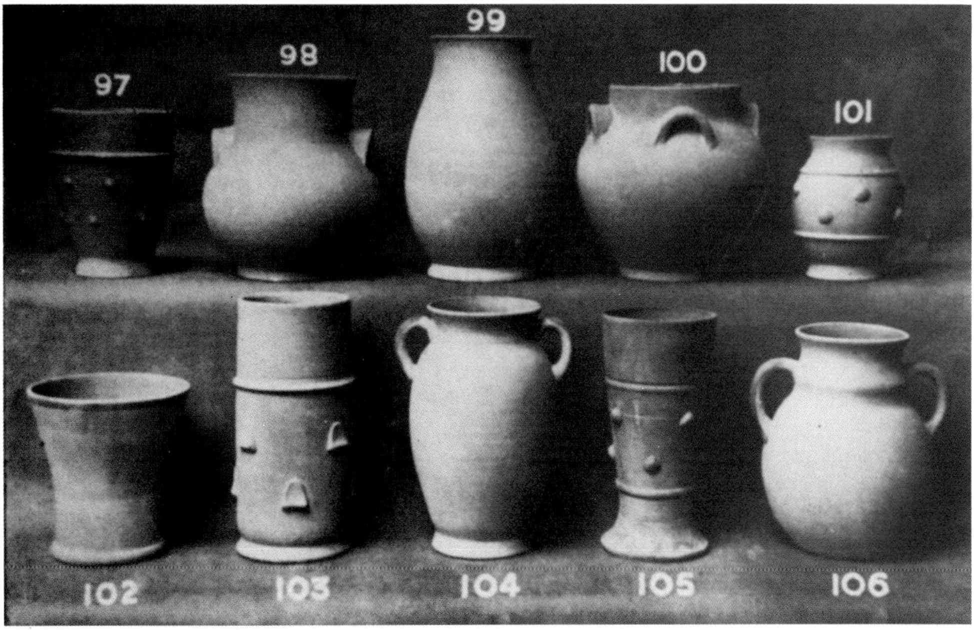

Plate 79

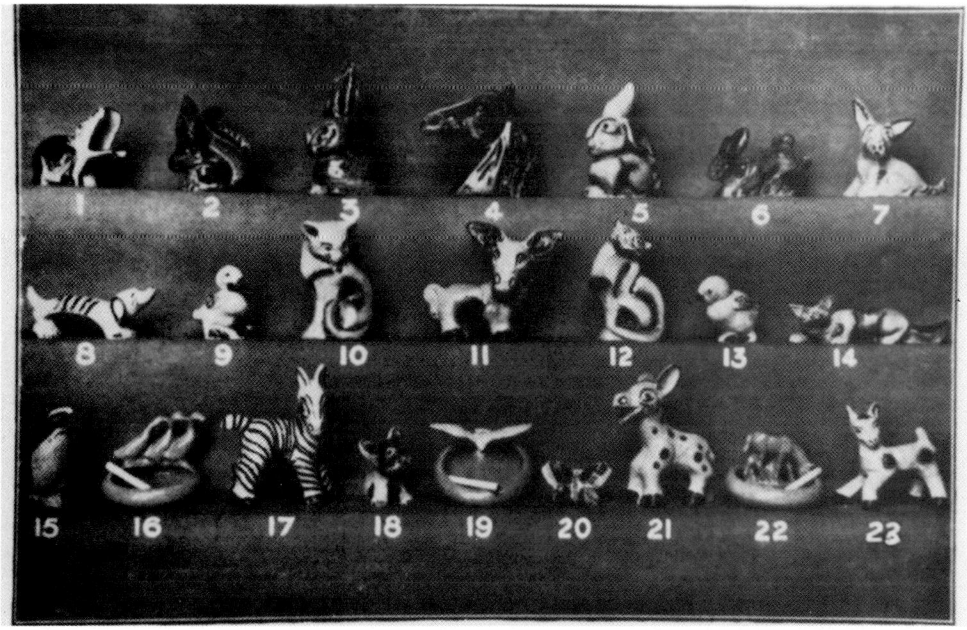

Plate 80

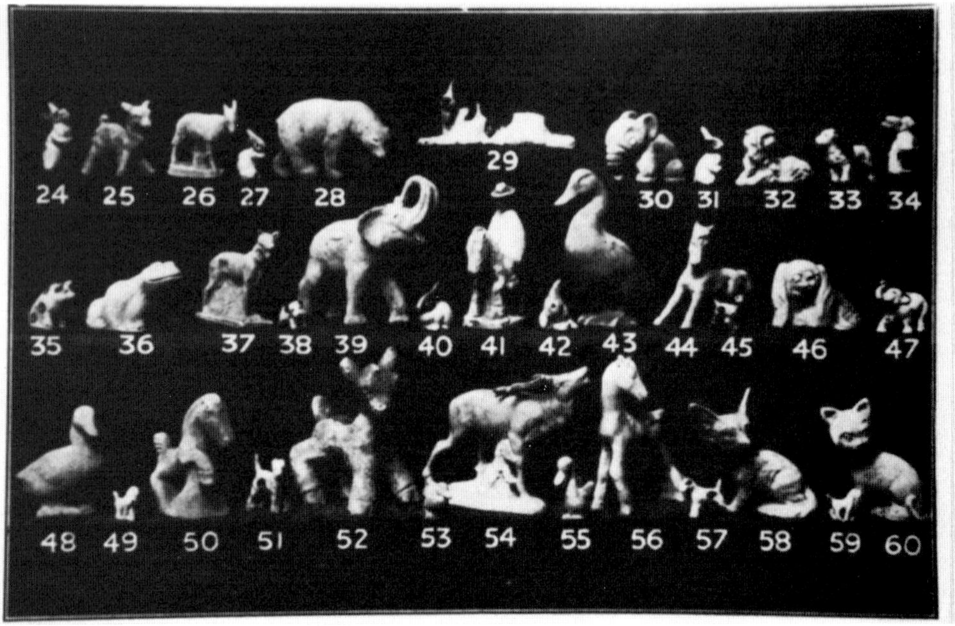

Plate 81

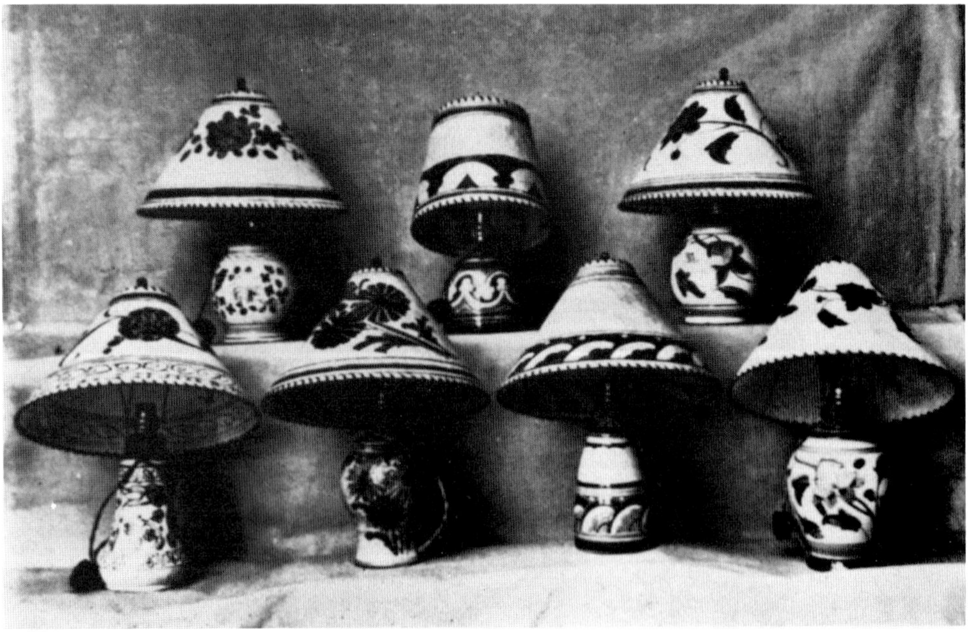

Plate 82